how to write lyrics

how to write lyrics

Better Words for Your Songs

Second Edition | Revised and Updated

Rikky Rooksby

Backbeat Books

Guilford, Connecticut

Backbeat Books

An imprint of Globe Pequot, the trade division of
The Rowman & Littlefield Publishing Group, Inc.
4501 Forbes Blvd., Ste. 200
Lanham, MD 20706
www.rowman.com

Distributed by NATIONAL BOOK NETWORK

Cover design by Paul Palmer-Edwards
Book design by Tom Seabrook

Library of Congress Cataloging-in-Publication Data available

ISBN 978-1-4930-5615-6 (paperback)
ISBN 978-1-4930-5616-3 (e-book)

contents

» To Paul Ashton-Bridges, for remembering the words, and much else.

preface to the second edition

"I can't think of anything to write..."

Has this thought crossed your mind, just when you need a lyric for a song you're composing? It happens to most songwriters at some point.

No aspect of songwriting causes more frustration than writing lyrics. It's a common scenario: you have the chords together, a melody to sing, an arrangement, but no words. So often, lyrics get left to the final stage of writing a song. Throughout the history of popular music, a lyric is scribbled at the last minute, often in the studio, and vocalists end up singing words they didn't exactly want to say, didn't like, or didn't mean.

Do you find yourself repeating phrases from other songs, using clichés, and searching for rhymes? Are you always writing about the same topics, perhaps the same themes, as everyone else? Do your lyrics seem obscure to others? After a gig, is your audience posting comments such as, "Great music, but I can't understand the lyrics"?

How to Write Lyrics has helped songwriters to write better lyrics, expand their awareness of the craft of lyric writing, and develop their own style, images, and themes. In it, there are suggestions for how to:

- draft a lyric
- rework an old or discarded lyric
- expand your sense of what a lyric can do
- write new types of lyric
- avoid obscurity
- become more aware of variations in style.

This book takes you deeper into lyric writing to grasp common techniques and subjects. Seeing what others have created in lyrics during the past 60 years will evoke opportunities to recharge your creative approach. There are many tips and ideas that can find new life in your own lyrics, and pages of encouragement, whatever your style of music.

You don't have to read *How to Write Lyrics* sequentially. Dip straight into any section of interest.

Do you have a half-complete lyric that's missing a section? Look through these pages and find an idea to complete it.

Stuck writing about the same subjects? Browse the many titles for some alternatives.

Short of inspiration? Open *How to Write Lyrics* at random and see what is brought to your attention.

Rikky Rooksby
Oxford, England
Winter 2021

how to use this book

The book has two parts. Part 1 is an instruction manual that takes you through all the major aspects of lyric writing, and is split into nine sections. Section 1 describes how to start a lyric. Section 2 provides 30 strategies for finding inspiration and avoiding so-called "writer's block." Section 3 takes you from a simple sketch through to a polished final draft, and includes specific examples of revising and redrafting. Section 4 looks at the magic of titles, and section 5 considers techniques that affect lyric writing line-by-line. Section 6 deals with how lyrics generate pictures through metaphors and similes, and surveys the commonest imagery in songs. Section 7 examines storytelling, point-of-view, and character. Section 8 discusses some broader issues to do with lyric writing that shape where you direct your songwriting. Section 9 is a gallery of different types of lyric, explaining how they work and are constructed.

Part 2 is split into two sections. Section 10 is a sourcebook of themes, citing hundreds of songs according to their subject matter, as a source of inspiration: find them on the web and see how leading lyricists have handled those subjects in the past. There is a mixture of singles and album tracks from bands and singers from the 1950s to the present day. The sourcebook also gives a sense of which themes have been most popular, and which are perhaps overdone or have become clichéd. This will help you invent titles that are sharper and more interesting than the average. Section 11 contains a number of insightful interviews with some famous songwriters who reflect on their own individual methods and experiences.

Titles alone can inspire songs; they can remind you of a song you know that might initiate a new song of your own. These are not definitive listings. It is inevitable, given the millions of songs in circulation on vinyl, CD, MP3, streaming services, advertising, and on TV and film soundtracks, that each reader of *How to Write Lyrics* will think of different examples. For the subjects that have the most interest, you could compile your own lists. Lyrics have never been more accessible. In decades past, the only way to get them was to buy sheet music. Today, vast numbers of copyrighted lyrics can be found online at lyric websites and all over YouTube.

How to Write Lyrics is part of a multi-volume series on songwriting. To find out more on chord sequences, melody, guitar chords and tunings, and writing songs on keyboards (especially if you're a guitarist), seek out the new edition of *How to Write Songs on Guitar* (2020), *The Songwriting Sourcebook* (2011), *Riffs* (2010; revised 2021), *Chord Master* (2004; revised 2016), *Melody* (2005), *How to Write Songs on Keyboards* (2005), *Arranging Songs* (2007), *Songs and Solos* (2014), and *How to Write Songs in Altered Guitar Tunings* (2010). Information about these titles can be found at www.rowman.com and www.rikkyrooksby.com.

finding inspiration, learning the craft

making a start

> Sometimes I finish the lyrics the month before we go into the studio. But for the most part, 90 percent of them are done at the last minute."
>
> **KURT COBAIN TO *GUITAR WORLD*, MARCH 1999**

> When I look at our first ten years, I just hear unfinished work, lyrics we never finished because we ran out of studio time."
>
> **BONO TO *MOJO*, OCTOBER 2004**

> I did the tune first and wrote words . . . later. I called that 'Scrambled Egg' for a long time. I didn't have any words to it."
>
> **PAUL MCCARTNEY TO *ROLLING STONE* ON "YESTERDAY," JANUARY 1974**

> Some songs come quickly and some songs take forever. 'Sherry' [Four Seasons, US #1 in 1962] was a quickie. It took 15 minutes. I was ready to leave for a rehearsal we were having, and I sat at the piano and it just came out. Not having a tape-recorder in those days, the only way I could remember it was to put a quick lyric to it and remember the melody and the words together. I drove down to rehearsal humming it, trying to keep it in my mind. I had no intention of keeping the lyrics. To my surprise, everybody liked the lyrics so we didn't change anything."
>
> **SONGWRITER BOB GAUDIO TO FRED BRONSON**

Writing lyrics requires completely different skills to those used in other aspects of songwriting. No wonder so many people find it a struggle.

Lyric seems to be the hardest word

For many, composing lyrics is the most challenging aspect of songwriting. If this is true for you, you're in good company. Noel Gallagher of the British group Oasis told *Guitar* in May 1996, "The music side of it is easy—it's the lyrics I can't stand writing." A few songwriters deal with this issue by forming a partnership with someone who can supply words to their music. The common division of labor in songwriting partnerships is along the music/lyric divide: one person composes the music, the other writes the words. Think of Burt Bacharach (music) and Hal David (words); or Elton John (music) and Bernie Taupin (words); or John Barry (music) and Leslie Bricusse or Don Black (words). Occasionally, a songwriter who usually creates both words *and* music might leave the writing of the lyrics to someone else. Brian Wilson asked Tony Asher to write lyrics for the classic *Pet Sounds* and Van Dyke Parks to do the same for *Smile*. But the majority of songwriters write music *and* lyrics singlehandedly.

It was in the 1960s that the separate roles of performer and songwriter often became fused, primarily owing to the success of the Beatles and a growing awareness of how much money could be earned through songwriting copyrights. Before that, there was often a team of creative people with individual roles behind a hit song. Each person in the team only needed to excel at one thing. So, don't think there's anything wrong in seeking a partner to share the burdens of songwriting.

> *Everybody's a singer/songwriter now, but not everybody should be; not everybody can do all of these things, and yet everybody does. And that's why I think music has gone downhill. It used to take three—a great lyricist and a great musician and then a great singer. Like with Frank [Sinatra], and that's why that stuff is so enduring—because you had three gifted people doing it. Now you've got people, they're not really a great singer or a great writer or a great musician doing it, so the standards have dropped severely."*
>
> **JONI MITCHELL TO *MOJO*, AUGUST 1998**

Writing lyrics involves shaping the meaning of something that, if left as instrumental music, would stay undefined; there is a change in the level of expression. Lyrics are more specific than music. That's one reason why (to play with an Elton John title) for many songwriters, "lyric" seems to be the hardest word.

Picture this scene: a songwriter at the piano, or with a guitar, plays with chords and creates an emotion and atmosphere that is creatively inspiring. This songwriter invents a melody to go with the chords and this mood. Then comes the moment where words are required, and that means getting specific. This sad- or happy-sounding chord progression must now direct its general sadness or happiness to a *particular* human situation. A lyric is the place where the emotional suggestions of pure music are defined into concrete human concerns and events. It's like a process of translation, from one medium into another. The general musical mood is focused by a lyric into a context, a voice, a human drama.

But what if you don't have anything in mind? It happens to everyone, including professional songwriters. Around the time of his album *The Soul Cages*, Sting admitted he had found the recording difficult because, though the music came easily, the ideas in his head at the time would not have led to suitable lyrics. The solution came from drawing on memories of his childhood and youth in Newcastle, in the north of England.

A second reason why writing lyrics is often problematic is because it requires different skills to those used for composing. A good lyricist has a multifaceted sensitivity to language. He or she can write memorable phrases, spot a potential hook or good first line, rhyme competently, handle metaphors and images, and reshape a phrase while retaining its sense. A lyricist has an ear for words that are awkward to sing, or too abstract or obscure, and knows how to organize a lyric around a character, an emotion, a story, or an idea so it makes sense to a large audience, even if its origin was personal.

Such language-oriented skills are not automatically granted just because you are a good singer, guitarist, keyboard player, or composer. For most songwriters, it's necessary to acquire these skills. *How to Write Lyrics* will help you to do that.

> *It's a great luxury—at least for a lyricist—to write to [recorded] tracks because you have a much better sense of what the musical mood of the song is. If you're writing with a person who plays piano and they're sitting at the keyboard playing, they may have a whole different sound in their head from what you have in your head when you hear what they play . . . although in some ways, it's a little more demanding because you're now having to fit into something that's complete whereas when you're writing lyrics to a song that has no real arrangement done to it yet, theoretically, what you write can influence what that turns out to be."*

TONY ASHER ON WRITING WITH BRIAN WILSON,
AS QUOTED IN "THE MAKING OF *PET SOUNDS*"

" *The way I write is to sit down with the guitar and keep on writing until it's finished. I've never written a set of lyrics independently of the song. I have to have an idea for the melody and then I'll choose words that sing well. I'm not proud of seeing the lyrics written out, usually, because they need the music to back them up."*

CHRISSIE HYNDE OF THE PRETENDERS TO *MELODY MAKER*

" *The rhythm of the words is more important to me than the sense at that [initial] stage . . . 'In the Air' was improvised like that, and so were songs like 'I Don't Care Anymore,' 'Take Me Home,' 'Sussudio.'"*

PHIL COLLINS TO *MELODY MAKER* ON IMPROVISING NONSENSE

" *Depending on whether a song starts with a melody or starts with lyrics, you know if it starts with a melody you just keep playing the melody over and over until you get it down and just throw in any lyrics that fit the verbal flow."*

NATHAN FOLLOWILL OF KINGS OF LEON TO TRIPLE J, FEBRUARY 2009

Which comes first, music or words?

A lyric can be written at any stage in the songwriting process. Each stage has advantages and disadvantages. You can write a lyric first. It doesn't have to be complete; a few lines and images could be enough to sing when working on the chord progression and melody. Some people find a title as soon as they get an inspiring musical idea, and this title maintains the song's identity and dominant emotion until it is finished. Some writers develop a lyric with the music: sitting, guitar in hand, writing down lyric ideas and chord ideas, or at a keyboard. It's a matter of whatever works for you.

The advantage to starting with a complete lyric is that it can be easier to sing a melody and decide on its timing and rhythms with meaningful words. Lyrics written first can be worked on until they make sense, have memorable lines and images, and are easily set to music because they are singable and don't have awkward phrases or line lengths.

Whichever way you decide to do it, it is a good discipline to keep a notebook and work up ideas so there is a stock of finished lyrics to fall back on.

Another method is to think of words as you invent the melody, or to write lyrics when the music is finished. This could even mean leaving it as late as having the backing track recorded and ready. In this case, the music may inspire a set of good lines; on the other hand, you will have to return and edit the track if the lyric requires it.

What kinds of lyric are there?

Lyrics can be classified in many ways, especially according to subject matter, as is done in section 10. But at this point we need a more general answer to the question.

Here are four fundamental types of lyric:

- *Feeling lyric*: expresses emotions, moods, atmosphere.
- *Thinking lyric*: expresses an idea, insight, realization, truth, falsity.
- *Experiencing lyric*: expresses a story, a sequence of events, time-dependent.
- *Contemplating lyric*: observes, describes, an object or objects, a scene.

These categories are not mutually exclusive. A single lyric could cover all four. But a lyric will tend to gravitate toward one of these, and a songwriter may have a temperamental bias to write more songs of one type than the others.

Most songwriters lean toward the feeling lyric, if only because emotion is the greatest spur to creativity. If we bring in other types of lyric, such as the confessional, comic, satiric, protest, or romantic lyric, you can see that these are subsidiary; they can be experienced through any of the four main types. This is one aspect to lyric writing that it may help to keep in mind.

> *It was . . . Rob [Collins, keyboards], and a microphone in the middle of the room, and I just sang the first thing that came into my head, based on the sort of mumbo jumbo feeling you get from like a huge crush on someone. Basically, that simple. I just had, like, 'not the same as everybody else' and 'why talk to her?' written down . . . and that was the way it was left. It was supposed to . . . get a feel of the song but it just ended up being the song. It was completely spontaneous."*
>
> **TIM BURGESS OF THE CHARLATANS TO *MELODY MAKER* ON**
> **THE RECORDING OF THE BAND'S SONG "SUBTITLE"**

Simply write

There are times when writing a lyric is easy. Sometimes, songwriters have an urgent sense of what they want to sing about. Perhaps the likeliest time for this to happen is when they're in love. As Rufus Wainwright once told *The Word* magazine, using the metaphor of a volcano, "When you have a crush on someone, when you're moved by someone's physical presence, lyrics come like Mount St. Helens, songs come out of your ears!"

This can lead to attempts to be spontaneous in the studio, so that a lyric is improvised during recording. One example of this "wing-it" approach would be U2's "Elvis Presley and America," where Bono's first-take improvised melody and mostly garbled lyric were left unchanged when the song was released on the album *The Unforgettable Fire* (1984).

The listening public has often been largely unaware of the hit-and-miss nature of so many lyrics. Cream's "Badge," for instance, got its title because of a misreading of the word "bridge" on a piece of paper.

The hope in such situations is that inspiration will strike. In 1998, Willie Nelson told *Mojo* magazine, "Writing is—I don't know—an instinct, an intuitive thing, you have to be in a receptive mood. Sometimes an idea comes along, and you have no control over it. It just overwhelms you, so you just sit down and get on with it."

Such inspiration will quickly fill a blank page with jottings—complete phrases, incomplete phrases, lines that rhyme, lines that don't rhyme, isolated similes or images, maybe a title. This is what I term a "sketch," and it can be as haphazard as you like.

Here's the important point: once the sketch is done you are no longer looking at a blank screen or sheet of paper. This makes a big psychological difference.

The hardest part of lyric writing is to get past the intimidating inertia of that blank paper. Once there is a sketch, you have surmounted that horrible feeling of, "What am I going to write? I can't think of anything." The sketch can be expanded, rewritten, and generally fiddled with. Gradually, through a series of drafts, decisions are made about the most effective beginning of the lyric, what will be its conclusion, how many lines make a verse, which lines belong to a chorus or a bridge, what is the title, et cetera.

But songwriters don't always feel inspired. So, what to do when you have no theme in mind and can't think of what to write? The answer is to do anything that will result in a sketch—anything that gets you writing. Nothing inhibits creativity more than the struggle to start. You need to find a way round this that suits, as an artist stuck for ideas might simply throw paint at a canvas to initiate a painting. It usually helps to move into a playful state of mind, willing to experiment and not too concerned with what the outcome may be.

One exercise is to write from the present by asking yourself:

- Where are you?
- What can you see, hear, smell?
- How are you feeling?
- What's been on your mind?
- What time of day, week, season is it?
- What happened yesterday?
- What's supposed to happen today?
- What would you like to happen tomorrow?
- What do you think likely to happen tomorrow?
- What's been on the news?
- What's going on in the lives of your partner, friends, family?
- What music have you been listening to recently?
- What do you like about it?

Write anything about any of these things. Don't evaluate what you put down. Just write. The fear of getting stuck can be inhibiting. But if you can develop the ability to play your way into a creative flow, you will find the process of songwriting more pleasurable and more productive.

30 ways to find inspiration

> *Ideas, titles for songs, I would definitely do at home because I would watch the news, the goings-on in the world, movies and listening to conversations between people on the street or in a restaurant. I was always looking for material. . . . When you're a songwriter, you're always very observant of the world around you.*

LAMONT DOZIER OF THE MOTOWN SONGWRITING TEAM
HOLLAND-DOZIER-HOLLAND TO SEAN EGAN

> *Lyrics usually come to me in the morning, in the first 15 minutes of the day, or when I'm out in the middle of the night. I carry a notebook, and I'll write a line down in a bar, then maybe the next day I'll look at it and think, Ah, that's interesting, I'll put this in a song.*

ALEX TURNER OF ARCTIC MONKEYS TO *NEW YORK MAGAZINE*, AUGUST 2018

The inspiration for a lyric can come from many sources. As Ed Sheeran explained to *Interview* magazine in 2011, "My inspirations came from love, life and death, and viewing other people's situations." It is said that Roy Orbison wrote one of his biggest hits, "Pretty Woman," when his wife Claudette went out one afternoon shopping. Orbison asked Claudette if she needed any money, but fellow songwriter Bill Dees interjected, "A pretty woman never needs any money." Dees was struck by the phrase, thinking it would make a good title. Meanwhile, Paul McCartney got the title for the Beatles' "Eight Days a Week" from a casual remark by a taxi driver on the way to a recording session.

Inspiration can come from an idea, a feeling, a phrase, a title, a person (real or imagined), or a story (true or fictional). You can start with a clear theme or none; with words, images, or different types of statement; and let the theme arise from them.

Joanna Newsom has said of her song "Divers," "It's a little simplistic for me to say that I write down the images that are in my mind, because it's not like I just have a frozen image that I'm illustrating with the language. But it's maybe a set of . . . visual imperatives and feelings and ideas that feel connected to me, and feel like they're waiting to be connected."

From eavesdropping to watching TV, there are many well-tried techniques that can help you overcome the inertia of the blank page. Here are 30 strategies to try.

1 Listen to people talking

> *I get ideas from almost everywhere, but especially from supermarket queues—I have a talent for eavesdropping, and it's amazing what you learn waiting to pay for your fruit juice."*
>
> **MORRISSEY TO *MELODY MAKER*, 1987**

2 Write a single, evocative phrase

Neil Tennant of the Pet Shop Boys claims that most of his lyrics begin with a phrase he's jotted down or an idea for a title.

3 Keep a small notebook and pen in your pocket

Write down ideas immediately as they occur.

> *I write passing thoughts, overheard conversations, discovered quotations, advertising signs, mumbled threats, and words of kindness and endearment, on scraps of paper. Sometimes I mutter them into Dictaphones or record them on my answer-machine when there is not even an eyebrow pencil in hand in order to commit them to the page."*
>
> **ELVIS COSTELLO TO *THE WORD*, FEBRUARY 2005**

> *It all usually starts with a riff on a guitar, and then I decide I want to write about something, and I look through my notebooks and find all the phrases and rhymes. I constantly write down things I like, like "bereft and adrift." If I'm missing one line I just flick through my notebook and there's one there."*
>
> **EVAN DANDO OF THE LEMONHEADS TO *MAKING MUSIC*, 1996**

4 Sketch a lyric in a public place

Bob Dylan is just one of those who would sit in a coffeehouse for days at a time, looking at the other customers, making up things about them and writing down whatever came into his head.

Nowadays the public space can be a virtual one. Social media, if used wisely, can also be a source of lyric ideas, either through comments people make or images supplied to your feed via membership of groups likely to post pictures of artistic or historical subjects. These arrive in random ways, and occasionally they may form an unexpected but colorful juxtaposition that will start a lyric.

5 Listen to music to alter your frame of mind and encourage a receptive mood

Write down the thoughts, feelings, and pictures the music evokes. Brian Wilson famously wrote the whole of the "Mount Vernon and Fairway" song sequence from the Beach Boys' *Holland* (1973) while listening to Randy Newman's *Sail Away* album from the previous year over and over again.

Listen to songs in a language you don't know and write down phrases that the unfamiliar sounds suggest. K. T. Tunstall's "Suddenly" was written in thirty minutes after the singer had been meditating on the cover of Patti Smith's album *Horses*.

6 Glance through a newspaper or a magazine

Paul McCartney once said that the first line of his Beatles lyrics often came from reading a book or looking at newspapers.

7 Put your pen down and go to your guitar or keyboard

Make some music first.

> *You get ideas for songs from all sorts of situations. I just start playing the piano and the chords start telling me something. Lyrics for me just seem to go with the tune, very much hand in hand."*
>
> **KATE BUSH TO *RECORD MIRROR*, FEBRUARY 1978**

8 Write with the TV on but your back to it, so you can't see the picture

Keep an ear open for odd phrases you could use, or that collide with what you're writing in fruitful ways. John Lennon got the idea for "Good Morning, Good Morning" from a TV ad that was on in the background as he sat at the piano.

9 Watch the TV with notebook and pen

Manic Street Preachers' Nicky Wire has said he writes "mostly when it's raining or dark, usually after ten at night. I get a lot of inspiration from watching TV."

> *At night... [John Lennon] loved to channel-surf, and he would pick up phrases from all the shows. One time, he was watching Reverend Ike, a famous black TV evangelist, who was saying, 'Let me tell you guys, it doesn't matter, it's whatever gets you through the night.' John loved it and said, 'I've got to write it down or I'll forget it.' He always kept a pad and pen by the bed. That was the beginning of 'Whatever Gets You Thru the Night,' an American #1 and UK Top 40 hit for John."*
>
> **MAY PANG TO *RADIO TIMES*, DECEMBER 2005**

10 Write randomly

Use the first things that come into your head. This could be prose; keep going until you have filled every line of the page. Then look for the nugget.

> *Lately, I get in a room by myself. No telephone, no TV, not much to look at. I usually by writing down random phrases. Maybe I'll start writing about a certain subject and there's a phrase that strikes me, so I'll spin off from that."*
>
> **DAVID BYRNE OF TALKING HEADS TO *MELODY MAKER***

> *'Madame George' is a stream-of-consciousness thing, as is 'Cyprus Avenue.' Both those songs came right out. I didn't even think about what I was writing. There are some things that you write that just come out all at once, and there's other things that you think about and consider where you'll put each bit."*
>
> **VAN MORRISON TO RITCHIE YORKE ON HIS 1968 ALBUM *ASTRAL WEEKS***

> *I often sit at a typewriter and knock out stream-of-consciousness stuff; it helps clear the head, but often brings forth ideas for songs and so on."*
>
> **PETE TOWNSHEND OF THE WHO TO *ROLLING STONE*, NOVEMBER 1977**

11 Travel by the transportation of your choice and watch the world shift to reveal new things

During June 2020, long car drives from an apartment in New York up to the Catskill Mountains inspired Robin Pecknold of Fleet Foxes to write lyrics for the band's fourth album, *Shore*. He recited the lines into his phone or wrote them down when parked. This produced 15 lyrics in about a month.

Tori Amos's 2017 album *Native Invader* was partly inspired by spending time in the Smoky Mountains, an area linked to her maternal grandfather. In an interview with *Songwriting* magazine, she observed, "Taking pilgrimages to places that might break the routine can shake things up a bit and trigger something that will help them [the muses] to find me."

> *I've written most of my best songs driving on a long journey, scribbling lyrics on cigarette packets whilst steering."*
>
> **NEIL YOUNG TO *VOX*, NOVEMBER 1990**

> *I wrote 'Black Hole Sun' in my head driving home from Bear Creek Studio in Woodinville, a 35-to-40-minute drive from Seattle. It sparked from something a news anchor said on TV and I heard wrong. I heard 'blah blah blah black hole sun blah blah blah.' I thought that would make an amazing song title."*
>
> **CHRIS CORNELL OF SOUNDGARDEN TO *UNCUT*, AUGUST 2014**

12 Imagine an ending or a punch line, and work backward from it

What needs to happen or be said to get there? Stephen Sondheim says that he finds it useful to write backwards, starting with "a climax, a twist, a punch, a joke."

13 Punch the clock: write on a regular, timetabled basis

Pretend you're a Brill Building songwriter expected to knock out songs every day. Randy Newman worked for years in an office from nine to five. Chris Difford of Squeeze consciously imitated him by establishing an office near his home. Nicky Chinn and Mike Chapman disciplined themselves to start work at 10am every day, beginning with a title and working from there.

St. Vincent (Annie Clark) has said that she approaches her work as a musician "as I would a day job. If you're a writer, you have to write. If you're a musician, you have to make music. I wrote a lot of [*St. Vincent*] in a shed behind my friend's house in South Austin." Bryan Adams has also stressed continual effort: "A songwriter writes songs all the time, whereas just writing a song can be done by anyone, anytime." The more songs you write the more you will improve.

> *I would say, you can never do enough gigs and you can never do enough songs ... every opportunity you can, write a song. The more you write tunes, the better they will become."*
>
> **ED SHEERAN TO *INTERVIEW*, DECEMBER 2011**

14 Cross-fertilize: try writing more than one lyric at a time

> *Lyrics are manna from heaven, and you have to interpret them. I always have three or four songs going at once. It's more competitive than confusing; they fight for my attention."*
>
> **RUFUS WAINWRIGHT TO *THE WORD*, MAY 2007**

15 Think of a childhood memory and either write about it or take the core feeling of that memory and project it into an imaginary situation

Describing a childhood stay in a hospital overlooking the Thames to *Q* magazine in 2005, Ray Davies of the Kinks recalled, "I remember looking at the river and thinking how happy I was to be alive. Waterloo Bridge has featured so prominently in my life that I have taken potential girlfriends there just to see how it felt."

> *I had an uncle who used to tell me stories. It seems to me now his sole purpose in life was to scare me witless. A recurring character in his stories was this spider-man. When I was about six or seven, he used to try and scare me and my sister, arriving late at night and whispering. He was my bogeyman."*
>
> **ROBERT SMITH OF THE CURE TO *MELODY MAKER* ON "LULLABY"**

> *A lot of early Move lyrics came from a book of fairy stories for adults that I wrote at school. It ended up in a folder in my bedroom, and I drew on it for songs like 'I Can Hear the Grass Grow' and 'Flowers in the Rain.'"*
>
> **ROY WOOD OF THE MOVE TO *MOJO*, JANUARY 2007**

16 Go out and watch what goes on in stores

I was looking for something for the kitchen in New York, in one of those long stores with cookers and fridges and microwaves and a wall of TV sets all tuned to MTV. There were these guys who delivered the kitchens, and there was this one who had his own little audience and he was going on. I sneaked behind the microwaves and just peeked through, then I went and borrowed a pen from one of the shop assistants and sat down in the kitchen display and just wrote down the things he said."

MARK KNOPFLER OF DIRE STRAITS TO Q ON WRITING "MONEY FOR NOTHING," JANUARY 1989

Hudson's was hip, the biggest and best department store in downtown Detroit. The holiday hustle and bustle . . . got me to feeling a little better. I avoided the toys and baby department, heading straight for the jewelry counter. Picked out some pearls for Claudette. 'They're beautiful,' I told the saleslady. 'Just hope my wife likes them.' 'I second that emotion,' said Al [Cleveland, fellow Motown songwriter]. What a funny phrase, I kept thinking on the way home, dodging in and out of the holiday traffic. That afternoon we wrote the song."

SMOKEY ROBINSON, *SMOKEY INSIDE MY LIFE*

17 Then, when you've finished eavesdropping on the sales assistants, go buy a book

I went into a shop and picked [Peter Reich's A Book of Dreams] off the shelf, and really liked the title and the picture on the front. I'd never bought a book before which I hadn't known anything about; I just felt I'd found something special. And nine, ten years later, I reread it and it turned into a song."

KATE BUSH TO *MOJO* ON WRITING "CLOUDBUSTING," NOVEMBER 2005

Sometimes a word or a turn of phrase excites me. I'll see a word and think, Hmmm. That's a cool word. Like 'hipshot,' that's a cool word. I think I used that in a song once. That's why I like reading. I'm hoping through osmosis I'll become a better writer, since you have to read a lot if you want to be a good writer."

CARL NEWMAN OF THE NEW PORNOGRAPHERS TO *SONGWRITERS ON PROCESS*, FEBRUARY 2015

18 Keep a notebook by your bedside, in case inspiration strikes in the middle of the night

Freddie Mercury of Queen used to scribble ideas at night without even putting the light on.

> *It was 3am when Bobbie Gentry woke up, inspired to write a song for her first Capitol album. A sentence scribbled on a pad of paper supplied the seed: 'Billie Joe McAllister jumped off the Tallahatchee Bridge.'"*
>
> **FRED BRONSON ON THE ORIGINS OF BOBBIE GENTRY'S 1967 US #1 "ODE TO BILLIE JOE"**

19 Play some favorite songs by other people to get yourself into a different frame of mind

Many famous songs were inspired by their writers hearing other people's songs and hoping to emulate them. Barry Mann and Cynthia Weil got the inspiration for "You've Lost That Lovin' Feelin'" from the Four Tops' "Baby I Need Your Loving." Brian Wilson's "Don't Worry Baby" was inspired by his love for the Ronettes' "Be My Baby."

> *By attacking [Love's] 'A House Is Not a Motel' or 'Seven and Seven Is' in a rehearsal room, I've actually found the means to start writing my own songs again. I always carry a notepad, pencil, rubber, and a French penknife, in a little Shure microphone bag, and these old songs have given me back [inspiration], and now I'm scribbling all the time."*
>
> **ROBERT PLANT TO *MOJO*, DECEMBER 1994**

20 Go for a walk around an art gallery

> *He did every gallery, every statue, every monument, took the imagery from that experience and turned them into songs. All those songs' characters came from that."*
>
> **JEFF DEXTER TO *MOJO* ON MARC BOLAN'S MYTHOLOGICAL SONGS WITH TYRANNOSAURUS REX**

21 Find an exciting title from a film

Browse a copy of *Halliwell's Film Guide* (or similar). It's optional whether you watch the film or just work with the title.

> *It's about a relationship being a very finely balanced thing that can be easily thrown off by a third party. The whole thing really came from a line in The Godfather, during some family argument, where Marlon Brando says, 'Don't interfere, it's between a man and a woman.'"*
>
> **KATE BUSH TO *NME* ON THE INSPIRATION FOR HER SONG "BETWEEN A MAN AND A WOMAN"**

22 Free associate to some music and record what you say

Mike Stoller once recalled that he would hammer away at the piano while Jerry Leiber paced around the room shouting out lines and phrases that came into his head. Anything promising would be worked on. They wrote "Hound Dog" in that way. It took only ten minutes.

23 Turn on the radio, at home or in the car

Hear accurately *and* inaccurately. John Gourrier, writer of the 1968 John Fred and the Playboys' hit "Judy in Disguise (with Glasses)," invented his song's title after mishearing the Beatles' "Lucy in the Sky with Diamonds" as "Lucy in *Disguise* with Diamonds." Bobby Hart's lyrics for the Monkees' 1966 hit "Last Train to Clarksville" were sparked by a mishearing of the Beatles' "Paperback Writer" as "take the last train."

> *It's always coincidence [that gets creativity moving]. You hear a song on the radio and hear just the word that you've been looking for for three months, or you go to a movie and get something going on in your mind . . . all these fluke things that happen that turn into good songs."*
>
> **PER GESSLE, WRITER OF "JOYRIDE," A US #1 FOR ROXETTE IN 1991, TO FRED BRONSON**

24 Have an emotional crisis (this method carries a health warning)

> *I was arguing with my girlfriend. I said, 'Stop in the name of love,' and we both started laughing and stopped arguing. I said, 'What did I say?' and she said, 'Something about stop in the name of love.'"*

LAMONT DOZIER TO SEAN EGAN ON WRITING THE SUPREMES HIT

25 Become a new person . . . or a little bit of a new person

Bruce Springsteen once said that a new song requires a new idea, and a new idea comes from being a new person. Not a *wholly* new person, but a person with new psychological growth.

26 Write with members of your band, using a random strategy

> *'Hallucinating Pluto' came out of this game we sometimes play when we're writing. It's called Exquisite Corpse—the Surrealists invented it, I think. They'd do it with a drawing: one person would draw a head, then they'd fold the paper, and the next person would then draw in a torso. We do that with our lyrics. Everyone writes three or four lines . . . it leads you to a place you wouldn't normally go."*

KEITH STRICKLAND OF THE B52'S TO *MOJO*

27 Read the lyrics, and listen to the music, of the pre–rock 'n' roll era

That was a time when the craft and purpose of lyrics was perceived differently. Or go outside the Anglo-American tradition to songs from other countries.

> *I was listening to Noel Coward last night—incredible, incredible craft, incredible wit, incredible social commentary with humor. Stylistically, the language is a bit more formal than certainly this generation would understand. But beautiful and correct, and internal rhyme, and so much skill and so much to say without being heavy."*

JONI MITCHELL TO *MOJO*, AUGUST 1998

> *In the past . . . there was more talent and there was more intelligence when it came to writing a lyric. There was more depth of feeling . . . [the present] generation was brought up on TV. They didn't read as much as our generation did."*

BARRY MANN TO SEAN EGAN

28 Find someone to write with

Lyrically, it doesn't come as naturally as the music. When you do an album it's 12 sets of lyrics and it's quite intense, so I enjoy writing things with other people to see what they bring out in me."

IAN BRODIE OF THE LIGHTNING SEEDS TO *MELODY MAKER*

As far as my songwriting is concerned, I believed in working with anyone who had something to offer and although I had some regular writing partners like Mike Valvano and Morris Broadnax, I'd work with virtually anyone."

MOTOWN PRODUCER CLARENCE PAUL TO THE *YTF* NEWSLETTER

29 Write a group of lyrics around a theme, story, or concept

The older I get, the more sense it makes to write several songs about the same subject, and the LP [Stevie Wonder's The Secret Life of Plants] taught me that a good title is an important launch pad for any project . . . I just don't think there's the space sometimes to deal with the whole of a subject in a single song."

PADDY MCALOON OF PREFAB SPROUT TO *MOJO*, MAY 1997

I didn't want this to be the type of double album that's about randomness. I almost felt like I had to be more rigorous in a way, so that the themes and the songwriting pointed in the same direction."

EZRA KOENIG OF VAMPIRE WEEKEND TO *PITCHFORK* ON THE BAND'S 2019 ALBUM *FATHER OF THE BRIDE*

30 Write more than you need—perhaps in prose—and then edit it down

If there are four verses in a song, I'll write 24 verses, then almost line by line I'll go them and cross them out: that's too clever, that's too stupid, that's too arch, that's too cute . . . and then with the detritus I'm left with I put a song together— which might lead to things that are disjointed, unclear, or whatever, but which would be, if not illuminative of a condition, expressive of it."

GREEN GARTSIDE OF SCRITTI POLITTI TO *MELODY MAKER*

from sketch to final draft

> " *Don't let the critic become bigger than the creator. Don't let it strangle you. Go ahead and say, 'I saw this girl / She was the best girl in the world.' Let it go. Put a string of stuff together. Go ahead.*"
>
> **RANDY NEWMAN TO *THE WORD*, 2008**

After you've started a lyric, the next stage is to shape, clarify, strengthen, and finally polish the words until you have something that is coherent and self-sufficient and will fit your music.

Silence the perfectionist within

If you want to write and don't feel inspired, recognize there is an outer and an inner aspect to the initial difficulty. The outer aspect is the inertia that blank paper or a blank screen embodies. The inner aspect is the perfectionist voice most of us have in our heads. This is the internalized critic who, in Newman's words quoted above, must not be allowed to become greater than the creator. In an interview with Beats 1 about her songwriting, Lorde revealed, "As a young songwriter, I would put a lot of pressure on myself. I'd write a line and then aggressively backspace . . . I would just censor myself so heavily. I felt like there wasn't room for me to write a bad song or write something that didn't necessarily fit with my vibe or whatever."

In my experience, the worst scenario is to have to write a lyric on a particular theme (for instance, if writing on commission, or for a story). Your inner critic will provide a stream of unhelpful comments, along the lines of "that's stupid," "that's been done before," "that's not very interesting," "you'll never find a rhyme for that," "it's not as good as the one you wrote last week/month/year," (and last but not least) "that's not perfect." But there is a simple phrase that will stop that inner voice interfering with your creativity: *Shut up, I'm not done yet.* You write a cliché—so what? *Shut up, I'm not done yet.*

Here are some tips to keep self-censorship at bay:

- Never sit chewing your pencil, consciously rejecting anything that falls short of what you think is sheer brilliance.
- Don't reject the first line that comes—write it down and keep going.
- Don't reject ideas and phrases as "not good enough" or "done before" until you have written a page or so.
- If necessary, write anything to get going. You may write a couple of pages before anything good forms. Eventually it will.
- Don't set a rhyme pattern too early in the draft, but if rhymes occur naturally, leave them in.
- Don't let the search for a rhyme hold up the initial flow of thoughts and images.

To summarize: when you sketch a lyric, just write. Clichés can be cut later. The sketch process is like panning for gold. Few prospectors ever waded into shallow water and immediately picked up gold. You may have to sift a certain amount of mud to get the couple of gold nuggets that will be the basis of a good lyric. Don't worry about the mud.

> *I'll start at about midnight and go through until about seven in the morning, writing sheet after sheet, and when I look at it it's garbage ... my ego is constantly getting crushed, you know? 'Eight hours, no sleep and that's the best I can come up with?' ... But a day or two later, at some point it'll happen. I could be chopping carrots and, bang, there's a line—and I stop what I'm doing and start writing and it all just flows out."*
>
> **MAXI JAZZ OF FAITHLESS TO *MELODY MAKER***

> *Hitsville had an atmosphere that allowed people to experiment creatively and gave them the courage not to be afraid to make mistakes. In fact, I sometimes encouraged mistakes. Everything starts as an idea and as far as I was concerned there were no stupid ones. 'Stupid' ideas are what created the lightbulb, airplanes and the like."*
>
> **BERRY GORDY TO *PLAYBOY* ON THE MOOD AT HIS**
> **MOTOWN RECORD LABEL IN ITS 1960S HEYDAY**

Unforeseen gifts: the virtues of spontaneity

Sometimes a frustrating writing session, from which it seems that nothing good has materialized, is the prelude to a later breakthrough. Creativity is about experimenting, thinking laterally, being spontaneous. Much can spring from a momentary, off-the-cuff action.

Of the writing of their international hit "I'm Too Sexy," Richard Fairbrass of Right Said Fred remembered:

> We took a tea break, and the computer was playing this loop round and round, and right out of the blue—I can't tell you where it came from—I started singing, "I'm too sexy for my shirt" and we all fell about laughing. Fred . . . didn't think we should be frivolous. He thought we should crank on and do our serious music. So, Rob [Manzoli] and I convinced Fred [Fairbrass] after three or four days that we should pursue it. And I couldn't get that top line out of my head.

Before it was called "I'm Too Sexy," the song was called "Heaven," and its theme was a serious one: looking forward to the afterlife and leaving behind of the problems of the here and now.

Kings of Leon's hit "Sex on Fire" has a similar backstory. Nathan Followill told an Australian radio station, "It was actually going to be 'Set Us on Fire,' but one of the sound mixers in the studio walked in as we were playing and said, 'Sex on Fire,' huh?" and it just kind of became a running joke and we stuck with it."

Cut-ups

A cut-up is a method for generating a sketch if you can't initially write one yourself. It won't *create* a lyric for you, but it can act as a stimulus. It provides raw material to refashion as the dripping of paint on a canvas might for an artist. As an avant-garde literary technique, it was pioneered by William Burroughs, and is related to the art technique of montage.

There was a vogue for "indeterminacy" technique in the arts in the 1960s, because it was (questionably) felt to have an authenticity that conscious intention lacked. The most famous cut-up lyric in rock is probably David Bowie's "Moonage Daydream," with its squawking pink monkey bird.

This is how cut-ups work:

- Choose two or three pieces of writing: your own discarded lyrics or poems, prose from a novel or short story, nonfiction prose, advertising copy, newspaper articles.
- Copy the words onto paper, so you can cut them into individual phrases.
- Put them in a box, shake it around, and pull them out one by one, arranging them into phrases.

The results will be peculiar, funny, startling, silly, nonsensical, and evocative juxtapositions of words, which constitute a sketch. You can then turn them into grammatical phrases in the first draft.

A productive cut-up provides some imaginative phrases and possibly a theme. A more refined approach would be to choose texts that were thematically related, like three famous poems on political freedom, or growing roses. You might experiment with texts written in different eras; simply even out any discrepancies of language in the final draft, such as archaic or obscure words.

Tools of the trade

Writing lyrics hardly requires the technology of audio recording, but there are a few tools of the trade, and finding which work best for you matters. Consider the materials for capturing your sketch. Songwriters often say that, for them personally, there is a world of difference between lined or unlined paper, narrow or wide feint, margin or unmargined, loose-leaf, spiral-bound, large or small, blue ink, black ink, hard pencil, soft pencil, and so on. Everyone has a preference.

I find there's something easeful and "organic" about writing sketches and drafts on paper with a soft, sharp pencil rather than ink. As for paper size and rule, narrow, feint paper keeps more lines in front of you at a time, especially if it's letter-sized, though that won't fit in a jacket pocket (a smaller notebook might).

I tend not to write on a computer screen until I'm nearly finished, when the typescript confers a dispassionate perspective that assists polishing the lyric. Perhaps a word processor encourages the wrong part of the brain at the beginning. When reaching for inspiration, you need to look inward, into your imagination, not outward at a screen.

If you can write melody in conventional music notation, a book with lines on one side and music staves on the other, such as Janis Ian used, is handy. Blank guitar chord boxes on one side of a notebook are useful, so you can write the chords down for the song (crucial with altered tunings, where the shapes are not conventional). I also find in drafting that I write out the lyric from start to finish *each time* I redraft, including lines I'm not changing, because it keeps the conscious mind occupied with the mechanical business of copying what's already there, so new ideas can pop up from the unconscious to fill in blanks or improve phrases.

If during a later draft you need to reconsider a single word or phrase, because it isn't what you want to say, the best tool of the trade is a thesaurus. This is a reference book that gives equivalent or closely related words (known as synonyms) from which to select one that is a better fit.

When sorting out rhymes, you will find a rhyming dictionary extremely helpful. You can even use it to provide a group of effective rhymes before you start writing. Exact meanings of words can be checked in a decent dictionary, while books of quotations and proverbs are good sources for finding common phrases. In each case, the book in question now has equivalent internet website proving the same information.

> *A computer is only of use to me to type a final legible draft . . . I find that, despite the variety of fonts available, the ordered appearance of the computer screen kills the rhythm of the written word. Sometimes the page needs to be tiny and crumpled. Sometimes it must be vast and pristine."*
>
> **ELVIS COSTELLO TO *THE WORD*, FEBRUARY 2005**

> *I like to write on notebooks. I generally use the computer a little later on, to move verses around."*
>
> **LEONARD COHEN TO *MOJO*, NOVEMBER 1997**

> *I love reference books that help me with words, dictionaries of slang, superstition, phrase and fable, the Book of Knowledge, things that help me find words that have a musicality to them."*
>
> **TOM WAITS TO *PLAYBOY*, MARCH 1998**

Writing a sketch (the "spell state")

When writing a sketch, keep going until you get tired, your attention breaks, or you run out of lines. During this phase of the process, it often feels like a spell has been cast over you. Stay in it as long as possible. This feeling indicates that unconscious and intuitive parts of the mind are in play. In the "spell state," you lose awareness of time and surroundings; concentration develops and deepens.

One of the rewards of any creativity, this state gives a sense of returning to your center, a curious power, a potent balance, such as exhibited by a tightrope walker. Poets and writers often describe it as being possessed by a greater energy. In this state, if ideas go in an unexpected direction, let them. It could be that your sketch will result in two or three sketches, rather than one. Make that decision later.

If you already have a tune or a chord progression, playing this over, or in your mind, or listening to an instrumental recording, can help bring ideas forward and keep you in the spell state.

 I usually start with a conversational line and don't stop till I get to the end. I don't worry about whether it's any good or makes sense. Then I review it all."

CHRIS DIFFORD OF SQUEEZE TO *THE WORD*

A first look

When the spell state fades, like a glider drifting in to land, stop, take a break, make a drink, then glance over your scribbles. What have you got to work on?

- Notice lines that stand alone, and others that connect for four, five, or six lines at a stretch—enough to make a verse. Does this point to how long the verses will be?
- Look for lines that could fit together.
- Look for potential patterns of phrase. These could determine the structure of the lyric. (An obvious example is a list lyric.)
- Some single lines will suggest ways in which they could be developed.
- What theme, story, or mood is emerging? If there's more than one, discard either the less interesting of them or the one for which there are fewer lines. It might provide the bridge of the song, where a contrast is needed.
- Scan the sketch for a memorable phrase or image that could be the song's

title, and therefore shape the chorus. This phrase may sum up what the song is about.

- Where will the song start and end? Sufjan Stevens has said, "Within songs you want to create scenes, establish setting, and develop the narrative around conflict." Look for what might be a memorable first line, though this can be developed later—first decide where the lyric is going to begin, in terms of content. If the song is a story, where does the story begin? Take the first line you have and then rework it to make it striking in a later draft.
- See if you can decide whether this lyric will have a rhyme scheme and, if so, what kind. It is a good idea to bring rhyme in as early as you can if you're going to have it. Trying to turn a later, unrhymed draft into a rhymed lyric can be difficult, and may produce a stilted effect.

After the sketch comes the first draft.

The first draft

Drafting is the process of rewriting a lyric sketch to shape, clarify, and finally polish it. The first draft is when you begin to edit and select from the rough material, laying out an initial structure that starts the lyric through the remaining drafts. This structure may be subject to further change later on.

I don't call the sketch the first draft, because the sketch is a different process, driven by inspiration, not by selective editing of something now written. With the first draft, you continue the inspiration of the sketch but go on to supplement, rephrase, and eliminate. This is also a creative process, and it should be conducted in as inspired a frame of mind as you can, so that new ideas can feed in.

It is desirable to write the first draft as soon as possible after the sketch. That way, you stay in touch with the first inspiration. It is a good idea to write as many drafts in one sitting as are needed, to get the basic content and form of the lyric. Precise corrections and polishing can wait for another day, because by then the fundamentals are in place. If the inspiration is there, your first sketch may be coherent enough to be a first draft in itself.

To avoid unhelpful and possibly destructive self-censorship, reserve judgment about your sketch. Don't be too critical, and don't agonize over single words. Go for overall sequence, imagery, and basic theme. Scrutiny from your critical faculties should come in only with later drafts.

The time to agonize over a single noun, verb, or adjective is when the lyric has been through a number of drafts. More important is finding the central energy of the lyric, as this is the theme that people must connect to even if they don't understand it.

The central energy of a lyric is most often located in:

- a chorus
- a repeated refrain (if it doesn't have a chorus)
- a first line and/or a title
- a last line of the verse.

As an example of "central energy" in a lyric, think about the Beatles' "All You Need Is Love" (no doubting what *that* song is about) or the climax phrase/title in "Born to Run." Call to mind a few of your favorite songs and look for where this central energy is verbally expressed.

If the sketch won't yield anything coherent, no matter how you look at it, put it aside and write another one, launching from a different inspiration. If there's no more creative juice, leave it and do something else that benefits your music.

Keep your unused sketches. At a later date, halfway through another lyric, you might find lines that can be salvaged. Or, with the passage of time, you'll revisit a sketch and find a way to rework it.

> *I've found that for most of my songs, I write ten verses. I just write and write and write, trying to find the voice of the song. Because when you start with the music, you don't know what the song is about. You're waiting for something to tell you."*

CARL NEWMAN OF THE NEW PORNOGRAPHERS TO
***SONGWRITERS ON PROCESS*, FEBRUARY 2015**

> *I was walking around this little Danish town north of LA that was totally empty and listening to this instrumental ['Everything to Everyone'] on repeat. The music was so addictive. I opened up an email to myself and started writing. The original version [of 'Not in Kansas'] is about 10 minutes long and it's got 17 more stanzas."*

MATT BERNINGER OF THE NATIONAL TO *PITCHFORK*, MAY 2019

> *It's a discipline, like exercising. It's very difficult to get to the nub of what you want to say in three minutes when you want to say hundreds of things. You have to use an editorial system and say in two lines three pages' worth of ideas."*
>
> **RAY DAVIES OF THE KINKS TO *MOJO*, FEBRUARY 2005**

Further drafts

Continue drafting for as long as it takes to get a coherent lyric. If your initial sketch and draft provide a lot of material, there may need to be some drastic cutting. The original sketch of Jimi Hendrix's 1967 hit "Purple Haze" ran for pages and had to be boiled down to three verses and a bridge. After two or three drafts, you may need only to reconsider the odd word here and there. If you already have music for this lyric, check each draft against the music to see if the words fit or are singable.

When a draft is nearly a finished lyric, type it up on a computer. At this late stage you should strive for objectivity. Seeing the words in cold type on a screen (or printed), no longer in your own handwriting, depersonalizes them. This helps you to see the effectiveness of the lyric and what might need changing.

Finally, a cooling-off period is advised. Return to the lyric after a few days and see how it looks. You may find a problem can be fixed then that couldn't be solved before. If you go on to compose the music for this lyric, the music might dictate changes (such as the song having too many verses, or too many lines in the chorus). Not all songs can be or are composed and written in a short space of time.

A revision in action

Here's a short example of the thinking that can occur during revision from one draft to another. Consider this opening verse, from a song called "In the Dark of the Year":

> *Found myself alone with her in the dark of the year,*
> *Together by the fireside we talked and sipped our beer.*
> *"This house is haunted," she laughed with flashing eyes.*
> *A spell was cast, I didn't care if it was truth or lies.*
> *In a garden of moonlight, full moon in the trees,*
> *She moved like a shadow, but I was at my ease.*
> *Our recognition proved this is not fool's gold:*
> *When the sale came, our hearts were already sold.*

Notice the AABBCCDD rhyme scheme, which is a popular pattern. This verse has a reasonable first line—it gives us two characters, a time of day or season, and a title, and it sets off a story. However, there are problems with it. The first problem is "sipped our beer," which sounds artificial—it's there for the rhyme. The first line has to be as it is, because "year" is part of the title, so it's line 2 that needs to change. Another blemish is line 5 having two references to the moon, one of which is redundant. The second is better because it is more visual. The "but" in line 6 is good because it is unexpected. But lines 7 and 8 are also problematic—first because of the jump to present tense, and second because of an unprepared metaphor of a "sale." What is this sale? It looks like it is only there to set up the rhyme of "sold" with "gold."

Here's a revised version of the same verse. It isn't great, but it's serviceable:

> *Found myself alone with her in the dark of the year,*
> *Together by the fireside we talked as we drew near.*
> *"This house is haunted," she laughed, and flashing eyes*
> *Cast a spell, I didn't care if it was truth or lies.*
> *In a garden of midnight, full moon in the trees,*
> *She moved like a shadow, but I was at my ease.*
> *The things we didn't say were like breath in the cold:*
> *Looking for a treasure that wouldn't prove fool's gold.*

A final polish

The 19th-century historian Thomas Carlyle once described genius as "the infinite capacity for taking pains." What seems like pure inspiration is often be the result of hard work. Even at a late stage, what looks like a finished lyric could be improved further. Here's Alex Turner of the Arctic Monkeys, speaking to *New York Magazine* in 2018: "I would keep adding or changing words forever if somebody didn't stop me, and that only seems to be getting worse as time goes on. I trust our producer, James Ford, to tell me when I'm not making things better anymore. In the studio, I do like to work on lyrics right up until the last possible minute."

Since some people think lyrics don't matter, or that audiences don't listen to them, this might be considered an artistic ambition beyond what is necessary. The controversy over Bruce Springsteen's 1980s anthem "Born in the USA" (was it anti-American, gung-ho patriotism, or both at once?) is a cautionary note about how a lyric can be misinterpreted. Springsteen always said that the song was not ambiguous: it only required people to listen to the verses as well as the chorus.

As a songwriter who has followed popular music for decades and surveyed internet discussions of songs and their lyrics, I can assure you that if there is a way for your audience to interpret your lyric away from what you meant—even to the point of concluding it is saying the opposite of what you thought—they will. All you can do is conduct a damage-limitation exercise and close off a few avenues of potential misunderstanding.

The last revising touch could be a significant change, such as altering the hook line and title. Thin Lizzy's hard-rock track "The Boys Are Back in Town" was originally called "GI Joe Is Back in Town," but bassist and singer Phil Lynott changed it because it didn't sound right. The change was significant, because it meant the song was no longer about a character but could now be interpreted as being about the band itself. It could simply be changing a "but" to a "yet."

 I worked for two or three nights just to find one line that was right. There were so many alternatives but only a few were right for the song."

KATE BUSH TO THE *KBC* NEWSLETTER ON "HOUDINI"

Time to stop

Conversely, there is also artistic judgment in knowing when to *stop* revising. Over-refine, or attempt too much ingenuity, and you could lose the freshness of a lyric's earlier drafts. Sometimes, the fault in a lyric lies too deep to change without starting again, like a human hair trapped in the glaze on a pot. Superficial changes can't always alter such a blemish.

A related skill is the ability to see that an idea is not worth pursuing. This takes experience. Songwriters have different views on the question of spontaneity versus craftsmanship. Pete Waterman believed, "The best art is always naïve. If I find myself working for a long time on an idea, I abandon it."

Sometimes it is a matter of self-awareness—knowing that you are too tired, distracted, or disinclined, to sketch or redraft. As Madonna once said, "When that happens, you have to stop and go out or something. Go to a movie . . . there are times when you just have to let it alone. And go get some inspiration. Ultimately, you can't force it. But there is a certain amount of discipline required."

From sketch to final draft

"White as Alaska" is a rock song that initiated an album unified by imagery and metaphors drawn from the Cold War to give a melodramatic treatment to themes of a failed love affair. Just as a song can have a primary metaphor that unifies the lyric—rich enough in itself to generate many lines, ideas, feelings, and scenarios—so an album of songs might be unified in a similar way. The choice of such a "global" metaphor depends on your own interests and connections between them, and also the style of music. In the lyric, Alaska is a geographical symbol but also at a certain moment in history full of drama and conflict. The sketch shows an initial list of images of Cold War confrontation.

Sketch: "White as Alaska"

Cold and white as Alaska

A climate of suspicion and fear

I've got my missiles pointed at you

But you won't know they've no warheads[1]

We laid waste to a continent[2]

And innocence was gone

And now beneath each winter sea

We cruise the depths alone[3]

Who was it cut the hotline, who killed

I get no such number on the red telephone

The years roll by and so I live on

In a climate of suspicion and fear

[1] The first indication that the imagery is hostile on the surface, but underneath the emotion is more to do with love.

[2] The continent is an image for a relationship that is in some way destroyed.

[3] The word "depths" here suggests submarine patrols.

Draft 1: "White as Alaska"

Chorus

Cold and white, cold and white as Alaska[1]

The people that we were are exiled far below[2]

Through the dark blue keep a vigil through the

  deep[3]

Love that's radioactive you can still detect today[4]

The crackle of uncertainty: half-life, half-love,

  half-way.[5]

They'll let you in at the border, let you cross the

  line[6]

No-one now will recognize the photo from that

  time

The papers are all in order, the code is sleeping

  dogs lie[7]

The heart has a capital welcome for such a

  beautiful spy[8]

And when I dial that number

No-one lifts the receiver[9]

Don't believe the cables—in public I'm a deceiver[10]

Yet when I dial that number no-one lifts the

  receiver[11]

1 Alaska is a symbol of a wild, northern, cold territory, and also a place of proximity between two countries.

2 The relationship is in the past: the ex-lovers and their old selves.

3 "Dark blue" is the ocean and thus submarines.

4 "Radioactive" is one of a number of nuclear references. It implies a situation still infected by love.

5 Wordplay on the meaning of radioactive "half-life."

6 The image of a "border" fits a lyric that has a geographical metaphor as its base.

7 "Let sleeping dogs lie" is a proverb: don't stir up things that could cause trouble.

8 The word "capital" here has a double meaning. The imagery in these lines suggests the world of espionage.

9 A potential rhyme is noted.

10 These were attempts to explore the "hotline" image for relations between the ex-lovers.

11 At this stage, there is a single line for the chorus, but otherwise the lines do not connect, except at the vague level of imagery. The lyric as yet has no shape, no stanza form, no narrative. This changes in the second draft.

Draft 2: "White as Alaska"

Chorus

Cold and white, cold and white as Alaska[1]

I've got my missiles fixed—pointed at you[2]

The vigil is still kept—down in cold blue

The people that we were—exiled far below

Radioactive love—crackles yet[3]

Half-life, half-love, half-way—everyday

They will let you in—at the border[4]

Let you cross the line—from that time

No-one will know—those lovely eyes

The password: sleeping dogs lie

For such a beautiful spy[5]

White between you and I[6]

Give the heart as bait—in the climate

Of suspicion and fear—I'd have you near[7]

A wasted continent—whose intent?[8]

Against love these crimes, who cut the line?

Still I dial the number—no receiver[9]

1. Note the repetition, as this is set off as a hook line.

2. An attempt at shortening the lines, balancing them, and grouping into threes (tercets).

3. This stanza of five lines carries forward several lines but revises and compresses them.

4. Being "let in" at the border suggests the speaker's hope of a reconciliation.

5. The absent ex-lover is cast in the role of the spy.

6. A snow image.

7. Another line with an internal rhyme.

8. More compression and rhyming of earlier ideas. Importantly, these lines have a distinct rhythm. Once this rhythm appears, it can shape future lines in the drafts.

9. This line is still not working, and the reference to calling a number gets dropped.

1 The stanzas settle down into quatrains with an internal rhyme.

2 The verb "decays" enriches this line.

3 "Old" replaces the earlier "no." The meaning is an outdated guardedness.

4 This line is a variation of the last line of verse 1. A winter sky suggests a bleak view.

5 In this stanza, "close so dear," "love," "lovely," and "cry" all indicate the tragedy of the situation is that underneath the feelings are still warm. The wall (as in Berlin) is declared to be "absurd."

6 This is a powerful image of reconciliation.

7 Notice the near repetition of these lines, which gives the stanza additional musical drama. If the sleeping dogs still cry, they are not quite as asleep as they appear.

The final stanza provided titles for two more songs on the album: "A Kiss in Berlin" and "My Lovely Spy."

Final draft: "White as Alaska"

Verse 1

Wasted continent not my intent,[1]

Innocent of crime—who cut the hotline?

Old suspicion and fear lingers ever near,

Such a winter sky freezes you and I.

Chorus

Cold and white, cold and white as Alaska.

Verse 2

Radioactive yet, a nuclear debt.

Half-love decays, half-life, half-way.[2]

Missiles are armed with old warheads,[3]

Such a winter sky above you and I.[4]

Verse 3

Smuggle close so dear at the frontier,[5]

Love will let you in, a kiss in Berlin.[6]

This wall is absurd, here's the password:

"Sleeping dogs still lie," my lovely spy,

Sleeping dogs still cry between you and I.[7]

" *[W. H.] Auden used to say: the poem is never finished, it's abandoned. At a certain point you've done all you can to bring it into existence and if you go a little further you start ruining it so you pull back.*"

LEONARD COHEN TO *MOJO*, NOVEMBER 2001

" *There's a song I really wanted to put on this record [I'm Alive] called 'Alive in the World.' It's really good. But there's this one moment, this one line, and it's the kind of line that can be shouted out over the battlements, that can be inscribed on something permanently, that's got to actually stand, like an emblem—and I don't know what the line is. It's the kind of line that you can't just throw off. So I couldn't finish the song.*"

JACKSON BROWNE TO Q, DECEMBER 1993

Rewriting an old lyric

The skills you develop getting from a sketch to a draft, and then from a first or second draft to a final version, can be applied to rescuing older lyrics. It is a common perception among songwriters that lyrics date faster than the music. If you have written songs for any length of time, it is normal to find your earlier lyrics feeble, immature, and/or incoherent, or that you have changed your mind about the topic. That young woman or man you met at that party who intoxicated you for a month and half a dozen songs of rapture, then turned out to have feet of clay and a capacity for giving you grief. Now you can't stand those lyrics, but you still like the music.

Of course, since your audience won't know how things turned out, they may be happy to hear those rapturous love songs with their original words. How things turned out doesn't matter to them; what they hear are songs of being in love. This is a first lesson in the artistic justification of insincerity. However, if there was something false, or inauthentic, or self-deceiving, in the emotion from which the song came, then that may have rubbed off on the lyrics. In which case (and not because things didn't turn out the way you hoped) it might be time for a salvage operation. Rather than scrap the song, go back and rescue the lyric. This, after all, is the age of recycling.

Sometimes it is a matter of adjusting a few words and phrases but retaining the overall content. But at its most thorough, rescuing a song from a bad or immature lyric means throwing away the original words and writing new ones.

This is easier said than done, because you have to find new words, maybe a new theme, for music that will, initially, remind you of the old words. The process may even change the music itself.

Some odd things happen in this creative territory—the emotion from the old scrapped lyric can hang over into the new one, with no apparent sign of where it comes from. Sometimes the change is about adjusting the emotional balance in a lyric, being fairer to the subject, covering your tracks, or making things less personal or less obscure.

As an insight into revising and rewriting a lyric, you could search out John Lennon's revision of "Child of Nature" into "Jealous Guy," George Harrison's rejected stanza from "While My Guitar Gently Weeps," or the two versions of Bruce Springsteen's "Stolen Car." This haunting song was originally released on his double album *The River*, but the four-CD box set *Tracks* has an earlier version with a lyric twice as long. The website www.leonardcohen.com has original drafts of songs such as "Suzanne" and "Joan of Arc" in Cohen's own handwriting, and with all his crossings-out.

Rewriting in practice

Let's end this section with a recast lyric from my own archive. In this instance, a love lyric called "She Says She'll Never," which was inspired by a photograph and a spoken remark, is turned into a less personal song about Marilyn Monroe and an imagined alternate life. It shows how phrases, rhythms, rhymes, and stanza form can be carried over to a recasting but take on a new meaning. The music in both versions remained essentially the same.

"She Says She'll Never"

Spectral beauty reflected in the window[1]

In front of me I watch, I see her:

The folds of a dress, one foot

Tilted rakishly back on its heel.[2]

Small shoe, strong mind, some blues[3]

No one else, long time waiting;

Small hands, love-kind? Some chance![4]

She puts me in and out of focus.

The girl is reflected in the glass,

She must know I'm free of the past.

I've held her close in dream, held her in my sleep:

Red hair with mine, head on my shoulder.

The girl reflected in the glass

She says she'll never fall in love.[5]

Flesh and spirit to whom I'm bound

She stands behind me and I can't turn around.[6]

She says she'll never fall in love.[7]

1   The term "spectral" means like a ghost. The woman in the photo appears as a reflection. She has taken a photo of herself.

2   These are details seen in the photograph.

3   The chorus phrasing is highly compressed. The heel image leads to "small shoe." Her small stature contrasts with her "strong mind."

4   "Small hands" parallels the earlier shoe image. The speaker hopes for kindness but realizes this is unlikely.

5   Chorus 2 has a dramatic assertion—also the title—which, if true, means the speaker has no chance of winning her.

6   The moment has passed. Despite feeling linked to her, he cannot go back. This last line is repeated several times.

7   The coda repeats the title.

In the new version below, the imagery of a woman being photographed is reworked and made historical. Monroe has been the subject of many popular songs, most notable Elton John's "Candle in the Wind." Many of these songs focus on the end of her life. "Pacific Morning" imagines instead an alternative history for the actress in which she never becomes famous but lives a longer life as a private citizen. It was inspired by some of the photographs of Monroe by André de Dienes. (A matching song might be composed reflecting on the fate that took him all the way from Hungary to this meeting.)

"Pacific Morning"

Verse 1

Youthful beauty [reflected in] captured by the

    camera:[1]

In front of him you smile wild and sweet.[2]

Blown hair [orphan] auburn brown,

    without a golden name,[3]

California waves wash your feet.[4]

Chorus 1

Picture a life unknown to the world[5]

In green and quiet towns:

Such eyes, life's kind;

Only he puts you in and out of focus.[6]

Pacific morning.

1. The earlier version in brackets is replaced by the alliterative "captured" / "camera."

2. "In front of me" becomes "In front of him."

3. Early photos of Monroe show her with brown hair. Both "auburn" and "orphan" are apposite words.

4. The state is mentioned as the location of the photos by the Pacific.

5. The "picture" is an invitation to imagine this other life with no fame.

6. Only the photographer alters the focus, not any other persons or powers. Monroe is more free at this point to be herself.

Verse 2

Politicians and actors, all the motley crew . . .[1]

Here at least the future must wait its turn.[2]

This morning's laughter light within your eyes—

More lovely than the legend that will end it.[3]

Chorus 2

No dreams, silver screen, or reaching hands,[4]

No flashbulb fireworks.

Flesh and spirit will soon be bound[5]

The sea advances and you can't turn around,[6]

You can't turn around.

The sea advances and you don't turn around,

The sea advances dark with fame—a heavy

    crown[7]

And you can't turn around.

Pacific morning.

1 Looking forward to the life she will lead when famous. "Motley crew" is sarcastic and satirical.

2 But that is the future, not this Pacific moment caught in the photographs.

3 Celebrated as she later was, perhaps she is just as beautiful in these earlier times.

4 These things will happen, but not yet.

5 Fame will be a constraining force.

6 The sea represents the future and destiny, advancing all the time, which it seems she cannot escape.

7 Repetitions elaborate on the image and add meaning to it.

the magic of titles

> *The songs have titles that read like paperback novels."*
> **MELODY MAKER REVIEW OF PROCOL HARUM'S *A SALTY DOG*, JULY 1969**

> *I'm like anybody else with the title. I purely wrote whatever I got out of it. I didn't have any problems with thinking it was, like, gay men or anything. I just loved the meter, I just loved the shapes of the words."*
> **JIM CAPALDI OF TRAFFIC TO *MOJO* ON "THE LOW SPARK OF HIGH-HEELED BOYS"**

A strong title can do wonders for a song, whether providing its initial inspiration or summing up its theme and mood. It can even help you structure your writing.

For many songwriters, the initial spark for a lyric is a title. In my own songwriting, I've always reserved a page in each notebook for writing down titles. I thought this was a personal thing, but in researching this book, I have been impressed by how many songwriters also say they value titles, and therefore what a significant role the title takes in lyric writing.

Many writers use a title as the seed from which to develop a song lyric. The US band Fountains of Wayne wrote three songs for their debut album in 1995, and then spent a week in a New York bar making lists of titles to see if they could turn them into songs. There are very good reasons for valuing titles:

- Never underestimate the power of a good title. It can by itself inspire you to write a lyric. Keep a list of potential titles for songs.
- A title can stabilize the theme or mood of a song until you get around to writing the whole lyric and music.
- A title can inspire your listener. If you're writing a batch of songs for an album, imagine picking up the finished CD or vinyl and glancing at the titles. This is what people will do in a music store or surfing the web. A title may persuade someone to stream or download a song out of sheer curiosity.

- Titles are the first point of contact with your music for artist management and record companies when they see your demo. Before they've heard a note of music, they'll see the title. What effect will the titles have?
- Have your titles been used before? Led Zeppelin were not the first to title a song "Stairway to Heaven." Neil Sedaka released a single by that name in 1960. But, let's face it, no one else is going to write a better "Stairway to Heaven" than Led Zep's, so discretion suggests you leave that title (and others of a similar fame) alone.

You might, however, use a cheeky variation on a famous song, as in the case of "Somebody to Shove" instead of "Somebody to Love," or "Baby's in Smack" instead of "Baby's in Black."

- If they belonged to someone else's songs, would your titles make you curious to hear the music?
- Do your titles have individuality? Do they stir your imagination? Do they establish a certain tone or style? Consider "Baby I Want Your Love," "Another Day," "Sun Is Shining," or "Blue Sky." These and other similar titles have been used many times; they're not exactly inspiring. An unimaginative title may indicate unimaginative music.
- Be clever, be memorable, be relevant to your lyric.
- Unless you're writing a concept album, don't have too many similar titles on an album, and make sure two from the same mold don't follow each other in the sequencing. Roy Orbison's album *In Dreams* (1963) had "In Dreams," "Dreams," "All I Have to Do Is Dream," and "Beautiful Dreamer." Maybe that's too many "dream" titles for one album.

Having a good title early on when writing a lyric matters because *where* it comes in the lyric has a significant effect on the structure. A title may determine the first line, the last line of a verse, or the shape of the chorus. The strongest position for a title is in the chorus where it functions as the hook of the song. As such, it is likely to be sung quite a few times during the song and will stick in listeners' minds. At the beginning or end of the verse, or at the end of alternating lines it could function as a refrain.

Commenting on his lyric for "I Say a Little Prayer," Hal David noted that the title would ordinarily fall in the chorus, but he chose to put it in a "less obvious place," the middle of the verse.

A witty title that isn't very singable won't make a good chorus. Think about where in the lyric you want to put the title, or even if it is going to be there at all. "Desperado," "Eight Miles High," and "Everybody's Talkin' at Me" are three songs with the title as the first phrase of the lyric. If the title isn't anywhere in the song, listeners would have to remember the title not from the song performance but from the DJ saying afterward, "That was 'Amber Sunlight Days' by the Fire Department." The title is the label by which people remember your song. Make it catchy and it will lodge in their minds.

To illustrate the quote above about Procol Harum's titles, consider "Quite Rightly So," "She Wandered Through the Garden Fence," "Magdalene (My Regal Zonophone)," "Shine on Brightly," and "In Held 'Twas in I."

Choosing a title

The title should indicate what the song is about, its mood or emotion, or something about the central event or story. Occasionally, you may want to title a song by a phrase that isn't in the song itself but describes the theme. Otherwise, if the title isn't obvious, look through your lyric and either choose a phrase that would make a good title or think of one that encapsulates the song. The incompleteness of a title can itself be a deliberate hook.

Some song titles use brackets to add information, which means the song can be known by its long and short forms. You can develop a personal style of song title, as Bob Dylan did in the mid-1960s when he wrote "Queen Jane Approximately" and "Positively Fourth Street." These stand out because of the unusual choice placement of the adverbs "approximately" and "positively," which give the titles ambiguity and energy. "Queen Jane" and "Fourth Street" would be much less interesting!

Finally, try not to overamplify. This does for our sensibilities what sticking your head in a PA stack does for your ears. Take Curtis Lee's title "Pretty Little Angel Eyes." Okay, we get it—she's cute, and you like her a lot. Still, those eyes don't have to be pretty *and* little *and* angelic! Bruce Springsteen has sometimes been guilty of this, referring, for example, to "a pretty little girlie." "Girlie" is already a diminutive without adding "little."

Types of title

Here is a selection of *styles* of title. This is not an exhaustive catalogue, and some titles belong to more than one of the categories, but it provides valuable templates. Some of them you may already have used. These categories show you how to unpack the implications of a title, to understand how your own title ideas can set up a lyric. This assists the process of writing a sketch.

> *Marvin [Gaye] was a sex symbol from the start. That gave me the idea to encourage the writers to create 'You' type songs where he could sing directly to the women. 'YOU're a wonderful one'... 'YOU are my pride and joy.'... He even recorded a song just called 'You.'"*

> **BERRY GORDY**

Pronouns

These are titles that have "I," "you," "he," "she," "they," and "our" in them, often with the word "love" there, too. They are very popular, especially in mainstream songwriting. They immediately establish the presence of persons and invite us to identify with them. We can imagine we are being addressed, or that the singer is speaking for us to someone else we wish to address. These titles often reveal the dynamic in the relationship(s) in the song. The Motown song catalogue is full of them, and there are many in the early songs of the Beatles. Probably the most overused of these is "I Want You," a title used by Bob Dylan, Squeeze, Elvis Costello, Madonna, the Beatles, Basement Jaxx, Marvin Gaye, Kings of Leon, Mitski, Savage Garden, Bon Jovi, Marian Hill, and many more.

» Here are some examples from Motown songs: "I Was Made to Love Her," "I Know I'm Losing You," "You Keep Me Hanging On," "I Heard It Through the Grapevine," "How Sweet It Is to Be Loved by You," "It's Wonderful (to Be Loved by You)." And from the Beatles: "She Loves You," "I Want to Hold Your Hand," "And I Love Her," "From Me to You," "I Saw Her Standing There," "You've Got to Hide Your Love Away," "You Won't See Me," "I Want to Tell You."

Personal statement

A variation on the pronoun title is where it makes a specific statement about the speaker, the "I." This sets up the lyric as an explanation of this initial statement and its consequences. Consider a title like "I'm Gonna Make You Love Me." It prepares us for a lyric explaining *why* the speaker has to *make* the other person love him or her, how they intend to do it, what they hope will happen, and so on.

» *The Beatles, "I Feel Fine," "I Call Your Name," "I Am the Walrus," "I Need You," "I'm Down," "I've Got a Feeling"; George Harrison, "If Not for You"; Bob Dylan, "It Ain't Me Babe"; the Who "I Can See for Miles"; the Monkees, "I'm a Believer"; David Bowie, "John, I'm Only Dancing"; Kaiser Chiefs, "Everyday I Love You Less and Less"; Jason Mraz, "I'm Yours."*

Conditional

A conditional song title adds a word or phrase which makes the statement depend on something else—a piece of information, an event, a cause or a fear. These titles exploit words like "if," "can," "can't," "don't," "just," "when," "then," "after," "ain't," "be," "because," "from," "here," "how," "keep," "let." They make the title dynamic because it functions like half of an equation, with the other half implied or stated in the lyric. Chicago's "If You Leave Me Now" sets up an expectation of finding out the consequence posited by the title. Bruce Springsteen's "Out in the Street" could have been titled (after its chorus) "*When I'm* Out in the Street," which has a different emphasis.

» *The Beatles, "When I Get Home," "If I Fell"; Trini Lopez, "If I Had a Hammer"; Tim Hardin, "If I Were a Carpenter"; the Jimi Hendrix Experience, "If 6 Was 9"; Harold Melvin and the Blue Notes, "If You Don't Know Me by Now"; Elvis Presley, "I Just Can't Help Believing"; the Temptations, "Just My Imagination"; Patti Smith, "Because the Night"; Percy Sledge, "When a Man Loves a Woman"; Fleetwood Mac, "Don't Stop"; Beyoncé, "If I Were a Boy"; Arctic Monkeys, "When the Sun Goes Down"; Kelly Clarkson, "Because of You."*

Titles with verbs

Since verbs denote action, they give a title energy. This covers very general verbs like "come," "get," "give," "hold," and well as verbs like "run," as in Bryan Adams's "Run to You." In titles such as these, the speaker, or another character, is doing something. The lyric can develop from this action, its cause, its quality and consequence.

» *The Beatles, "Ask Me Why," "Carry That Weight," "Drive My Car," "Fixing a Hole"; the Supremes, "Come See About Me"; Billy Ocean, "Get Out of My Dreams, Get into My Car"; Spencer Davis Group, "Keep on Running"; Snow Patrol, "Run"; HAIM, "Don't Save Me"; Tame Impala, "Breathe Deeper."*

Descriptive

Some titles are plain descriptions. They might be the name of a person, place, time, or an event. They are apt not to be as dynamic as other titles, though they are usually clear in meaning. To make a title dynamic, or give a hint as to the theme, add a word that suggests a mood, action or event. The Beatles didn't write a song called "Strawberry Fields," it was "Strawberry Fields *Forever*." That "forever" is a glimpse of the speaker's feelings toward the place. A traditional descriptive title might have the word "ballad" in it, as in "The Ballad of John and Yoko," to signify a lyric that tells a story.

» *The Beatles, "Birthday" (time), "Christmas Time (Is Here Again)" (time), "Penny Lane" (place); the Small Faces, "Itchycoo Park" (place); the Kinks, "Waterloo Sunset" (time and place); Crosby, Stills, Nash, and Young, "Marrakesh Express" (journey and place); the Bee Gees, "New York Mining Disaster 1941" (place, event, and time); Ocean Colour Scene, "The Day We Caught the Train" (event and time); the 1975, "The Birthday Party" (event and time).*

Opposites

One potent form of title is that which embodies some kind of opposition. Such a title indicates the lyric may be about conflict, and the struggle to bridge the tension between the terms. Pushed far enough, this can lead to outright paradox rather than simple contrast (see below).

» *The Beach Boys, "Heroes and Villains"; Free, "Fire and Water"; James Taylor, "Fire and Rain"; the Faces, "Glad and Sorry"; Paul McCartney and Stevie Wonder, "Ebony and Ivory"; Joni Mitchell, "Shadows and Light"; the Corrs, "Love Gives Love Takes"; the Beatles, "Hello Goodbye," "Within You, Without You"; Johnny Cash, "I Forgot to Remember to Forget"; U2, "With or Without You."*

Propositions

A proposition title is one which sets out an idea, rather than an action or feeling. Such titles are often versions of proverbs, or catchphrases that express current opinion. They may be offered as a corrective or as a consolation.

Although the use of "you" in these suggests a speaker introducing the idea to an audience, the song might also be addressed to the self. The lyric should explain the proposition and why it is important to the speaker, usually describing an experience which led to its adoption.

» *The White Stripes, "I Think I Smell a Rat"; Adele, "Turning Tables," "Right as Rain"; Queens of the Stone Age, "Go With the Flow"; the Hives, "Hate to Say I Told You So"; the National, "The System Only Dreams in Total Darkness"; the Doors, "People Are Strange"; the Yardbirds, "You Can't Judge a Book by the Cover"; the Rolling Stones, "You Can't Always Get What You Want"; Mary Wells, "Let Your Conscience Be Your Guide"; Marvin Gaye and Tammi Terrell, "You Ain't Living Until You're Loving"; the Temptations, "Everybody Needs Love"; Smokey Robinson and the Miracles, "I Don't Blame You at All"; the Korgis, "Everybody's Got to Learn Sometime"; the Beatles, "All You Need Is Love"; Gordon Lightfoot, "If You Could Read My Mind."*

Questions/interrogative form

A title can invite curiosity if it asks a question, makes a demand, or addresses someone. Such a question requires scene-setting and explanation from the lyric. In this sense, these titles are pregnant with narrative.

» *The Beatles, "Do You Want to Know a Secret?," "You Can't Do That"; Travis, "Why Does It Always Rain on Me?"; Buzzcocks, "Ever Fallen in Love (with Someone You Shouldn't've)"; the Clash, "Should I Stay or Should I Go?"; Dire Straits, "Where Do You Think You're Going?"; the Beach Boys, "Wouldn't It Be Nice"; Jeff Buckley, "Lover, You Should've Come Over"; the Moody Blues, "Go Now"; Jet, "Are You Gonna Be My Girl?"; Lenny Kravitz, "Are You Gonna Go My Way?"; Arctic Monkeys, "Do I Wanna Know"; Sam Smith, "How Do You Sleep?"*

Repetition

Many titles use repetition, which helps the title/hook lodge in people's minds. Repetition is verbal rhythm and therefore well-suited to a chorus; it can also emphasize a word. The commonest repetition in a title is where words are repeated twice or three times as in Abba's "Money Money Money" or "Gimme! Gimme! Gimme! (A Man After Midnight)." A pleasing variation is where a word is repeated in a modified form, as with Fleetwood Mac's "Dreamin' the Dream," Hole's "Softer, Softest," or Travis's "The Last Laugh of the Laughter."

» *Repetition by two: the Beatles, "Cry Baby Cry," "She Said, She Said"; the Monkees, "A Little Bit Me, a Little Bit You"; Bob Dylan, "Lay Lady Lay"; Bob Marley, "No Woman, No Cry"; Smashing Pumpkins, "Tonight, Tonight"; David Bowie, "Rebel Rebel"; the Undertones, "Really Really"; Genesis, "Follow Me, Follow You"; Abba, "Knowing Me, Knowing You"; the Youngbloods, "Darkness, Darkness"; the Strokes, "The End Is the End"; Black Eyed Peas, "Boom Boom Pow."*
» *Repetition by three: the Who, "Run Run Run"; the Hollies, "Stop Stop Stop"; the Damned, "Neat Neat Neat"; Wings, "Hi Hi Hi"; the Beatles, "Long Long Long"; Teenage Fanclub, "Dumb Dumb Dumb"; James Brown, "It's a Man's Man's Man's World"; Johnny Cash and Bobby Bland, "Cry Cry Cry"; the Beach Boys, "Fun Fun Fun"; Paul McCartney, "Say Say Say"; the White Stripes, "Take Take Take"; Destiny's Child, "Bills, Bills, Bills"; Lady Gaga, "Boys Boys Boys."*
» *Repetition by four or more: KC and the Sunshine Band, "(Shake Shake Shake) Shake Your Booty"; Abba, "I Do I Do I Do I Do I Do."*

Alliteration

Titles that repeat a word also feature alliteration. This is an effect of words starting with similar consonants. Alliteration is a linguistic device valued in poetry because it stresses the sounds of words, thus bringing them closer to the condition of music. In moderation this can be appropriate for a lyric.

» *Madonna, "Maluma Medellin"; Stone Roses, "Sugar Spun Sister"; k. d. lang, "Constant Craving"; the Who, "You Better You Bet," "Anyway, Anyhow, Anywhere"; Scott Walker, "Plastic Palace People"; 10,000 Maniacs, "Tension Makes a Tangle"; Jim Stafford, "Spiders and Snakes"; the Zombies, "Sticks and Rolling Stones"; Smokey Robinson and the Miracles, "Darling Dear"; Gene, "Sick, Sober and Sorry"; Van Morrison, "Slim Slow Slider"; AC/DC, "Dirty Deeds Done Dirt Cheap"; Heaven 17, "Penthouse and Pavement"; Donovan, "Sunshine Superman"; MIA, "Paper Planes"; Semisonic, "Secret Smile."*

Rhyming

Another way of making a title memorable is to include a rhyme. This was popular in 1950s rock 'n' roll songs.

» *The Beatles, "For You Blue," "Helter Skelter"; the Smiths, "Frankly Mr. Shankly"; Shorty Long, "Function at the Junction"; Bill Haley and the Comets, "See You Later Alligator," "Razzle Dazzle"; Iron Maiden, "Bring Your Daughter to the Slaughter"; Little Richard, "Good Golly Miss Molly," "Tutti Frutti"; Badfinger, "Name of the Game"; Marshall Crenshaw, "Someday, Someway"; Donovan, "Mellow Yellow"; the Pixies, "Indie Cindy"; Faith Hill, "This Kiss."*

Wordplay

Wordplay in a title takes many forms. Sometimes, a lyric generates inadvertent wordplay by virtue of the fact that different words share the same sound and can only be told apart when read, known as a homonym. Did the Moody Blues sing about *nights* or *knights* in white satin? Did the Hollies sing about someone gasoline alley *bred* or a foodstuff, gasoline alley *bread*? Why did Elvis want to return to Zenda? (Homonyms are a specific category of the larger phenomenon of the "mondegreen" where a lyric is misheard, often with hilarious results.)

Conscious wordplay in titles goes from puns, riddles, *non-sequiturs*, double meanings, incomplete phrases, and variations on catchphrases, all the way to outright paradox. Use it to tease your audience. Meat Loaf famously declaimed that he'd do *anything* for love, but he wouldn't do *that*. This enticed listeners to concentrate, to see if the lyric explained what "that" was. Fleet Foxes' "A Long Time Past the Past" uses "past" as a verb and then as a noun.

Here's Ezra Koenig of Vampire Weekend on "Step": "The chorus is just a series of little phrases: 'The gloves are off, the wisdom teeth are out.' That's a collage, two little cliched phrases stuck together that creates a feeling, maybe about ageing, maybe about a relationship to music. But it's a feeling that is bigger than its units."

The Beach Boys' *Pet Sounds* album cover brought out a double meaning in the word "pet," which could also mean "favorite," since the band are pictured feeding animals. Elvis Costello developed many early song lyrics by exploring double meanings, using phrases like "High Fidelity" and "Needle Time" from the world of recorded sound and applying them to relationships. Both Costello ("Love for Tender") and Louis XIV ("Illegal Tender") have played with the financial meaning of "tender." Here are examples of wordplay titles, taking paradox first. Some titles play on a famous other work, such as the Cramps' "The Creature from the Black Leather Lagoon."

Paradox

A paradox is a statement that links two ideas in a way that is logically contradictory. An example would be, "Those who would find their life must lose it." These titles may not all be strict paradoxes, but they provoke our curiosity by asking the question, "How can that be?" Look through the titles here and see if you grasp what the paradox is in each case. In some it is easy to see that there is a drama lurking behind the title, which explains the lyric theme.

» *Adele, "Set Fire to the Rain"; Simon and Garfunkel, "Sound of Silence"; Stereophonics, "Hurry Up and Wait"; the Strokes, "Alone, Together"; Fleetwood Mac, "Before the Beginning"; Frank Sinatra, "Glad to Be Unhappy"; Joy Division, "Love Will Tear Us Apart"; Vanessa Williams, "Colors of the Wind"; Laura Nyro, the Fifth Dimension, "Wedding Bell Blues"; David Byrne, "Tiny Apocalypse"; the Beautiful South, "I Love You But You're Boring"; the Kendalls, "Heaven's Just a Sin Away"; Smashing Pumpkins, "Bullet with Butterfly Wings"; Katy Perry, "Hot 'n' Cold."*

Ambiguity

These titles arouse our curiosity because they don't tell us all we need to know to make sense of them.

» *Undisputed Truth, "Smiling Faces Sometimes"; Love, "Seven and Seven Is," "Alone Again Or"; the Beatles, "Love You To," "And I Love Her," "And Your Bird Can Sing," "That Means a Lot"; Buffalo Springfield, "For What It's Worth"; the Wallflowers, "The Beautiful Side of Somewhere"; Third Eye Blind, "Semi-Charmed Life"; St Vincent, "Birth in Reverse."*

Wordplay with common phrases

Most of these work because the listener recognizes the title is playing with a well-known phrase. For example, Billy Ocean's "When the Going Gets Tough, the Tough Get Going" is a popular saying where the first "tough" is an adjective, but the second is a noun referring to a group of people; the first "going" is a noun describing a set of conditions, the second is a verb. Ocean didn't have to change anything; the wordplay was in the phrase to begin with.

» *The Beatles, "Eight Days a Week"; Stevie Wonder, "Yester-me, Yester-you, Yesterday"; Smokey Robinson and the Miracles, "I Second That Emotion"; Brian Eno, "Seven Deadly Finns"; Electric Prunes, "I Had Too Much to Dream (Last Night)," "Get Me to the World on Time"; Suede, "Animal Nitrate"; Def Leppard, "Armageddon It"; Robbie Williams, "Ego a Go Go"; Joan Armatrading, "Me Myself I"; the New Pornographers, "The Bleeding Heart Show"; Fall Out Boy, "The Kids Aren't Alright."*

Imagery

A title might also be based around an image. This could be visual (another example of a descriptive title) or a simile/metaphor, or it could have a symbolic meaning. It might take the entire lyric to explain what that is. The Motown hit "The Onion Song," credited to Marvin Gaye and Tammi Terrell, compares the world to an onion, whereas in the Beatles' "Glass Onion," the same image is a satire on misguided interpretations of their songs.

The image in a title can have its roots in the songwriter's desire to conceal the autobiographical roots of a song. Of "Norwegian Wood," John Lennon once told *Rolling Stone*, "I was trying to write about an affair without letting my wife know I was writing about an affair, so it was very gobbledygook. I was sort of writing from my experiences, girls' flats, things like that."

» *Cream, "Sunshine of Your Love"; the Supremes, "Up the Ladder to the Roof," "Reflections"; Martha Reeves and the Vandellas, "Live Wire"; the Drifters, "Up on the Roof"; Bob Dylan, "Tangled Up in Blue"; David Bowie, "Always Crashing in the Same Car"; Captain Beefheart, "A Carrot Is as Close as a Rabbit Gets to a Diamond"; Supergrass, "Sofa (of My Lethargy)"; the Marvelettes, "The Hunter Gets Captured by the Game"; Father John Misty, "Hangout at the Gallows"; the National, "Pink Rabbits"; Purple Mountains, "Snow Is Falling in Manhattan."*

Similes

Similes by their very nature are propositional. A simile in a title asserts that [x] is like [y], and the presumption is that the lyric will explain this. As the following titles show, one of the most popular terms to feature as [x] is "love." Songwriters have created many similes for love, and they will continue to do so.

» *Gene Vincent, "Love Is a Bird"; Martha Reeves and the Vandellas, "(Love Is Like a) Heat Wave"; Pat Benatar, "Love Is a Battlefield"; Magnetic Fields, "Love Is Like a Bottle of Gin"; Bob Dylan, "Like a Rolling Stone"; Neil Young, "Like a Hurricane"; the Verve, "Life's an Ocean"; the Supremes, "Happy (Is a Bumpy Road)"; Johnny Cash, "Dark as a Dungeon"; 10cc, "Life Is a Minestrone"; 10,000 Maniacs, "Like the Weather"; Coldplay, "Hurts Like Heaven."*

Slang

One direct method to signal your "hipness" to the audience is to use slang (as long as it's this year's slang—anything much older will sound outdated). This may win you brownie points with a sector of the market, but it risks alienating others or limiting the number of artists who would feel able to cover the song. Street slang dates quickly. As with bold haircuts, to be fashionable today is to be a hostage to posterity—but since popular songs are often seen as ephemeral, maybe this doesn't matter. Examples are deliberate misspelling ("-er" endings become "a," as in "flava") and substituting numbers and for words in text-message form ("R U Rite 4 Me").

» *Laura Nyro, "Stoned Soul Picnic"; Squeeze, "Cool for Cats"; Wayne Fontana, "Groovy Kind of Love"; T.Rex, "Life's a Gas"; James Brown, "Papa's Got a Brand New Bag"; Mel and Kim, "Uptown Top Rankin'"; the Beach Boys, "I'm Bugged at My Ol' Man"; the Prodigy, "Serial Thrilla"; Love, "Bummer in the Summer"; the Offspring, "Pretty Fly (for a White Guy)"; Extreme, "Get the Funk Out"; Smokey Robinson, "Baby That's Backatcha"; Gwen Stefani, "Hollaback Girl."*

The "no-title" title

Sometimes it seems songwriters can't think of what to call a song, and they don't find one before the recording deadline. The result is titles like this:

» *Elton John, "This Song Has No Title"; Robert Plant, "Mystery Title"; Status Quo, Bassnectar, "Mystery Song"; Heaven 17, "Song with No Name"; Blur, "Song #2"; Smashing Pumpkins, Eminem, Interpol, Rex Orange County, Simple Plan, and others, "Untitled"; Snob Scrilla, "The Song with No Title."*

Variations on "Strawberry Fields Forever"

To illustrate the effects of contrasting title styles, here is a set of variations on the title of the Beatles 1967 classic, to show how the same image could be presented in a variety of ways to match the categories described in the preceding pages.

» *"I Love Strawberry Fields" (pronoun); "Strawberry Fields" (descriptive name); "The Ballad of Strawberry Fields" (narrative); "Strawberry Fields Forever Fields of Strawberry" (inversion); "Funky Strawberry Fields" (buzz word); "Like a Strawberry Field" (simile); "Strawberry Fields of Uncertainty" (metaphor); "Strawberry Fields Possibly" (grammatical wordplay); "(Shall We Go to) Strawberry Fields?" (question); "Strawberry Fields and Stone Pavements" (opposites).*

The original title could be classified as a proposition, and it has alliteration.

Cliché

A cliché is an expression that no longer (to use a cliché) cuts the mustard. Once it was evocative, but no longer. Clichés are phrases that are like dead spots on an instrument: they lack resonance. But there are ways of rescuing a clichéd title. One is to take a word like "beautiful," which has occurred with positive associations in titles like "Beautiful Stranger/Dreamer/Losers" and join it to something unexpected, as in "Beautiful Screw-Up."

Here are some overused, maddeningly unimaginative song titles. If they ever meant anything, they don't anymore.

» *"Love Song"; "My Song"; "Song for You"; "This Song"; "Alone Tonight"; "Lonely Nights"; "Money"; "Fade Away"; "Baby Blue"; "Just Another Day"; "Time"; "Sea of Love"; "Love Is Here"; "Blue Sky"; "Behind the Lines"; "Together Forever"; "Shine On"; "Wind of Change."*

To test a song title, type it into a website like www.soundcloud.com and see how many results come up. I would suggest using them only if you're being funny or ironic. The track listing from hell would be any album that had more than a third of its tracks named with these titles. Do yourself a favor—avoid them and think of something fresher. Scan your lyric for a more memorable phrase.

In the internet era, the more individual a title, the fewer competing examples will come up on a search. Ideally, you want a song title that has been never or hardly used before. Then it will be easy to find when people search for it.

A track-list recipe

Cliché titles are so prevalent, there are many mainstream albums whose track listings can be partially predicted with this list. Given there might be 12 songs on an album, try finding a title featuring:

- a number
- a girl's name
- the name of a street
- the word "day"
- the word "rock"

- the word "lonely"
- the word "fire"
- the word "sky"
- "sunrise," "morning," or "sunset"

- "rain" or "sun"
- "heart" and/or "together"
- the word "fade."

This is apparent when browsing CDs from the mainstream rock/pop/soul areas. Music that belongs to a subgenre will have a different set of title styles, because subgenres in popular music are partly differentiated from the mainstream by lyric themes and images. Heavy-metal bands do not sing lyrics about loving their pet dogs; teenage pop stars do not sing songs about sacrificing goats.

Spot the genre

Genre-defining titles can be as predictable in their own way. To demonstrate the relationship between genres, titles, and themes, here is a quiz. Below are nine make-believe albums—see if you can guess the genre of each album from the titles alone. The genres are Motown/soul, US punk rock, indie rock, black metal, hard rock, folk, disco, UK punk rock, and blues.

» **ALBUM A** *"When I Was a Blacksmith"; "Sailor's Lament"; "The Miller's Daughter"; "By the Stream"; "Ballad of Rough Johnny"; "Herd My Cows"; "Rover's Song"; "Four Candle Inn"; "Highwayman"; "Bessie's Jig."*

» **ALBUM B** *"On the Road"; "Marauder Blues"; "Ambushed"; "Roll the Dice"; "Want Your Love"; "Rock the House"; "Sweet Jane"; "Motel Squeeze"; "I'm Gonna Love You All Night Long"; "Movin' On."*

» **ALBUM C** *"Get Down Tonite"; "Dance All Night"; "Party Party"; "Funky Hour"; "Mirrorball"; "Boogie Till You're on the Floor"; "Dance With Me"; "Strut Your Stuff"; "Go-getter"; "Shake Your Body."*

» **ALBUM D** *"Blitzville"; "Biology Lesson"; "I'm So Tired"; "Dabba-Rabba-Wabba"; "Glued to You"; "Broke a String, Robbed a Bank"; "Dumber Than the Rest"; "Starch Head"; "Stealin' Wheels"; "I Wanna Chew Gum."*

» **ALBUM E** *"Under the Flyover"; "I Hate the Thin Blue Line"; "There's No Union, Jack"; "Blowing Up the Palace"; "Soho Bondage"; "Bored, Bored, Bored"; "Couldn't Get a Witless"; "Adolf in Downing Street"; "Lewisham Rub-a-dub Dub"; "Mission Creep."*

» **ALBUM F** *"Annihilator"; "Torture Chamber"; "The Lonely Death of Eleanore Grace"; "Book of Shadows"; "Spectre from the Abyss"; "Satan Needs Your Surrender"; "Blood and Black"; "Sweet Nothing"; "End Point."*

» **ALBUM G** *"This Morning I Have Done Time"; "Born on a Bad Day"; "Son of a Gun"; "You Got Me Runnin'"; "Barrelhouse Hour"; "North Train Shake"; "Shakedown Mama"; "Life Mistreated Me"; "Deal Me a Hand, Lord"; "Gonna Leave You Woman."*

» **ALBUM H** *"Not All There"; "Frequent Flyer"; "Sincerely, I Don't Think"; "Gauze"; "Tailspin"; "Square Root of a Fractional Effort"; "Claustrophobia Download"; "Merely Browsing"; "Synchronize"; "Magenta No. 4."*

» **ALBUM I** *"Keep Your Loving for Me"; "Darlin' Come Back to Me"; "My World Revolves Around You"; "Everything's a Rose (Since You Loved Me)"; "in Times Like These"; "All Through the Night (I'm Thinking of You)"; "Josephine"; "Whichever Road I'm on Leads to You"; "Ain't Nothing I Can Do About It; When the Key Turns the Lock."*

Answers: A = folk album, B = hard rock, C = disco, D = US punk rock, E = UK punk rock, F = black metal, G = blues, H = indie rock, I = Motown/soul.

techniques and craft

> I write the verses and get to the chorus and it's like, 'How do I sum up what I'm trying to say here?'"
>
> **SKIN OF SKUNK ANANSIE TO *MELODY MAKER***

> It is bad writing that ruins rhymes—not lists of words that do or do not rhyme."
>
> **JIMMY WEBB**

As much as inspiration, writing good lyrics depends upon proficiency in the techniques and skills that will bring your songs to life.

Writing a first line

Having discussed titles, the next step is to consider the two places where a title is often placed, namely the first line and the chorus. Whether they contain the title or not, many lyrics have evocative first lines to seize the listener's attention. Often, a good first line can make the rest of the lyric flow. Experiment with writing provocative first lines for their own sake and see if you can develop a lyric from the situation they set out.

Here are some good approaches for a first line:

- Pose a question ("Where were you? Today you never came").
- Make a conditional statement—one that includes words like "if," "why," "because," "how," "only," et cetera ("If I knew then what I know now").
- Describe an action ("Faced the ceiling when the day came to").
- Quote a conversation, or say something to someone ("That wasn't what you said last time we met").
- Describe a place and time ("He grew up in a Midwest town / Where you could walk the streets at night").

- Introduce a character performing an action ("Billy turns off the light for another day").

Song sections: verse, pre-chorus, chorus, bridge

How many sections does a lyric have? The simplest form would be a verse of four, six, or eight lines and a refrain of one or two lines, as is often found in folk music, with simple accompanying music to match.

Many traditional blues songs have a three-line verse where lines one and two are the same:

> *Woke up this mornin' and the sky was blue,*
> *Woke up this mornin' and the sky was blue.*
> *Lookin' for a change in the weather, and then I found you.*

> *I hate to see the evening sun go down*
> *Said I hate to see that sun go down*
> *'Cause my baby, he upped and left this town.*

Most popular song lyrics have at least two sections: a verse and a bridge, where the bridge contrasts to the verse but is not the place where the theme is summarized; or a verse and a chorus. Many Beatles songs have a verse/bridge (or A+B) form, from early ones like "You're Going to Lose That Girl," which has a short bridge that is always the same, to later ones such as "While My Guitar Gently Weeps," which has two lyrically different bridges.

A chorus is the center of a lyric's energy, as well as the music's energy. In the chorus, you declare what the song is really about. Your verses lay out aspects of what the context is for the concentration of energy in the chorus.

Choruses are usually shorter than verses. Up to four lines for a chorus is standard. If you write too many lines in a chorus, the title might get lost, and there could be a problem maintaining its musical punch. Put your most focused, most memorable phrases into the chorus.

Chorus lyrics tend to be simpler in meaning (though not less profound) than verses, because more complex, nuanced phrases are likely to get either lost or check the flow of the music at that point. In many songs, verses are about talking, reflecting, or describing, whereas choruses are about concluding or metaphorically asserting—and it's hard to assert a complex phrase or idea in a short space.

Song sections do not have set numbers of lines in the way the poem form of the sonnet has 14 lines. Verse length depends on how long your lines are and the tempo. In a slow ballad with long lyric lines, there might only be two or three lines to a verse because it takes as much time to sing them at that speed as it would to sing a 12-line verse in a faster song. Verses explain the overall situation and color in some of the details. In a narrative song, the verses carry most of the plot; the chorus will supply the meaning of it, if there is one, or pose questions of it.

In a more extended lyric, there might be a pre-chorus appended to the verse immediately before the chorus. A pre-chorus is a couple of lines of lyric that advance on from what the verse has described and set up the chorus's appearance. Where verses change, pre-choruses lyrically remain the same. This introduces an additional element of lyric repetition apart from what is in the chorus. The pre-chorus can almost function like a refrain or an extra hook. It can also stand alone between a bridge and a last chorus, so that you don't have to insert another verse.

Bridges contain some sort of contrast with what is stated in the verse and chorus. A bridge can be the section of the lyric where alternatives are explored, or where something happens that sets the scene for the closing verse and/or chorus. The Beatles' "Back in the USSR" has a bridge that introduces the attractions of Ukraine and Moscow girls into a lyric whose verses are mostly descriptive of travelling to Russia, and therefore supply a reason why you might want to go.

These basic sections can be twisted and changed in many ways. Many songwriters will say that it is a common experience to find the lyric itself dictates its form. Sometimes a song can have an opening couple of lines and music that are not repeated later in the song. They form a little curtain-raiser of their own. This happens in the Miracles' "Shop Around" and the Beatles' "Here, There and Everywhere," which Paul McCartney later told *Mojo* magazine "was our homage to the standards of the '30s and '40s, which John and I both admired. They often had a preceding verse before the song proper started." The same admiration of earlier songwriting led them to craft a bridge lyric that is only completed by the first word of the next verse.

Rhyme

Songwriters have contrasting views on rhyme and how necessary it is. In practical terms, after the issue of finding inspiration to write a lyric in the first place, rhyme is probably the next obstacle for songwriters. Nothing seems to put a spanner in the works so effectively as being stuck for a rhyme or getting trapped into hideous rhyming clichés such as fantasy/reality, fire/desire, love/above.

Rhymes become clichéd when used too often. The overused rhymes are always the obvious ones—the ones that come to mind when you're up against a deadline to finish a song. There is even a common phrase for such predictable rhymes: "moon/June rhyming," which Joni Mitchell included ironically in "Both Sides Now," and Yoko Ono once deployed as an insult when comparing John Lennon's lyrics with Paul McCartney's.

Cliché rhymes make your lyric say things you don't want to say. A word like "fire" is a good example. Before you know it, you're "reaching for desire" or trying to "get higher," or calling someone a liar, or putting them on a pyre, just to have a rhyme. Put "dreams" at the end of a line and someone will soon be "coming apart at the seams," whether you want that or not.

Poor rhymes can also blemish a lyric for other reasons. They can seem contrived, which makes the lyric sound insincere, though contrivance is a subjective thing, or bathetic, where there is a sudden lurch from serious to silly. A good example is Des'ree's "Life," where the singer decides she would rather have a piece of toast than see a ghost, as that's what she fears most. The change of register is disastrous.

Why rhyme?

If a lyric does not have to rhyme, what can be said for and against the use of this technique?

- The presence of rhyme gives a lyric an appearance of logic and structure.
- Lines that rhyme can have extra authority (especially in a couplet).
- Where a lyric has to be more assertive—as in a comic, satirical, or protest song—it benefits from the emphasis rhyme gives.
- Rhyme also makes lines easier to remember. Memorizing a poem that rhymes is much easier than remembering one that doesn't.

The disadvantages of rhymes are that:

- they seduce you into using clichés to make them fit
- they tempt you to overuse the same rhymes
- they can put your words in an ungrammatical and awkward order
- they lead you to say things you didn't mean to say, or that are not relevant to the theme.

Consider this couplet:

> *When I was born, I heard a gun*
> *And then I knew my race had begun.*

"Had begun" is a lyrical cliché that often appears as an awkward line ending merely to complete a rhyme. And in what sense is growing up a "race"? The metaphor of a "race" is often used nonsensically, as here, for something which might be a competition but isn't against a clock in the strict sense.

Here's another syntax problem caused by rhyme:

> *My love's a machine with a heart of gold,*
> *Take a look behind glass, to you I must be sold.*

Ordinarily, we'd say, "I must be sold to you," not the tortured "to you I must be sold," which awkwardly inverts the phrase and gives it an archaic tone.

Make rhymes work for you

Here are some guidelines to avoid the pitfalls of rhyme:

- Don't put a word on the end of a line for which there aren't many effective rhymes. Classic troublemakers are "love," "world," "field," "heart," "room," and "moon."
- Avoid obvious rhymes—this means some that come to you during a sketch.
- Avoid archaic forms like "thee" instead of "you" to clinch a rhyme, unless the style of the lyric makes such diction appropriate.
- Always have a rhyming dictionary or website to hand.

- Circumvent the problem of finding rhymes by adapting some from another song and write a new lyric with them. The rhymes need not be in the same order, but you could retain the shape of the verse and chorus (and bridge, if there is one).
- Start a lyric sketch by first choosing a few interesting rhymes from a rhyming dictionary and write phrases to fit them.
- Don't rely on spelling alone—some words rhyme even though spelt differently: jokes/coax, wear/chair, brown/noun.
- Keep rhyme schemes simple. Use alternate rhymes, where every other line is rhymed, in a verse and bridge; save couplet rhyming, where each pair of lines rhyme, for a chorus or the end of a verse where the emphasis might be more fitting.
- Don't force your way out of a rhyming problem by mangling tenses, as Bob Dylan once did when he used "knowed" instead of "knew," and Neil Diamond when he devised "brang" instead of "brought" to rhyme with "sang."

Verses do not have to have identical rhyme schemes. Two four-line verses might sound okay with lines two and four rhymed, with a third verse rhymed ABAB— an increase of rhyme to give the third verse added weight. But a rhyme scheme quickly establishes an expectation in the listener that it will be followed. Breaking this expectation can create an unwanted anticlimax.

A special version of this technique is to insert an internal rhyme in a lyric where there hadn't been one before, as in this line:

At the ball their hearts in thrall to a smile like a disease.

For examples of multiple rhymes in a single line, see Bruce Springsteen's debut album *Greetings from Asbury Park* (especially "Blinded by the Light"). Used sparingly, internal rhyme can be handy to end a chorus, as Travis do in "Driftwood," which rhymes "find/bind/grind" in a single line.

Multiple rhymes on the same sound create an impression of artifice because they draw attention to themselves. This works fine in certain types of song, such as comic numbers (where the artifice becomes funny) or satires (where it feels like hard-edged sarcasm or threatening). Take, for example, this Dylan-esque stanza with quadruple rhyme:

Once upon a time you spun a line
That it would be fine, commit no crime, so you said.
You could take a shower at any hour,
It was in your power to make goodness cower until it bled.

For the real thing, see Dylan's "Like a Rolling Stone" or "Just Like a Woman," with its chorus of "aches/makes/fakes/breaks"; or, among other writers, Jackson Browne's "The Pretender" and U2's "Bad." In the Beatles' "While My Guitar Gently Weeps," repeated multisyllabic rhymes make the song's statements portentous.

The genre where rhyme works differently is rap/hip-hop and its derivatives. Here, multiple consecutive rhyming on the same sound signifies and enacts the skill, authority, assertiveness, and aggression of the vocalist. The artifice is reconfigured not as the breaking of an aesthetic illusion but the rejection of it. As a general point, rap and hip-hop elevated the importance of the lyric, often extending it and making it the main focus of a recording, with a corresponding reduction of the musical content, including melody.

Perfect versus imperfect rhyme

In the past, some songwriters believed rhymes should be perfect ("strong/along/wrong"). In practice, few songwriters now worry about this, and there is one obvious reason why imperfect or approximate rhymes may not matter.

Most vocalists are not especially clear in their enunciation (hence comical mishearings of lyrics, known as "mondegreens," which can be found gathered in books like Gavin Edwards's *Scuse Me While Kiss This Guy* and *When a Man Loves a Walnut*).

Often, the last syllable of a word in a vocal performance is hardly audible. So, rhyming "mind" with "time" in a lyric is perfectly okay, because the vowel sound *i* counts more than the words' terminations. That means imprecise rhymes are frequently met with in lyrics:

- *alone / home*
- *stones / cloned*
- *rage / days*
- *name / rain*
- *down / shout*
- *line / time*
- *young / fun*
- *gained / remain*
- *tree / need*
- *free / succeed*
- *nursed / worse*
- *hate / cake / ache*

These shouldn't be confused with "half-rhymes" like "powder/hunger," where only the final syllable rhymes. Approximate rhyme enables something like Sting's ingenious "cough/Nabokov" rhyme in the last verse of "Don't Stand So Close to Me."

Rhymes can also be squeezed out of mispronunciations and colloquial words, such as "warn yer" with "corner," and "do yer" with "hallelujah." in "Big Yellow Taxi," Joni Mitchell rhymed "museum" with "see 'em," and the Ramones rhymed "tell 'em" with "cerebellum." Such contractions once looked crude, but in some contexts, as a change of register, they can be playful and expressive.

Most rhymes were labeled "masculine"—that is, stressed and single-syllable. The so-called "feminine" rhyme involves a two-syllable word, the second syllable of which is unstressed, as in "flowing/growing." A single or two-syllable word can complete a two- or three-syllable rhyme and vice versa:

- *tambourine / cream*
- *suspicion / exhibition*
- *action / satisfaction*
- *ended / suspended*
- *state / congregate*
- *spectacularly / perpetually*

There are many of these in Tony Christie's "Amarillo" ("dawning/morning," "pillow/willow," "ringing/singing"), no doubt because the title lends itself to double-syllable rhyme.

Parallel phrasing

Alongside verse, chorus, and bridge structures, here's another useful structuring device. One lazy way of generating a lyric is to use various types of parallel phrasing. This kind of lyric involves minimal creative output to get it started, and then it almost writes itself. I wouldn't advise using this technique often (it easily becomes tediously predictable), but it is okay occasionally. It involves writing a phrase and then retaining its structure, repeating the phrase with a variation, either in adjacent lines, or several lines apart. Here's an example:

> *Some days are full of promise,*
> *Some days never leave the ground;*
> *Some days are like an echo chamber,*
> *Some days don't have a sound.*

Roy Orbison's "Pretty Woman" does this to some degree, with phrases built on the title. Miranda Lambert's "Bluebird" uses phrases that join "I" with a noun: "I'm a turner," "I'm a giver," et cetera.

The technical rhetorical name for this when it happens in poetry is "anaphora"—phrases that parallel each other in the first part of a line. This is an easy technique, since the part of the phrase, which stays the same from line to line, nudges you to the next idea; and if you introduce alternate rhyming, the search for a rhyme often suggests the next line.

The longer you keep such a phrase going, the more it draws attention to itself—which may be undesirable. Imagine a song with three eight-line verses: twenty-four lines all commencing "some days"! It would be too repetitious. Avoid this by a break with the pattern, either by confining the repeated phrase to alternate lines or leaving it after four statements.

If it doesn't figure anywhere else in the lyric, parallel phrasing is effective in a chorus, where you want an increase of tension and focus. Clearly repeating a phrase with small variations can provide that.

» *Maroon 5, "Girls Like You"; Pink Floyd, "Another Brick in the Wall," "Eclipse"; the Police, "Every Breath You Take"; Sam Cooke, "What a Wonderful World"; the Byrds, "Turn Turn Turn"; the Velvet Underground, "Who Loves the Sun"; Ian Dury, "Reasons to Be Cheerful, Part 3," "What a Waste"; Coldplay, "Fix You"; Noel Harrison, "Windmills of Your Mind"; Michael Kiwanuka, "Black Man in a White World."*

The list lyric
A song that is a list by *content* doesn't necessarily have the same exact syntactical parallels, though some do. The list-driven lyric has an actual list of related objects, persons, or events. List songs include:

» *The Kinks, "Village Green Preservation Society"; the Stranglers, "No More Heroes"; the Plastic Ono Band, "Give Peace a Chance"; Madonna, "Vogue"; Ian Dury and the Blockheads, "Hit Me with Your Rhythm Stick," "Reasons to Be Cheerful"; the Beach Boys, "Surfin' USA"; Cornershop, "Brimful of Asha"; the Beatles, "Dig It"; Beyoncé, "If I Were a Boy."*

There is also R.E.M.'s "It's the End of the World as We Know It," which Michael Stipe said came from a dream in which he was the only person at a party whose initials were not LB. (The other guests included Lenny Bruce, Leonid Brezhnev, and Leonard Bernstein.) The tour de force of list lyrics is Tom Lehrer's "The Elements," which uses the periodic table from chemistry.

Nick Cave and the Bad Seeds' "There She Goes, My Beautiful World" namechecks St. John of the Cross, Karl Marx, Johnny Thunders, Dylan Thomas, and Philip Larkin. In the musical field, Van Morrison's "Cleaning Windows" refers to Leadbelly, Blind Lemon Jefferson, Sonny Terry, Brownie McGhee, and Muddy Waters, and Arthur Conley's "Sweet Soul Music" lyric is structured as a list of 1960s soul stars including Otis Redding, Wilson Pickett, and James Brown. A massive example of such listed allusions and names is Bob Dylan's epic song about the assassination of John F. Kennedy, "Murder Most Foul," released in 2020.

The refrain

One special form of repetition in a lyric is the refrain. A refrain would normally use the title of the song; a refrain that *isn't* the title might lead listeners to think it *was* the title.

A refrain can come anywhere in a lyric, though a standard location is at a verse end. The refrain could be a line that unlocks the meaning of what would otherwise be puzzling images. The Police's "King of Pain" enigmatically has only descriptive images in each verse, including a flag, a dead salmon, a black spot on the sun, and a hunted fox, with the backing vocals delivering the explanatory refrain that each stands for the singer's soul. Without it, we would not know the significance of the images.

Another example would be the function of the title of "I Say a Little Prayer" as a refrain in the verse; interestingly, it does not feature in the chorus. It is also possible to obtain shifting shades of meaning from a refrain throughout a song. To explore this further, read poems which have refrains and note how they work. Examples might include Dylan Thomas's "Do Not Go Gentle into That Good Night," James Laughlin's "O Best of All Nights, Return and Return Again," and W. B. Yeats's "Beggar to Beggar Cried."

One of the most striking instances of a refrain is Elvis Costello's "I Want You," in which almost every other line is punctuated by the title, which functions as a refrain (the song lasts for six minutes). The repetition is psychologically justified because it expresses the obsessional nature of the person in the song (though I can't avoid feeling that the songwriter enjoys the whole scenario with a perverse aesthetic pleasure that makes the song more theatrical than realistic).

Hyperbole and understatement

Hyperbole (exaggeration) is a stylistic feature of many lyrics. The more romantic the lyric, the more likely it will contain hyperbole. From the word "hyperbole" comes the slang term "hype" and the tautologous "overhype" ("hype" already contains the sense of "over").

You can spot hyperbole because it involves statements that are not literally true, as in the phrase, "What kept you? I've been here a century at least." It may have been put there consciously or unconsciously. It naturally arises in love songs as a way of describing extreme feelings; it's melodramatic and certainly eye-catching. It is so much the natural currency of popular music that an anti-hyperbole title like the Housemartins' "Five Get Over-Excited" is positively revolutionary—no one in the pumped-up world of pop, where everything is bigger than life, admits to getting overexcited about anything.

» *Coldplay, "Every Teardrop Is a Waterfall"; the Walker Brothers, "The Sun Ain't Gonna Shine Anymore"; David Ruffin, "My Whole World Ended (The Moment You Left Me)"; the Four Tops, "I'll Turn to Stone"; the Only Ones, "Another Girl, Another Planet"; Jesus and Mary Chain, "Nine Million Rainy Days"; Stevie Wonder, "Drown in My Own Tears"; Evanescence, "Bring Me to Life"; the Gap Band, "You Dropped a Bomb on Me"; Roberta Flack, "Killing Me Softly With His Song"; Blue Öyster Cult, "Cities on Fire with Rock and Roll"; Muse, "Supermassive Black Hole"; Savage Garden, "To the Moon and Back."*

Understatement is much less common in lyrics. Where hyperbole operates on a principle of "more is more," under-statement in romantic lyrics is the equivalent of "less is more." A lyric can be set up so that even a relatively moderate statement of affection could become very moving. Don't forget you have the power of the music itself to generate emotion, and the more emotional the music the more you can afford to restrain the lyric's overt declarations. The title of Paul McCartney's "Maybe I'm Amazed" is a great use of understatement, provoking us to ask, "What do you mean, *maybe*? If you are amazed, how could you be unsure?"

Here, the purpose of the understatement is to communicate the singer's feeling of having stumbled onto something magical.

Bruce Springsteen's "Night" is a thunderous rock song whose lyric states the intent to find one true love somewhere in the big wide world. Dire Straits' reflective "On Every Street" has the same theme but couldn't be more of a contrast in its understatement, lyrically and musically. They're both fine songs. But we hear more hyperbolic anthems than we do reflective, understated songs (a dynamically quiet song can of course also be full of hyperbole). A good rule is this: the more emotive the subject, the more understated, even indirect, you can afford to be.

Irony

Irony is a sophisticated writing technique. An ironic statement is intended to have the opposite meaning to its apparent one. Irony requires an active, alert, intelligent listener who will consciously reverse the apparent meaning of an ironic statement. If you think you have or can find such listeners, writing and performing ironic songs is an option. The point of the technique is that it offers the listener a gratifying aesthetic reward when the true meaning is realized, rather than having it stated outright.

The bigger your audience, the greater the percentage who take your songs at face value. They will think you mean what you *appear* to say. This is dangerous territory, especially in the era of Twitter mobs and social media pile-ons. Ironic songs could get two reactions, neither of which you want. If the irony is missed (and there are many who are very good at missing it, who will shoot first and ask questions later, if at all), many will take your lyric literally, making you a proponent of the very views you may be attacking, winning you mistaken friends and enemies.

Irony is also used to be cynical with the audience. For many bands, irony ends up (whether intentionally or not) as a "have your cake and eat it" strategy. Imagine writing a deliberately over-the-top arena-rock number called "Gonna Rock You All Nite" as a send-up along the lines of Spinal Tap. Play it mega-loud in an arena of beer-swilling headbangers. Half the audience takes the lyric at face value and misses the irony (allowing the band to feel patronizingly cleverer and "subversive," even as they take the money); the other half of the audience gets the irony, has a laugh, and feels "in" on the act. The band wins either way. The career of the Sex Pistols offers many examples of this.

Acronyms, initialisms, and anacrostic lyrics

In their pure form, these are pattern lyrics, where a word is spelt out letter by letter, often in a chorus. Ian Brown's "F.E.A.R" has a lyric of phrases whose first letters spell out the title word. In the Four Tops' "Still Water (Peace)," each letter of the word "peace" is taken as the first letter of the words "privilege," "ease," "absence," "calm," and "everlasting." Cream turned the phrase "she walks like a bearded rainbow" into the acronym "SWLABR."

Other examples of spelling out words include Ottawan's "D.I.S.C.O," Tammy Wynette's "D.I.V.O.R.C.E.," Al Green's "L.O.V.E.," John Cougar Mellencamp's "R.O.C.K. In the U.S.A.," Rhythm Syndicate's "P.A.S.S.I.O.N.," and Pulp's comically titled "F.E.E.L.I.N.G.C.A.L.L.E.D.L.O.V.E." Songs that use other well-known formulae include the Jackson 5's "ABC," Manfred Mann's "5-4-3-2-1," and Feist's "1234."

Wordplay

An element of wordplay makes a lyric entertaining and memorable. We have already seen how wordplay can be used in a title. Wordplay comes in many guises—repetition, puns, catchphrases, the deliberate distortion of clichés and proverbs, drawing attention to similar sounding words, and so on. The common factor is a momentary heightened increase of interest in the properties of language itself. That's why a lot of wordplay in certain types of lyric will make them sound insincere, as though the singer is more focused on getting off a good line than expressing an emotion. However, insofar as a sense of humor is not incompatible with deep emotions or maturity of outlook, a little wordplay can give a lyric sophistication.

Try working with two meanings of the same expression, such as the verb in "When he drove into her life, he drove her out of his mind." The first "drove" means driving a car (literal meaning); the second, to drive someone out of their mind, is a metaphor.

Wordplay becomes important in comic and satirical songs, but of itself is not always funny. In a song about beaches and surfing, the phrase "pipelines and pipe dreams" connects two different things—a pipeline is a type of wave, a pipe dream is a dream that stands little chance of coming true. Think of the repetition of the word "absolute" in Bowie's "Absolute Beginners," which is a form of wordplay, or the cumulative, rhythmic force of the 13 uses of "nothing" in the chorus of Gilbert O'Sullivan's "Nothing Rhymed."

The ability to generate wordplay in your lyrics is comparable to the discovery that you can write songs about other lives and experiences than your own. With wordplay, you are no longer stuck in a framework of literal and autobiographical meaning. However, once this animal is off the leash, it is easy to get dragged all over the place. The result can be a lyric that's full of clever wordplay but is also incoherent. Wordplay should serve the theme, not the other way round.

 I love the music but what the f***ing hell are you singing about? You want to be writing lyrics that a 16-year-old girl putting her makeup on can sing."
PRODUCER STEVE LIPSOM (ALLEGEDLY) TO XTC'S ANDY PARTRIDGE

Cliché

A cliché is a phrase that has been overused and has lost its original force. Clichéd images, metaphors, and similes are so worn they are almost invisible; they no longer function as comparisons. They represent a failure of vocabulary—the kind that results in highly generalized lyrics such as Razorlight's "Somewhere Else," with its repeated use of "just" and "really."

The good news about clichés is that—unlike in poetry, where a cliché unconsciously signals incompetence and poor technique—you can get away with them in commercial songwriting. This is partly because lyrics are often so banal that noticing the cliché is like looking for white ink on white paper—it has faded into the background—and the magic of music can make a cliché seem unimportant. Your songwriting peers may notice clichés, but then they're not providing your royalty checks. So, how careful you are depends on what sort of level of craftsmanship you aspire to, and what sort of audience you're after.

Unfortunately, clichés can take the form not only of words, phrases, or images, but also stereotypical situations, characters, and emotions. The traditional blues lyric that commences "woke up this morning" has become for many simply funny, not expressive. We have a strong sense that we know exactly the situation and the sentiment that will follow. It's too predictable.

It takes time to become sufficiently knowledgeable about a breadth of song history to spot if you are simply recreating a stereotypical song lyric. Avoiding specific phrases is easier. A cliché can be rescued if you use it ironically or deliberately foreground it in some way. Aerosmith did this when they took the phrase "falling in love" and used it as a song title "Falling in Love (Is Hard on the

Knees)." Giving a clichéd metaphor a comically literal meaning is a sure way to rescue it, if temporarily. Using such romantic language but not really meaning it makes a singer look rakishly witty and lyrically aware.

Here is a list of clichés in lyrics I would avoid. Much of the objection to this language is that it is imprecise and generalized:

- *no matter what they say*
- *this cold world*
- *cold as ice*
- *cuts like a knife*
- *backs against the wall*
- *down the line*
- *make a stand*
- *sands of time*
- *my heart beats like a hammer / drum*
- *share my load*
- *set me free*
- *fantasy / reality*
- *like a moth to a flame*
- *love tears us apart*

- *little miss*
- *pretty*
- *down on my knees (usually beggin' you please)*
- *walking down the street*
- *tonight*
- *make you mine*
- *blue as can be*
- *broken heart*
- *these four walls*
- *looking for some action*
- *sun and rain*
- *catch you when you fall*
- *guess I'm . . .*

Unusual vocabulary

Generally speaking, the vocabulary you employ in a lyric has to be pretty straightforward. The more commercial your ambitions, the truer this is. There are a number of reasons for this:

- Polysyllabic words can be awkward to sing.
- They can be hard to hear, especially at a gig.
- Using words that are unfamiliar to your audience might obscure the theme of your song.
- It might cause them to think that you're too clever or bookish.
- Do complex words fit in the genre of your music?
- Abstractions can make a lyric seem insufficiently grounded.

You are on safe ground if you include current colloquial expressions. This is one way to bond with a young audience, provided you're roughly the same age as they are. Different youth subgroups have their own slang.

Occasionally, songwriters use a rare word, as in these titles: the Monkees' "Propinquity (I've Just Begun to Care)," Clifford T. Ward's "Wherewithal," Oasis's "Acquiesce," Family's "Burlesque," Canned Heat's "Parthenogenesis" and "Nebulosity," Evanescence's "Tourniquet."

Sometimes, an unassuming word in the right place creates a special tone, as with Madonna's "I'd Be Surprisingly Good for You." The use of a foreign word or two can lend an air of sophistication. In the case of the Manic Street Preachers "Glasnost," it is the actual theme of the song, and there is no English equivalent word. Badly Drawn Boy derived "Donna and Blitzen" from the German phrase *donner und blitzen*.

Songwriters have also entertained themselves (and us) by inventing new words. The list below includes a couple of ten-ton-monster compound words!

» *Daft Punk, "Technologic"; Phil Collins, "Sussudio" (a word to represent a drum fill); R.E.M., "Ignoreland"; T.Rex, "Jeepster"; Donovan, "Barabajagal"; Iron Butterfly, "In-A-Gadda-Da-Vida" (derived from "in the garden of Eden"); Lisa Germano, "Tomorrowing"; Jethro Tull, "Aqualung"; the Beach Boys, "Cabinessence"; Roxy Music, "Pyjamarama"; David Bowie, "Moonage Daydream"; the Bluetones, "Autophilia"; Muse, "Screenager"; Megadeth, "Youthanasia"; Marillion, "Assassing"; Little Richard, "Tutti Frutti," "Awopbopaloobopalopbamboom"; Isaac Hayes, "Hyperboliesyllaciscequelalymistic"; Parliament, "Supergroovalisticprosifunkstication"; Sly and the Family Stone, "Thank You (Falettinme Be Mice Elf Agin)"; Red Hot Chilli Peppers, "Californication"; Destiny's Child, "Bootylicious."*

" *We should be on the lookout in our reading and conversation for that unfamiliar word with an intriguing sound, the one whose meaning we have always guessed at but about which we are not certain.*"

JIMMY WEBB

Nonsense

There are moments when nothing but pure nonsense will do. And if you've been accused of writing lyrics that are nonsense, why not go the whole hog? Nonsense syllables form part of the jazz "scat-singing" tradition, where a singer imitates the improvisatory freedom of an instrumental soloist. They also feature in more organized patterns in doo-wop and harmony singing. They suit more light-hearted songs.

Sometimes you might end up with a nonsense refrain left over from an early draft of a lyric, originally put there to fill a gap in a verse when you were working on a melody. Such refrains are good for audience participation—it's easy to sing along with a song when you don't have words to learn, as in the scat-singing refrains in Mungo Jerry's "In the Summertime," T.Rex's "Hot Love," and Neil Sedaka's "Breaking Up Is Hard to Do" ("come-a, come-a, down dooby-do down down") demonstrate. As Frank Zappa once pointed out, everyone in the world understands "la la la." At one time, the Eurovision Song Contest was full of songs with choruses that seemed to all go "bong-cheedle-cheedle-bong-doo-dee." Nonsense is an international language, you see . . .

» *The Beatles, "Ob-La-Di-Ob-La-Da" (and the long fade on "Hey Jude"); Manfred Mann, "Doo Wah Diddy Diddy"; the Police, "De Doo Doo Doo, De Dah Dah Dah"; Lulu, "Boom Bang-a-Bang"; Stevie Wonder, "Shoo-bedoo-bedoo-day-day"; Madonna, "Shoo-Be-Doo"; the Kaiser Chiefs, "Na Na Na Na Naa"; the Crystals, "Da Doo Ron Ron (When He Walked Me Home)"; the Rivingtons, "Papa-Oom-Mow-Mow"; Major Lance, "Um Um Um Um Um Um Um"; Roy Orbison, "Ooby Dooby"; Hanson, "Mmmbop."*

Proverbs and catchphrases

Proverbs, quotations, and catchphrases can contribute to a lyric. Dip into books of them and you will be surprised at how many you know, and how many can be adapted as lyrical themes, titles, or first lines. Even if you don't reproduce them straight, you can twist them by changing a word, introducing a pun, inverting their terms, or taking a term literally that was meant as a metaphor—as Billy Bragg did when he turned the phrase "milk of human kindness" into the milkman of human kindness who promised to leave an extra pint. This is funny and touching at the same time.

The point about these phrases is that they belong to everyone. Proverbs have been around for generations. The tip with a proverb is to find a way of changing it or deducing something from it that wouldn't normally follow, or write an ironic continuation, or even splice two incompatible proverbs together.

Take the proverbs "like the cat with the cream" and "dog in the manger." If we reverse the terms, we get the unsettling potential of "She's the cat in the manger / the dog with the cream." The proverb "too many cooks spoil the broth" is about people getting in each other's way. Reversing it produces "too many broths spoil the cook," which could mean that if you have to do the same thing over and over, eventually it gets to you. Or "you can lead a horse to water, but you can't make it think (or sink)," instead of the expected "drink."

» The Temptations, "Beauty Is Only Skin Deep"; Billy Joel, "Only the Good Die Young"; the Velvelettes, "Needle in a Haystack"; the Only Ones, "No Peace for the Wicked"; Jimmy Cliff, "The Bigger They Are, the Harder They Fall"; Thomas Dolby, "She Blinded Me with Science"; the Four Tops, "Still Waters Run Deep"; Badfinger, "Storm in a Teacup"; Bryan Adams, "Where Angels Fear to Tread"; David Gray, "Silver Lining"; Bo Diddley, "You Can't Judge a Book by the Cover"; the Fantastics, "Something Old Something New"; Ian Hunter and Mick Ronson, "Once Bitten, Twice Shy"; Frankie Goes to Hollywood, "The World Is My Oyster"; New Radicals, "You Get What You Give."

Catchphrases are invented every day by comedians and advertising agencies, for TV commercials, posters, and so on. Both can provide excellent titles and sometimes first lines (but don't infringe copyright). Keep watch for memorable slang phrases. Take the phrase "mission creep," popularized in the 1990s. In it, "creep" is a verb—to move forward slowly but inexorably—but "creep" is also slang for a person who makes you feel uncomfortable ("he's a creep"), as in the famous Radiohead song. Seeing those meanings is a basis for developing a song about a person on a mission.

Sometimes, bringing stock phrases together is enough to wake them up. Combining "cold light of dawn" with "harsh light of day" is more interesting than using them separately.

Modern catchphrases can make your song seem contemporary and streetwise, especially if you do something original with them. Some catchphrases are connected with drama or storytelling, like "meanwhile back at the ranch" or the traditional "once upon a time" (a song title by many, including Donna Summer and Simple Minds). If I used this as a title, I would seek an unexpected word or image to substitute for "time," as Lana Del Rey did for "Once Upon a Dream."

Another group are ordinary phrases taken from everyday life, sometimes instructions or warnings, that have potential metaphorical meanings, like the Manic Street Preachers' "Everything Must Go," Black Grape's "Shake Well Before Opening," and Whitesnake's "Slippery When Wet." Turning these phrases into songs seems to sometimes release energy in them.

» *Taylor Swift, "You Need to Calm Down"; Jethro Tull, "Later That Same Evening"; Sparks, "This Town Ain't Big Enough for the Both of Us"; Joss Stone, "Less Is More"; Donna Summer, "If You've Got It Flaunt It"; Aerosmith, "Don't Get Mad, Get Even"; Nick Lowe, "Cruel to Be Kind"; David Gray, "Dead in the Water"; Everything But the Girl, "Come Hell Or Highwater"; Radiohead, "Everything in Its Right Place," Manic Street Preachers, "There by the Grace of God"; Meat Loaf, "You Took the Words Right Out of My Mouth"; Elvis Costello, "Accidents Will Happen"; Coldplay, "A Rush of Blood to the Head"; Bonnie Raitt, "Nick of Time"; the Hives, "Hate to Say I Told You So"; La Roux, "In for the Kill."*

painting pictures with words

> " *The minute I wrote, 'Like a bridge over troubled water I will lay me down,'*
> *I knew that I had a very clear image. The whole verse was set up to hit that*
> *melody line."*
>
> **PAUL SIMON TO *MOJO***

> " *No one had ever said 'tracks of my tears.' The whole thought of tears was you*
> *wipe them away because they've left these tracks, y'know? I thought it was a*
> *good idea."*
>
> **SMOKEY ROBINSON TO NELSON GEORGE**

Lyrics are brought to life by the introduction of figurative language, in which you describe your subject by comparing it with something else. Figurative language and imagery stimulate the listener's imagination through vivid images that bring new insights and associations. A powerful metaphor, simile, or image can generate a whole lyric, as you explore the meaning of it. Sometimes this metaphor features in the title.

When Bruce Springsteen first sang "I'm on Fire" or the Kings of Leon "Sex on Fire," no fire marshal rushed to their rescue. The image wasn't meant literally. It was a metaphor: to be on fire with passion.

These songs were not the first (or the last) in the annals of popular music to express it that way. In many of Elvis Costello's early songs, the lyric is spun out of a nucleus of associated images and metaphors. Even if the meaning sometimes got derailed, it gave the lyrics a certain energy of their own in addition to that of the music.

The Four Tops' "Standing in the Shadow of Love," the Miracles' "Shop Around," Mary Wells's "You Beat Me to the Punch," and Jackson Browne's

"Sleep's Dark and Silent Gate," are all examples of this. There is also a tradition of enclosing the simile in brackets: "(Love Is Like a) Raging Fire."

Simile

Put simply, a simile is an explicit comparison in which the thing of primary concern at a given moment [x] is likened to something else [y] of secondary concern, often using the formula "[x] is like [y]." The purpose of the comparison is to explain something about the nature of [x]. So, one song tells us that love [x] cuts like a knife [y]. This isn't literally true, but a moment's reflection makes sense of it—the physical pain of being cut is an analogy for the way love can hurt our feelings.

Another song says that love is like a heatwave, or soft as an easy chair, or a person is like a hurricane. Some comparisons are so obvious they become clichés—a heart that beats like a drum, a passion that rages like a fire, something that shines like the sun or a star, are all clichés, whereas shadows that "stretch out like dead men" is not. (Such clichéd and far-fetched similes are effectively parodied in the Bonzo Dog Doo Dah Band's "Canyons of Your Mind" and 10cc's "Life Is a Minestrone.")

A great simile need not be visual. To say a woman's face is like a magnet, as Elvis Costello did in "Watching the Detectives," gives no idea of what she looks like, but it does tell you that her effect is powerful. In Radiohead's "Karma Police," an irritating man buzzes like a fridge.

Similes must make sense and not collide with each other, unless that is intentional. Romantic imagery about the sea brings this sort of problem. Be careful about saying "the waves of sadness wash over me" and then, a few lines later, "the peaceful ocean of happiness," because you're making water mean two opposing things.

Metaphor

Like a simile, a metaphor is a comparison between two things, but it is implicit, not explicit. The two things are brought closer together, almost identified with each other. This can be handy in a lyric where space is at a premium, but metaphor is also not as immediately clear as a simile.

"The soldiers went into battle like a herd of sheep" is a clichéd simile. "As sheep, the soldiers went into battle" is slightly shorter, but still a simile. "The soldiers were herded into battle" is a metaphor. They have been identified with the animals simply by the verb "herded."

Some verbs are connected, so often, with certain objects, the verb alone evokes it. Farmers *herd* sheep and cattle—creatures whose lives are not self-governed. This means we don't need to spell out the comparison between the soldiers and the animals; "herded" does it alone. Similarly, we could write "Your absence is like a wolf / hanging around my door" (simile) or, using a metaphor, "The wolves of your absence are hanging round my door." Or the more compressed, "Your wolfish absence hangs round my door."

It takes time to develop an awareness of metaphors working through verbs, since it is more obvious to think of them as nouns. Take the line, "Sun melts the frost off each whitened roof and fence." This has two problems: "whitened" is awkward to sing, and "melts" is a predictable verb. Better is "Sun smokes the frost off each roof and fence." The simile of "The sun evaporates the frost like smoke" is compressed into the verb "smokes."

A literal and a metaphorical meaning hinging on a single word can be pressed into a single line. Imagine two ex-lovers who meet again out of curiosity and rekindle (there's a metaphor!) a relationship: "Thinking it was safe to meet / and play with fire." To play with fire is a metaphor for taking a risk. A rock critic writing about Janis Joplin reaches for a metaphor to describe her husky vocals: "Hers was a voice flecked with rust." Both similes and metaphors can be momentary details, but they can also be extended to occupy a whole verse.

A metaphor can be a "local event" in a lyric, whose meaning does not extend further than a line or two. In the line "Radar wipes its tired eye," such a metaphor is a momentary decoration. Radar is naturally associated with an eye because it is a means of looking. The "wipe" is the sweeping beam that travels 360 degrees round the circular display. A metaphor might be carried through a whole verse, as happens in the lyric "Rainy Day Market" in section 9.

By contrast, a "thematic" or grand metaphor is a comparison that dominates an entire song. In fact, it is possible to write a song lyric entirely within a thematic metaphor (say, a civil war) and never say what the metaphor relates to. Thematic metaphors can unify a lyric, giving an overarching plan of reference. They can stiffen the emotion and stop certain subjects (like love songs) becoming sentimental or too plain. Such grand metaphors disguise personal themes yet keep the drama open to listeners who can place their own dramas in it.

Finding these requires the ability to see potential double meanings at work, and the relationship between surface meanings and deeper meanings. Take, for example, the phrase "crush depth." This refers to the point where a submarine's hull cannot take any more pressure from the ocean, resulting in a catastrophic failure. But the word "crush" also has a romantic meaning—to have a crush on someone is to be attracted to them.

A metaphor presents itself—the idea of getting into a relationship or attraction that takes you out of your "depth." A second metaphor, meaning "what you can handle." With this metaphor in mind, you could begin a sketch by writing down words and phrases that come to mind from this ocean metaphor.

A grand or primary metaphor is not always arrived at merely by compiling a list of wordplays based on a single idea. That may not create the important emotional foundation and instead only be an accumulation. The lyric "Trouble" in section 9 is an example, whereas a true foundational metaphor is seen in "White as Alaska" in section 3.

Like similes, over-ingenious metaphors can work in a comic situation. On the other hand, overelaborate metaphors can turn into the sort of allegory that is unintentionally funny.

A catalogue of imagery

Simile and metaphors are particular examples of imagery in songs. The following pages provide a catalogue of the most common types of imagery.

The weather

On Planet Pop, the weather is always a main topic of lyric conversation. The forecast is for heavy and persistent rainfall with outbreaks of thunder, but we should see sunshine later. Writing about the weather can be a way to avoid writing anything specific in a lyric at all. Nothing beats weather imagery for implying meanings in a vague, metaphorical way. This imagery is also the language of the unconscious in dreams, so it is deeply embedded in human consciousness.

If you reach for it, best avoid creating a homily—we don't need to be told "every winter must turn to spring," followed by a rhyme on "sing," as though it has only just struck you that one follows the other. Promising to shelter someone from the rain or the storm is a cliché, so those images need a touch of the unexpected to make them work. No one should ever write another song called "Wind of Change."

Buddy Guy's "Change in the Weather" and "Feels Like Rain" are examples of weather imagery lyrics. James Blunt's "Tears and Rain" is almost a tautology in the lexicon of pop. We know that rain is like tears, so it doesn't need to be spelled out. Similarly, Willie Nelson's "Blue Eyes Crying in the Rain" is too much. Refresh weather imagery by reversing its usual metaphorical associations. Passion and desire are normally associated with fire, but you could connect them with snow and ice.

Here's a breakdown of the metaphorical weather on Planet Pop, with associated meanings.

RAIN Love, life, redemption, tears, unhappiness, suffering, being happy regardless of what life throws at you, that which gives life and renewal.

» *Ed Sheeran, "Make It Rain"; Lady Gaga and Arianna Grande, "Rain on Me"; the Beatles, "Rain"; R.E.M., "I'll Take the Rain"; Ann Peebles, "I Can't Stand the Rain"; B. J. Thomas, "Raindrops Keep Falling on My Head"; Gordon Lightfoot, "Early Morning Rain"; Tom Waits, "Diamonds on My Windshield"; Gene Kelly, "Singing in the Rain"; the Temptations, "I Wish It Would Rain"; Carole King, "It Might as Well Rain Until September"; James Taylor, "Fire and Rain"; Garbage, "Only Happy When It Rains"; Turin Brakes, "Painkiller (Summer Rain)"; Bob Dylan, "A Hard Rain's A-Gonna Fall"; Travis, "Why Does It Always Rain on Me?"; the Move, "Flowers in the Rain"; Rihanna, "Umbrella."*

RAINBOWS Traditionally a symbol of hope, biblically a sign of God's covenant with humanity after the flood. Rainbows tend to appear after rain. An ephemeral transcendent vision.

» *The Marmalade, "Rainbow"; Mountain, "Sitting on a Rainbow"; Richard and Linda Thompson, "The End of the Rainbow"; Robbie Robertson, "Sign of the Rainbow"; Laura Nyro, "Broken Rainbow"; Judy Garland, "Over the Rainbow"; Kate and Anna McGarrigle, "Rainbow Ride"; the Rolling Stones, "She's a Rainbow"; Bill Nelson, "The Gold at the End of My Rainbow"; Dennis Wilson, "Rainbows"; the Love Affair, "Rainbow Valley"; Katy Perry, "Double Rainbow."*

SUNSHINE Happiness, love, joy, morning, summer, emotional warmth.

» *The Beatles, "Here Comes the Sun"; Stevie Wonder, "You Are the Sunshine of My Life"; Donovan, "Sunshine Superman"; the Beach Boys, "The Warmth of the Sun"; the Isley Bros, "Summer Breeze"; Traffic, "Paper Sun"; Bill Withers, "Ain't No Sunshine"; Cream, "Sunshine of Your Love"; Katrina and the Waves, "Walking on Sunshine"; the Velvet Underground, "Who Loves the Sun"; the Supremes, "Automatically Sunshine"; Elton John, "Don't Let the Sun Go Down on Me"; Fleet Foxes, "Sun It Rises"; Arctic Monkeys, "When the Sun Goes Down"; Tame Impala, "Sun's Coming Up."*

WIND Difficulties, adversity, change, resistance, natural force tending to motion, unknown forces of fate.

» *Van Morrison, "Full Force Gale"; Rod Stewart, "Mandolin Wind"; Scorpions, "Wind of Change"; Bob Dylan, "Idiot Wind," "Blowin' in the Wind"; the Byrds, "Hickory Wind"; Donovan, "Catch the Wind"; Neil Young, "Like a Hurricane"; Joni Mitchell, "Let the Wind Carry Me"; Nick Heyward, "Whistle Down the Wind"; Richard Thompson, "Mystery Wind"; Robert Plant and the Strange Sensations, "Let the Four Winds Blow"; the Jimi Hendrix Experience, "The Wind Cries Mary"; the Luminaires, "Gale Song"; Feist, "The Wind."*

CLOUDS/FOG Mystery, not being able to see, confusion, getting lost.

» *Joni Mitchell, "Both Sides Now"; Kate Bush, "Cloudbusting," "The Fog"; All About Eve, "In the Clouds"; Mercury Rev, "Nite and Fog"; Lindisfarne, "Fog on the Tyne"; Judy Garland, "A Foggy Day"; Kristin Hersh, "Fog"; Paul Weller, "Above the Clouds"; the Rolling Stones, "Get Off of My Cloud"; the Temptations, "Cloud 9"; Air, "Clouds Up"; One Direction, "Clouds."*

STORM/FLOOD Overwhelming emotions, dramatic events, conflict, loss.

» *Bob Dylan, "Shelter from the Storm"; Howlin' Wolf, "Smokestack Lightning"; Fleetwood Mac, "Storms"; the Doors, "Riders on the Storm"; the Jimi Hendrix Experience, "In from the Storm," Doves, "The Storm"; the Verve, "Stormy Clouds"; Led Zeppelin, "When the Levee Breaks"; Madonna, "Drowned World"; Bruce*

Springsteen, "Lost in the Flood"; Stevie Ray Vaughan, "Texas Flood"; Mumford and Sons, "After the Storm"; Lady Gaga, "No Flood."

SNOW/ICE Purity, burial, danger, skating on thin ice, emotional coldness, transformation of the ordinary world into enchantment.

» *Kings of Leon, "Velvet Snow"; Madonna, "Frozen"; Van Morrison, "Snow in San Anselmo"; Haircut 100, "Snow Girl"; Genesis, "Snowbound"; Also the Trees, "From the Silver Frost"; Josh Ritter, "Snow Is Gone"; Emmylou Harris, "Roses in the Snow"; Everything But the Girl, "Frost and Fire"; Sia, "Snowman."*

> *A butterfly caught up in a hurricane—the image suddenly came to me. I put the words in the song. I heard distant thunder, smelled the air just before the rain, saw lightning streak across the sky, felt the winds blow. Soft winds ... warm breeze ... a power source ... a tender force ... quiet storm ... blowing through my life ... I finally had the musical concept I'd been seeking since hearing [Marvin Gaye's] What's Going On. I also had a device for moving from one tune to another: the wind. I saw seven songs carried on the back of a breeze, blowing through the record from start to finish."*
>
> **SMOKEY ROBINSON ON THE GENESIS OF HIS ALBUM *A QUIET STORM***

Topography

The category of topography covers imagery based on the features of the physical world. This excludes specific named places. Traditional folk songs belong to societies and times where a landscape's terrain and features were greater obstacles than now. Such difficulties express psychological struggles, as in Rodgers and Hammerstein's "Climb Every Mountain."

People still use the cliché of the "urban jungle" for the city. Dido uses the metaphor of land as emotional territory and relationship in her song "This Land Is Mine"—with perhaps a nod to Woody Guthrie's "This Land Is Your Land," where the land image is not metaphorical but literal.

Along with landscape imagery go song lyrics that refer to maps and charts, such as R.E.M.'s "Maps and Legends" and Wire's "Map Ref. 41° N 93° W." These tend to be more artistically successful than yet another lyric about rivers that run (as proverbially they do) to the sea. Probably the greatest extended use of oceanic/

water imagery in rock is throughout the Who's concept album *Quadrophenia*.

Hank Williams, Woody Guthrie ... everybody has that landscape inside them, doesn't matter if you live in the city, it's a mythical landscape that everybody carries with them."

BRUCE SPRINGSTEEN TO Q, 1992

Initially I get just a natural image like sky, sea, sun, earth, and then something very domestic like washing. The juxtaposition of those things is endlessly interesting."

NEIL FINN OF CROWDED HOUSE TO *MOJO*, JUNE 1994

It sort of expressed to us the intensity [of] the feelings ... it sang well and it painted a nice image."

ELLIE GREENWICH, COWRITER OF "RIVER DEEP MOUNTAIN HIGH," TO SEAN EGAN

MOUNTAINS Aspiration, determination to overcome great odds, a place where you get a much broader perspective. They are often part of the hyperbole of love songs. When they fall into the sea this denotes the end of time, which is when he can finally stop loving her.

» *Diana Ross, "Ain't No Mountain High Enough"; Ike and Tina Turner, "River Deep Mountain High"; Kate Bush, "King of the Mountain"; Led Zeppelin, "Misty Mountain Hop"; U2, "One Tree Hill"; Aimee Mann, "Crawling Up a Hill"; David Bowie, "Up the Hill Backwards"; the Beatles, "Fool on the Hill"; Fats Domino, "Blueberry Hill"; Neil Young, "Sugar Mountain"; Goldfrapp, "Felt Mountain"; the Byrds, "Wild Mountain Thyme"; Fleet Foxes, "Blue Ridge Mountains"; Arcade Fire, "Sprawl II (Mountains Beyond Mountains)."*

RIVERS Change, the flow of time, an obstacle, redemption, benign waters of life, on a more human scale than the sea. Fountains, springs, and waterfalls are related images. They can also imply the journey through death to the afterlife.

» *Bruce Springsteen, "The River"; Al Green, "Take Me to the River"; Doves, "Caught by the River"; Neil Young, "Down by the River"; R.E.M., "Green Grow the Rushes," "Find the River"; Johnny Cash, "Big River"; Fats Domino, "Going to the River"; Fleetwood Mac, "Silver Springs"; Jimmy Cliff, "Many Rivers to Cross"; Tony Christie, "Yellow River"; Creedence Clearwater Revival, "Green River"; Travis, "Driftwood"; Henry Mancini, "Moon River"; the Band, "Up on Cripple Creek"; the Killers, "This River Is Wild"; Emeli Sandé, "River"; Justin Timberlake, "Cry Me a River."*

FIELDS Freedom, the wide-open outdoors, places of seduction, the fruitfulness of nature at times of harvest, battles if a war context.

» Gary Moore, "Out in the Fields"; Sting, "Fields of Gold"; the Beach Boys, "Cotton Fields"; R.E.M., "West of the Fields"; Big Country, "Fields of Fire"; Nanci Griffiths, "Fields of Summer"; Lenny Kravitz, "Fields of Joy"; Garnet Rogers, "Golden Fields"; Dreamtale, "Green Fields"; Bat for Lashes, "Winter Fields."

DESERTS AND PLAINS A barren place, emotional aridity, hardship, a tough journey, occasionally the exotic and/or the erotic.

» Maria Muldaur, "Midnight at the Oasis"; David Bowie, Martha Reeves and the Vandellas, "Quicksand"; Smokey Robinson and the Miracles, "The Love I Saw in You Was Just a Mirage"; America, "Horse with No Name"; the Coral, "Arabian Sand"; Screaming Trees, "Gray Diamond Desert"; Led Zeppelin, "Kashmir"; Nirvana, "On a Plain"; Rory Gallagher, "Out on the Western Plains"; Kings of Leon, "Cold Desert."

WOODS A tangled situation, being lost and far from civilization, magical encounters. Or the proverbial expression "We're not out of the woods yet." A jungle is a more brutal or exotic version of this meaning.

» The Cure, "A Forest"; Fleet Foxes, "Ragged Wood"; Paul Weller, "Wild Wood"; Tyrannosaurus Rex, "Find a Little Wood"; Robbie Robertson, "Go Back to Your Woods"; Don McLean, "Winter Woods"; Jethro Tull, "Songs from the Wood"; Taylor Swift, "Out of the Woods"; Bon Iver, "Woods"; Mercury Rev, "Black Forest (Lorelei)"; Johnny Burnette, "Setting the Woods on Fire"; Bruce Springsteen, "Jungleland"; Simple Minds, "Oh Jungleland"; Guns N' Roses, "Welcome to the Jungle."

ISLANDS/BEACHES Isolation, being cast away, solitude, escape, holiday, hot beaches, paradise. Castles made of sand are the best example of sand as representing all things transient. "Sands of time" is another cliché, connected to an hourglass.

» *The Springfields, "Island of Dreams"; Madonna, "La Isla Bonita"; Weezer, "Island in the Sun"; Elton John, "Island Girl"; Billy Bragg, "Island of No Return"; the Police, "Message in a Bottle"; CSNY, "Lady of the Island"; Kenny Loggins and Dolly Parton, "Islands in the Steam"; the Jimi Hendrix Experience, "Castles Made of Sand"; Stevie Wonder, "Castles in the Sand"; the Ramones, "Rockaway Beach"; the Shangri-Las, "Walking in the Sand"; Weezer, "Island in the Sun"; Lana Del Rey, "High by the Beach."*

SEA Hyperbolic imagery of romanticism. The metaphor of drowning is very popular. The sea can be of love (as it is in Fleetwood Mac's "Sara") or depression or eternity. Ships and sailing also figure for the journey of life.

» *Rod Stewart, "Sailing"; Pearl Jam, "Oceans"; Led Zeppelin, "Down by the Seaside"; Roxy Music, "Grey Lagoon," "Sea Breezes"; Robert Plant, "Down to the Sea"; U2, "Drowned"; the Who, "Sea and Sand," "Drowned," "I Am the Sea," "Water"; the Beach Boys, "Wreck of the Marie Celeste," "Surfin' USA," "Surfin' Safari," "Catch a Wave," "Surfer Girl"; Manic Street Preachers, "Ocean Spray"; All About Eve, "Drowning"; Lana Del Rey, "Marine Apartment Complex"; Avril Lavigne, "Head Above Water"; Lady Gaga, "Shallow"; Fleet Foxes, "Wading in Waist-High Water"; Coldplay, "Oceans," "Swallowed in the Sea"; DNCE, "Cake by the Ocean."*

The heavens

After the features of the earth, lyricists turn their attention to the sky.

THE SUN tends to be treated as the source of sunshine (i.e., as weather), rather than as a cosmic body, and symbolically is anything you shouldn't look at directly. It also represents hope and is the symbol of better times if it has temporarily set or gone behind a cloud.

» *Thin Lizzy, "The Sun Goes Down"; Elton John, "Don't Let the Sun Go Down on Me"; the Walker Brothers, "The Sun Ain't Gonna Shine Anymore"; Gordon*

Lightfoot, "Sundown"; Eric Clapton, "Behind the Sun"; Bob Marley, "Sun Is Shining"; the Cult, "Sun King"; Nanci Griffith, "The Sun, Moon and Stars"; TV on the Radio, "Staring at the Sun; the Libertines, "Don't Look Back into the Sun."

THE STARS signify eternity, devotion, unfathomable laws, fate, destiny, and in a more mundane way, celebrity.

» *Ed Sheeran, "All of the Stars"; Coldplay, "A Sky Full of Stars"; Nina, "Little Star"; Radiohead, "Black Star"; Rose Royce, "Wishing on a Star"; Madonna, "Lucky Star"; Lee Marvin, "Wanderin' Star; Portishead, "Wandering Star"; Albert King, "Born Under a Bad Sign"; Perry Como, "Catch a Falling Star"; Coldplay, "A Sky Full of Stars," Kendrick Lamar, "All the Stars"; the Wanted, "I'm Glad You Came."*

THE SKY itself is often symbolic of freedom and flying, and sunset and dawn have a special appeal for lyricists (see the entry on 24 hours in section 9).

» *The Allman Brothers, Patty Griffin, Ring of Fire (and others), "Blue Sky"; Jeff Buckley, "The Sky Is a Landfill"; Kate Bush, "The Big Sky"; Bob Dylan, "Under the Red Sky"; the Platters, "Red Sails in the Sunset"; Pink Floyd, "Goodbye Blue Sky"; ELO, "Mr. Blue Sky"; David Wilcox, "Blue Horizon"; Kanye West, "Touch the Sky"; Adele, "Skyfall."*

THE MOON as silver moonlight is the perfect setting for romance, but as a celestial body it is mysterious, "witchy," haunting. Under certain atmospheric conditions, the moon appears in other colors than silvery-white. It has been described in song lyrics as silver, yellow, red, blue, pink, and black.

» *Television, "Marquee Moon"; Elvis Presley, "Blue Moon of Kentucky," the Waterboys, "The Whole of the Moon"; Echo and the Bunnymen, "The Killing Moon"; Tyrannosaurus Rex, "By the Light of a Magical Moon"; Van Morrison, "Moondance"; Henry Mancini, "Moon River"; Matt Monroe, "Fly Me to the Moon"; the Rolling Stones, "Moonlight Mile"; Creedence Clearwater Revival, "Bad Moon Rising"; Norah Jones, "Shoot the Moon"; Janis Joplin, "Half Moon"; Brandy, "Full Moon"; the Microphones, "The Moon"; Phoebe Bridgers, "Moon Song." The White Stripes, "White Moon"; Ray Noble, "By the Light of the Silvery Moon";*

Rickie Lee Jones, "The Moon Is Made of Gold"; the Neville Brothers, "Yellow Moon"; Erykah Badu, "Orange Moon"; Paco Versailles, "Lilac Moon"; Nick Drake, "Pink Moon"; the Walkmen, "Red Moon"; Marya Stark, "Scarlet Moon"; Dan Norvan, "Turquoise Moon"; Carlo Buti, "Luna Verde (Green Moon)"; the Marcels, Beck, "Blue Moon"; the Cramps, "Blue Moon Baby"; Amy Stroup, "Purple Moon"; Blackmore's Night, "Under a Violet Moon"; Creeper, "Black Moon"; the xx, "Blood Red Moon"; Wilco, "Black Moon."

The lyricist's zoo

Animals provide a ready supply of images and metaphors for human life. They often have symbolic qualities granted to them—some already folklore, some grounded in observation of their behavior. There are many proverbial sayings that encapsulate the symbolic meanings given to animals, such as "cry wolf" or "black sheep of the family." This is also fertile territory for out-of-hand misanthropic attitudes and satire, notoriously in the Beatles' "Piggies."

The majority of songs with animal imagery are often not actually about the animals themselves; rare exceptions include Michael Jackson's "Ben" (about a pet rat) and the Who's comic "Boris the Spider." These lyrics range from popular animals such as birds, dogs, cats, horses, to the less common—see Stackridge's "The Indifferent Hedgehog" or Tame Impala's "Elephant."

BIRDS In the lexicon of popular song, there are probably more lyrics that mention birds than any other creature. Traditionally associated with freedom (hence "Free as a Bird"), the bird belongs to the sky, not the earth, and thus signifies the soul, or a free-living spirit. Bird imagery expresses the romantic desire for transcendence—think of "One Day I'll Fly Away," or "Love Lifts Us Up," with its mention of eagles. By virtue of its wings, the bird is symbolically related to angels. Songs nominally about birds are usually about freedom, innocence, rising above a situation, and escape.

» The Beatles, Emeli Sandé, Supertramp, "Free as a Bird"; Elton John, "High Flying Bird"; The The, "Sweet Bird of Truth"; It's a Beautiful Day, "White Bird"; Jimi Hendrix, "Night Bird Flying," "Little Wing"; Snowy White, "Bird of Paradise"; Siouxsie and the Banshees, "Painted Bird"; Neil Young, "Birds"; Miranda Lambert, Wings, "Bluebird"; Iron and Wine, "Flightless Bird, American Mouth."

Songbirds such as nightingales, blackbirds, larks and others are an easy metaphor for a woman singing (think of Eva Cassidy's *Songbird*) or the power of music itself, as in Norah Jones's "Nightingale," Carly Simon and James Taylor's "Mockingbird," Fleetwood Mac's "Songbird," Joe Cocker's "Bye Bye Blackbird," and the Beatles' "Blackbird." as singers, birds represent the romantic ideal of organic creativity—instantaneous, unreflecting, ever-renewing, and apparently effortless—as evoked across Kate Bush's album *Aerial*. In the act of singing, what a bird *is* and what it *does* are one. In human experience only rarely do we achieve states of consciousness where doing and being are blissfully one.

Swans are supposed to sing most expressively before their death, hence the phrase "swan song" when something is coming to an end. The mockingbird comes a close second to the songbirds in lyric mentions because it can satirize or imitate someone. Doves have their traditional Biblical meaning of peace. The seagull is linked with the freedom of the sea, owls represent wisdom, night, and far-seeing, and roosters carry a sexual connotation.

» *Buffalo Springfield, "Blue Bird"; R.E.M., "Swan Swan Hummingbird"; Seals and Crofts, Wilco, "Hummingbird"; Anne Murray, "Snowbird"; Prince, "When Doves Cry"; Kristin Hersh, "Cuckoo"; Joni Mitchell, "Black Crow"; Elton John, "Skyline Pigeon"; Bebop Deluxe, "Sister Seagull"; Canned Heat, "An Owl Song"; Steve Miller Band, "Fly Like an Eagle"; the Police, "Canary in a Coal Mine"; Donovan, "Three Kingfishers"; Manfred Mann, "Pretty Flamingo"; Willie Dixon, "Little Red Rooster"; Christina Aguilera, "Birds of Prey"; P. J. Harvey, "Seagulls."*

BUTTERFLIES Next to birds in the lyric menagerie come butterflies. Butterflies symbolize something beautiful, fragile, and ephemeral. There is a recognition that any attempt to capture and hold onto this living beauty is doomed to fail. The Mission's "Butterfly on a Wheel" alluded by title to an editorial in the *Times* of London in June 1967, following the drug trial of Mick Jagger and Keith Richards, though the song itself is about a young woman damaged by a love affair. The Muse song listed below refers to chaos theory—that a butterfly on one side of the world is part of a sequence of effects linked to hurricanes on the other.

» *Lloyd Cole, Lenny Kravitz, Crazy Town, "Butterfly"; the Four Tops, "Elusive Butterfly"; the Mission, "Butterfly on a Wheel"; the Verve, "Catching the Butterfly";*

the Jam, "The Butterfly Collector"; Paul Weller, "Amongst Butterflies"; Heart, "Dog and Butterfly"; Muse, "Butterflies and Hurricanes"; Massive Attack, "Butterfly Caught"; Lana Del Rey, "Happiness Is a Butterfly."

DOGS Symbolically, dogs are loyal but downtrodden, except in folksongs if they are sheepdogs; if they are black, they can symbolize depression (though not Led Zep's black pooch).

» Led Zeppelin, "Black Dog"; Nick Drake, "Black-Eyed Dog"; Robert Johnson, "Hellhound on My Trail"; the Stooges, "I Wanna Be Your Dog"; David Bowie, "Diamond Dogs"; Elvis Presley, "Hound Dog"; Monkees, "Gonna Buy Me a Dog"; the Rolling Stones, "Walking the Dog"; the Everly Brothers, "Bird Dog"; Tom Waits, "Rain Dogs"; Aerosmith, "Sick as a Dog"; the Beatles, "Hey Bulldog"; Cat Stevens, "I Love My Dog"; Fall Out Boy, "Alpha Dog."

CATS Cats are feline, independent, and sexy, and associated with women. "Cat" can also be slang for a person of either sex who is a happy-go-lucky, hip person.

» The Beatles, "Leave My Kitten Alone"; the Cure, "The Love Cats"; Harry Chapin, "Cat's in the Cradle"; the Stray Cats, "Stray Cat Strut"; the Kinks, "Phenomenal Cat"; the Rolling Stones, "Stray Cat Blues"; Elton John, "Honky Cat"; David Bowie, "Cat People"; Ted Nugent, "Cat Scratch Fever"; Beyoncé, "Kitty Kat"; Hot Chip, "Alley Cat."

HORSES Horses are powerful and sexy; donkeys represent the easily exploited— as in the colloquial "donkey work." There is a strand of sexual innuendo to do with riding animals such as ponies, horses, and even a camel (in Maria Muldaur's "Midnight at the Oasis"), for instance in the Rolling Stones' "Beast of Burden"; and another in the milking of cows, hence lyrics like "Milk Cow Blues" and the allure of the dairy maid in ribald folk songs.

» America, "Horse with No Name"; the Byrds, "Chestnut Mare"; P. J. Harvey, "Horses in My Dreams"; Free, "Ride on a Pony"; Racing Cars, "They Shoot Horses Don't They"; U2, "Who's Gonna Ride Your Wild Horses"; the Rolling Stones, "Wild Horses"; the Beatles, "Dig a Pony"; Lee Dorsey, "Ride Your Pony"; Canned Heat,

"Pony Blues"; Sleepy John Estes, "Milk Cow Blues"; Sandy Denny, "One-Way Donkey Ride"; Paul McCartney, "Ram"; Rainbow, "Black Sheep of the Family"; K. T. Tunstall, "Black Horse and the Cherry Tree"; Goldfrapp, "Ride a White Horse"; Mitski, "A Horse Named Cold Air."

FOXES Foxes are traditionally cunning, and the adjective "foxy" means sexually alluring and independent, as in the Jimi Hendrix Experience "Foxy Lady," Manfred Mann's "Fox on the Run," and Thin Lizzy's "Johnny the Fox." Hard-rock and heavy-metal groups are lyrically fond of anything that has a nasty bite or sting, such as snakes, scorpions, tigers, lions, wolves, et cetera. Predatory animals signify power, energy, and self-determination. Spiders are almost invariably mentioned in terms of their webs—an image for the laying of a trap in which someone might be caught, as in Coldplay's "Trouble" or Dream Theater's "Caught in a Web."

» *Survivor, "Eye of the Tiger"; the Tokens, "The Lion Sleeps Tonight"; Beck, "Paper Tiger"; Metallica, "Of Wolf and Man"; Duran Duran, "Hungry Like the Wolf"; Joni Mitchell, "Coyote"; Red Hot Chili Peppers, "True Men Don't Kill Coyotes"; Leadbelly, "Black Snake Moan"; Heart, "Barracuda"; Accept, "Fast as a Shark"; Radiohead, "A Wolf at the Door"; Shakira, "Shewolf."*

The heart—the emotional self

One of the hardest cliché metaphors to deal with is the word "heart." This is the universal term for referring to the seat of the emotions, and there isn't really a substitute. There are many phrases that reinforce it: "don't take it to heart," "he broke my heart," "lift up your hearts," "heartfelt," "hearts and minds," "heartache," "being hard-hearted," "a heartless thing to do," et cetera. The phrase "two hearts" is lyric shorthand for two lovers. To deliver something "straight from the heart" (a title used by Bryan Adams) is to speak with sincerity. The nearest might be "soul," but that has religious connotations.

As the symbol of romantic love, it is not surprising popular music is full of songs with hearts in them. Use "heart" by all means, but if you want to be a cut above the average, find something new you can do with it. Be aware of clichés like "heart of stone" (used by the Rolling Stones, Springsteen, and many others). In his famous poem "Lines Written a Few Miles Above Tintern Abbey,"

William Wordsworth (1777–1850) wrote of sensations felt "along the heart." We don't think of the heart as having an "along"; it's a great image that refreshes the heart reference.

» *Cilla Black, "Anyone Who Had a Heart"; Blondie, "Heart of Glass"; Neil Young, "Heart of Gold"; the Isley Brothers, "This Old Heart of Mine"; Bonnie Tyler, "Total Eclipse of the Heart"; Captain Beefheart and His Magic Band, "Ashtray Heart"; Kate and Anna McGarrigle, "Heart Like a Wheel"; the Magnetic Fields, "Cactus Where Your Heart Should Be"; Yes, "Owner of a Lonely Heart"; Eagles, "Heartache Tonight"; Elvis Presley, "Heartbreak Hotel"; Gene Pitney, "Something Got a Hold of My Heart"; U2, "Two Hearts Beat as One"; Christina Perri, "Jar of Hearts"; Kanye West, "Heartless"; the 1975, "Heart Out."*

Roses

When it comes to flowers in lyrics, roses have special status. They stand first for beauty; second for the price paid for beauty, because they have thorns (thus creating an association between red roses, blood, and problems in love); third for transient beauty. The rose garden is an image for a place of content and paradise, a place where nothing goes wrong—hence the proverbial "bed of roses."

Roses are probably the first flower that springs to mind when a songwriter looks for a comparison for how beautiful is his love, some way ahead of the foxglove or lesser-spotted meadowsweet. In this respect, song lyrics follow in the wake of centuries of poets.

Elvis Costello pointed up the rose as a symbol with his album title *Mighty Like a Rose*—an interesting title as it invites us to reconsider what concept of strength is being used to support the simile, since roses are not "mighty" in any conventional sense. Wings titled an album *Red Rose Speedway*, comparing the petals to a racing track.

» *Lynn Andersen, "I Never Promised You a Rose Garden"; the Damned, "New Rose"; Marv Johnston, "I'll Pick a Rose for My Rose"; Bobbie Vinton, "Red Roses for a Blue Lady"; Joni Mitchell, "For the Roses"; the Jam, "English Rose"; Mary Black, "The Thorn Upon the Rose"; Poison, "Every Rose Has Its Thorn"; Bon Jovi, "Bed of Roses"; Eurythmics, "Thorn in My Side"; Thin Lizzy, "Black Rose"; Aretha Franklin, "A Rose Is Still a Rose"; Seal, "Kiss from a Rose"; Outkast, "Roses"; A Perfect Circle, "Rose."*

Games of chance

Gambling and games of chance form a popular set of metaphors for song lyrics. There is an underlying assumption that life is itself a game of chance, or comparable to one, involving risk, so gambling expresses something about the human condition.

Since popular music loves an outsider, a gambler can be the subject of a lyric, as well as a metaphor. Gambling metaphors are especially popular with hard-rock and heavy-metal bands, possibly because bands who tour a lot kill time by (among other things) playing cards and betting. The figure of the gambler is often romanticized in popular culture. Gamblers are mostly portrayed as getting away with the risks they take.

A roulette wheel is associated with the idea of a wheel of fortune. Dice-throwing is a common lyric image, as in the cliché "the die is cast." Playing cards offer ready-made characters, since a pack contains court figures of jack, queen, and king. The suits have symbolic meanings—hearts relates to emotions; diamonds to money and gemstones; spades to power and death, because the suit is black. KC and the Sunshine Band punned a disco hit title with "Queen of Clubs." There is the expression "poker-faced," meaning to conceal your feelings, as used for a song by Lady Gaga.

A more sophisticated version of the card lyric refers to chess, which implies thoughtful strategy and the gradual conquest of another, as well as symbolic figures such as pawns, knights, kings, and queens (see the white queen/black queen mythology on the second Queen album). The pawn image is a cliché of protest lyrics.

» *Bob Dylan, "Queen of Hearts"; Motörhead, "Ace of Spades"; Ned Miller, "From a Jack to a King"; Wink Martindale, "Deck of Cards"; the Rolling Stones, "Tumbling Dice"; Neil Sedaka, "Solitaire"; the Cramps, "Domino"; Robbie Robertson, "American Roulette"; the Faces, "Pool Hall Richard"; Penetration, "Life's a Gamble"; Wayne Fontana, "The Game of Love"; Chris Isaak, "Wicked Game"; Wilco, "Casino Queen"; Lady Gaga, "Poker Face"; the Cardigans, "My Favorite Game"; Amy Winehouse, "Love is a Losing Game."*

Fire

The Prodigy, Sly and Robbie, U2, Scooter, the Jimi Hendrix Experience, and the Pointer Sisters are just a few of the artists who have recorded songs called "Fire," and there is fire imagery as a linking device throughout R.E.M.'s *Document* album. The other elements (air, water, earth) tend to be subsumed in weather or topographical imagery.

Fire imagery is tied up with desire, passion, sex, and the erotic. Someone you fall in love with was once colloquially known as your "flame." The image acknowledges the transience of romantic love, as a flame can only burn for as long as it has adequate fuel. Fire can also represent a trial or a test that may be purifying. In Christian myth, it is associated with purgatory or hell.

» *Bruce Springsteen, "I'm on Fire"; Crazy World of Arthur Brown, "Fire"; Elvis Presley, "His Latest Flame"; Free, "Fire and Water"; the Move, "Fire Brigade"; James Taylor, "Fire and Rain"; Billy Joel, "We Didn't Start the Fire"; Super Furry Animals, "Fire in My Heart"; Deep Purple, "Fireball"; the Prodigy, "Firestarter"; Cheap Trick, "The Flame"; the Bangles, "Eternal Flame"; Kings of Leon, "Pyro"; the National, "Fireproof"; These New Puritans, "Into the Fire"; Alicia Keys, "Girl on Fire."*

Color

Color imagery is strongly visual. Colors have important psychological effects—which is why we consider the colors in our homes and public spaces. Colors already carry associations that relate to moods or states of mind.

A color in a title can give the listener half an idea of what the song is about immediately. Looked at in a more pragmatic way, it also provides an instant starting point for the marketing of your song through any visual medium: adverts, record sleeves, posters, live performance and stage lighting, videos, and more. Imagine writing a song called "Flame So Blue"; your lighting technician has half the job done for that song straight off. (Notice how, in concert, bands use blue lighting for slower songs.) Consider the role the colors red and white play in promoting the music of the White Stripes.

Before surveying individual colors, remember that the word "color" itself, singular or plural, often crops up in song titles. Donovan wrote "Colours" by leading each verse off with a different color.

» *Petula Clark, Chicago, "Colour My World"; Cyndi Lauper, "True Colors"; Phil Collins, the Sisters of Mercy, Hot Chip, "Colours"; David Sylvian and Ryuichi Sakamoto, "Forbidden Colours"; Love, "She Comes in Colors"; the Icicle Works, "Love Is a Wonderful Colour"; the Colour Field, "The Colour Field"; Billy Ocean, "The Colour of Love"; the Men They Couldn't Hang, "The Colours"; Teardrop Explodes, "Colours Fly Away"; Counting Crows, "Colorblind"; Death Cab for Cutie, "A Lack of Color."*

An obvious type of color symbolism is based on a flag. Burning Spear's "Red, Gold and Green" alludes to the colors of Rastafarianism, and anything with red, white, and blue could be the USA or the UK or France. Red and blue also have left/right political connotations. In the Who's "Blue, Red and Grey" the colors represent dusk. (The multicolored rainbow can be found under weather imagery). It isn't always obvious what the color in a title refers to, as with the Band's debut *Music from Big Pink* (it was in fact a house).

Here are individual colors' associations and a selection of songs.

WHITE This color is associated with purity, innocence, snow ("white as the driven snow"); "white lies," which are forgivable; weddings; a white flag of surrender, as in Elvis Costello's "Wave a White Flag"; peace; the white man; a whitewash or a coverup; a whited sepulcher, meaning hypocrisy; illness; death.

» *Procol Harum, "A Whiter Shade of Pale"; Tomorrow, "My White Bicycle"; Billy Idol, "White Wedding"; Bing Crosby, "White Christmas"; Foreigner, "White Lie"; Dream State, "White Lies"; the Velvet Underground, "White Light/White Heat"; Big Star, "Life Is White"; Paul Kantner and Grace Slick, "White Boy"; Texas, "White on Blonde"; Meredith Willson, "My White Knight"; Clannad, "White Fool"; Sunscreem, "White Skies"; Taylor Swift, "White Horse"; Frank Ocean, "White Ferrari"; Coldplay, "White Shadows."*

BLACK The contrasting associations of the color black are, on the positive side, power, authority, mystery, sexual allure; on the negative side, tragedy, grief and mourning, hate, loss, death, and depression. A number of artists have recorded "black" albums, including Prince and Metallica.

Probably the most used song title with this color is "Fade to Black" (see Dire

Straits and Metallica, to name two), closely followed by "Black and Blue," a title used by Dio, Pearl Jam, Sevendust, and Rancid. In the gloomier corners of popular music (goth, grunge, metal), black is *always* the new black. To see things "in black and white" is to see them in polarized and simplistic terms, as implied by a title like Elvis Costello's "Black and White World."

» *The Rolling Stones, "Paint It Black"; Santana, "Black Magic Woman"; Soundgarden, "Fell on Black Days," "Black Hole Sun"; Death Cab for Cutie, "Black Sun"; Stephen Stills, "Black Queen"; Queen, "March of the Black Queen"; the Doobie Brothers, "Black Water"; Paul Weller, "Black Is the Colour"; Suede, "Black or Blue"; KISS, "Black Diamond"; Deep Purple, "Black Night"; Screaming Trees, "Black Sun Morning"; Janis Ian, "Black and White"; Pearl Jam, "Black"; the Black Keys, "Little Black Submarines"; the Cramps, "Colour Me Black"; Amy Winehouse, "Back to Black"; Thom Yorke, "Black Swan"; My Chemical Romance, "Welcome to the Black Parade"; Arcade Fire "Black Mirror"; David Bowie, "Blackstar."*

GRAY The associations of gray are more negative than with other colors. Black may be negative, but it often has a thrill with it; gray commits the ultimate pop sin of being plain or dull. Gray evokes boredom, mediocrity, conforming, uniformity, being suppressed, an overcast cast. Of hair, it means the dreaded first sign of aging (which can be dignified by replacing it with silver).

» *Madness, "Grey Day"; 10,000 Maniacs, "Grey Victory"; Family, "Mellowing Grey"; Richard Thompson, "Grey Wall"; Gene Pitney, "Blue Turns to Grey"; Visage, "Fade to Grey"; the Monkees, "Shades of Gray"; Grateful Dead, "Touch of Grey"; the Pretty Things, "Defecting Grey"; XTC, "Wrapped in Grey"; Caravan, "In the Land of Grey and Pink"; Joni Mitchell, "Two Grey Rooms"; Modest Mouse, "Grey Ice Water": Waxahatchee, "Grey Hair."*

SILVER The associations of silver are primarily something of value, money, something metallic, moonlight, age (silver hair, which could represent wisdom). If it's metallic, silver can represent the future; in TV commercials and sci-fi films, the future is often depicted as a world made up of gray and silver surfaces. There is also the proverb that every cloud has a silver lining, and to have a "silver tongue" is to be a persuasive speaker.

» *Echo and the Bunnymen, "Silver"; Mountain, "Silver Paper"; Hawkwind, "Silver Machine"; Jeff Beck, "Hi Ho Silver Lining"; the Rolling Stones, "You Got the Silver"; the Beatles, "Maxwell's Silver Hammer"; Genesis, "Silver Rainbow"; Sonic Youth, "Silver Rocket"; Andrew Kerr, "Silver Suitcases"; the Rolling Stones, "Silver Train"; Fleetwood Mac, "Silver Springs"; LCD Soundsystem, "Sound of Silver."*

GOLD Like silver, gold represents value, money, wealth, and in its own right wedding rings. It can also be a color of hair, the best of something (a "golden" age), a wisdom that should not be broken ("golden rule"), and fields at harvest time. Spiritually, it is something or someone who is dependable—as in Neil Young's "Heart of Gold." Proverbially, silence is golden, and there is a pot of gold waiting at the end of every rainbow.

The unwary in popular lyrics are left with "fool's gold" (a popular lyric title used by Thin Lizzy, the Stone Roses, and many others). Mythically, the figure most likely to spring to mind in connection with gold is King Midas, who was granted a wish to turn everything he touched into gold, then found this was a curse.

» *David Bowie, "Golden Years"; the Black Keys, "Gold on the Ceiling"; Sting, "Fields of Gold"; the Tremoloes, "Silence Is Golden"; Shirley Bassey, "Goldfinger"; the Beatles, "Golden Slumbers"; U2, "Silver and Gold"; Syd Barrett, "Golden Hair"; Freda Payne, "Band of Gold"; Fleetwood Mac, "Gold Dust Woman"; Dire Straits, "Love Over Gold"; Dio, "Golden Rules"; Razorlight, "Golden Touch"; Tina Turner, "Golden Eye"; Richard Thompson, "Gold Kisses"; Stevie Wonder, "Golden Lady"; Kacey Musgraces, "Golden Hour"; Kanye West, "Gold Digger."*

BROWN Like gray, in décor and fashion, brown is a color without especially strong or attractive associations. It implies conformity, dullness, and paper bags, but it is also the color of earth and therefore of fertility. It is most attractive for songwriters when an eye or hair color (for which brunette might also be used), or when linked to something else.

» *The Stranglers, "Golden Brown"; the Rolling Stones, "Brown Sugar"; June Tabor, "Shallow Brown"; James Brown, "Shades of Brown"; Lynn Miles, "Big Brown City"; Boney M, "Brown Girl in the Ring"; Roni Size and Reprazent, "Brown Paper Bag"; Billy Bragg, "Greetings to the New Brunette."*

RED Along with blue, red is the most likely color to turn up in a song lyric. Blue and red symbolize the two key emotional states in lyrics: passion and misery. They are linked with fire and water. The connotations of red are passion, blood (possibly murder), the heart, the emotions, sex, warning, and wine. To be angry is to "see red." Infrared is one end of the visible light spectrum. We speak of a "red-light district," and in the Police's "Roxanne" the young woman of the title plied her trade by switching on a red light. To be a "scarlet" woman is to be a sexual predator. Overnight flights are catching the "red-eye"; otherwise, to have red eyes may indicate crying. (Red rose songs are listed under roses; red clothing and shoes appear under clothing in section 10).

A "little red book" is understood to contain addresses and phone numbers of lovers, past and present. To see things through "rose-tinted glasses" is to idealize a situation. A "red herring" is a piece of information that is an unhelpful distraction. In a recording studio, a red light indicates the necessity for quiet, because a session is in progress. A "red letter day" is a special day on which something great has happened.

Variations on red include ruby and scarlet, both intensifications of red.

» *Spirit, "Red Light Roll On"; the Jimi Hendrix Experience, "Red House"; Nena, "99 Red Balloons"; Love, "My Little Red Book"; Split Enz, "I See Red"; the White Stripes, "Red Rain"; Neil Diamond, "Red Red Wine"; Robin Williamson, "Red Eye Blues"; the Incredible String Band, "Red Hair"; Kris Delmhorst, "Red Herring"; U2, "Red Light"; Limp Bizkit, "Red Light—Green Light"; Robert Johnson, "They're Red Hot"; Fiona Apple, Taylor Swift, "Red"; All About Eve, "Scarlet"; Cat Stevens, "Sweet Scarlet"; Joni Mitchell, "Shades of Scarlet Conquering"; Mercury Rev, "Vermilion"; Tommy James and the Shondells, "Crimson and Clover"; the Misfits, "Crimson Ghost."*

PINK Pink is a toned-down, less active, feminine color (check the social phenomenon known as "pinkification"); a more luxurious version of red; and also a skin color, and a color of the sky at dawn and twilight.

» *Alan Dale, "Cherry Pink and Apple Blossom White"; Aerosmith, the Cure, "Pink"; Nick Drake, "Pink Moon"; Psychedelic Furs, "Pretty in Pink"; Cherry Poppin' Daddies, "Pink Elephant"; AC/DC, "Sink the Pink"; Bruce Springsteen,*

"Pink Cadillac"; They Might Be Giants, "Stormy Pinkness"; Frank Ocean, "Pink + White"; the National, "Pink Rabbits."

ORANGE Orange is a rare color in song lyrics. It is notoriously hard to find a suitable rhyme sound when it is placed at the end of a line (though "syringe" is not bad), and this may have discouraged people from putting it in a title. It tends to appear either in protest songs about the deployment of the defoliant Agent Orange in the Vietnam war (see R.E.M.'s "Orange Crush") or as part of a riot of color in a psychedelic song. In recent years, it has become associated with the effect of wildfires in the USA.

» *Dandy Warhols, Kasabian, "Orange"; Depeche Mode, Kate Wolf, "Agent Orange"; Leah Labelle, Love, "Orange Skies"; Natalie Cole, "Orange Colored Sky"; Johnny Cash, "Orange Blossom Special"; Van Dyke Parks, "Orange Crate Art"; the Cocteau Twins, "Pink Orange Red"; P. J. Harvey, "The Orange Monkey"; Bob Dylan, the Band, "Orange Juice Blues"; Screaming Trees, "Orange Airplane"; R.E.M., "Orange Crush."*

YELLOW This color is primarily associated with sunshine and summer, blonde hair, corn, childhood, and is a favorite color for psychedelic songs. Apply it to something that isn't usually yellow to get a playful effect, as with the Beatles' "Yellow Submarine": yellow is bright, innocent, frivolous, so painting a submarine yellow is not something the military would go in for. Sometimes the word "lemon" is used as a substitute.

» *Coldplay, "Yellow"; Donovan, "Mellow Yellow"; the Beatles, "Yellow Submarine"; Joni Mitchell, "Big Yellow Taxi"; Phil Lynott, "Yellow Pearl"; Jackson C. Frank, "Yellow Walls"; Christie, "Yellow River"; Mitch Miller, "The Yellow Rose of Texas"; Haircut 100, "Lemon Firebrigade"; Dawn, "Tie a Yellow Ribbon Round the Old Oak Tree"; the Leaves, "Lemon Princess"; Randy Newman, "Yellow Man"; Stina Nordenstam, "Keen Yellow Planet"; Cardi B, "Bodak Yellow."*

GREEN The associations of green fall into quite distinct areas: it is the color of nature, of grass, the environment and the politics thereof; it also stands for money ("greenbacks"); for envy or jealousy (the green-eyed monster); and inexperience (to be green in judgement). To get the "green light" is to go ahead with a project. Ireland is described as the "Emerald isle." Something "evergreen" (see Barbara Streisand's song of this title) can weather all seasons, while to have "green fingers" is to have a talent for gardening.

» *New Order, "Everything's Gone Green"; Lorde, "Green Light"; Johnny Cash, "Forty Shades of Green"; Siouxsie and the Banshees, "Green Fingers"; Fleetwood Mac, "The Green Manalishi (with the Two-Pronged Crown)"; Nelly Furtado, "The Grass Is Green"; Tom Jones, "Green, Green Grass of Home"; the Jam, "Pretty Green"; the Lemon Pipers, "Green Tambourine"; Dinosaur Jr., "Green Mind"; Bonnie Raitt, "Green Lights"; Donovan, "Turquoise"; Mr. Big, "Green Tinted Sixties Mind"; Lianne La Havas, "Green and Gold"; Laura Mvula, "Green Garden."*

BLUE Along with red, blue is the most likely color to be found in a song lyric. When a popular lyric isn't passionate, it's sad . . . *blue*. So, "blue" is shorthand for a whole gamut of emotions that run from mild sadness to outright depression, until, as the Foo Fighters put it, "The Deepest Blues Are Black."

Blue is also the color of sky and ocean, of water, which have positive meanings, and of smoke. Blue lights are associated with the police and emergency services such as ambulances. Something that comes "out of the blue" is a complete surprise. Blue can signify electricity, and there is a generic character called "Baby Blue" who crops up in many songs. "Blue-sky thinking" is free and imaginative. (I have not included titles where "blues" implies a style of music.)

» *Bob Dylan, "It's All Over Now, Baby Blue," "Tangled Up in Blue"; Prince, "Blue Light," "Computer Blue"; Nick Drake, "Way to Blue"; Janis Joplin, "Little Girl Blue"; Joni Mitchell, "Blue"; Madonna, "True Blue"; Tommy James and Shondells, "Crystal Blue Persuasion"; the White Stripes, "Blue Orchid"; Kate Campbell, "Fade to Blue"; Paul Mauriat, "Love Is Blue"; Laura Nyro, "Mr Blue"; R.E.M., "Electron Blue"; Ella Fitzgerald, "Born to Be Blue"; Icehouse, "Electric Blue"; Lana Del Rey, "Blue Jeans"; Jorja Smith, "Blue Lights."*

PURPLE This color does not feature often in lyrics because it is not an everyday color. Purple is associated with royalty and wealth, and it can also function as a color of twilight. Related colors are violet and indigo. Ultraviolet is the opposite extreme of the visible spectrum of light to infrared. Purple's most famous use in popular music is Prince's song and film *Purple Rain*. This title has the psychedelic aura set by Hendrix's "Purple Haze" in 1967. Perhaps, too, Hendrix inspired Robert Plant of Led Zeppelin to give his "Living Loving Maid" on the second Led Zeppelin album a purple umbrella.

» *Stone Temple Pilots, "Purple"; Van Morrison, "Purple Heather"; Sheb Wooley, "Purple People Eater"; Tempo and April Stevens, "Deep Purple"; Marvin Gaye, "Purple Snowflakes"; Joni Mitchell, "Turbulent Indigo"; Frank Sinatra, "Mood Indigo"; Babes in Toyland, "Bruise Violet"; Peter Gabriel, "Indigo"; U2, "Ultra Violet (Light My Way)"; Stevie Nicks, "Violet and Blue."*

Eyes

We speak of "making eye contact," of seeing eye to eye, of eyes as the "windows" of the soul, and of lovers who gaze into each others' eyes. So, it's not surprising that many song titles have "eyes" in the title. Occasionally, it's not just love that gets in the eyes. Jackson Browne wrote his 1970s hit "Doctor My Eyes" when he had an eye infection, the Platters lamented that "Smoke Gets in Your Eyes," Richie Havens offered "Eyesight to the Blind," and Sam Cooke even dared to say "I'd Rather Go Blind."

In proverbial usage, to be "green-eyed" is to be jealous (hence Less Than Jake's "Green Eyed Monster"), and to be "wide-eyed" is to be surprised and/ or innocent. Combining eyes and color is a favorite song-title ploy. The most popular eye color is blue, with brown and green close behind. Blue also allows for a play on the meaning "sad," hence Crystal Gayle's "Don't It Make My Brown Eyes Blue."

For lyrical ingenuity about eyes, consider the phrase "luggage eyes," which occurs in T.Rex's "One Inch Rock." Marc Bolan explained to *Beat Instrumental*, "At first I was thinking she had eyes with bags beneath them . . . then I thought, *Why not 'luggage eyes'?*"

» *Art Garfunkel, "Bright Eyes"; Roxy Music, "Angel Eyes"; Eagles, "Lyin' Eyes"; Dusty Springfield, "I Close My Eyes and Count to Ten"; the Supremes, "When the Lovelight Starts Shining Through His Eyes"; the Who, "Behind Blue Eyes"; Coldplay, "Green Eyes"; Fleetwood Mac, "Emerald Eyes"; Chuck Berry, "Brown-eyed*

Handsome Man"; Everly Brothers, "Ebony Eyes"; Silversun Pickups, "Lazy Eye";
Billie Eilish, "Ocean Eyes"; Taylor Swift, "Eyes Open"; the Weeknd, "In Your Eyes";
the War on Drugs, "Red Eyes."

> *There's a point in every writer's life where they've got to look hard and long at*
> *the stock images they use."*

NEIL FINN OF CROWDED HOUSE TO *MOJO*, JUNE 1994

This survey of popular lyric imagery, though not exhaustive, will encourage thought about well-used images and your own lyrics. Have a look at your writing for common images that you repeat. If they are obvious or clichéd ones, consider developing your own.

If you are a more experienced songwriter, look for images that are distinctly yours. These may be part of your fingerprint as a songwriter, but check they aren't overused either.

SECTION 7

telling a story

> I wanted to make it feel like you meet somebody. The Nebraska stuff was like that. You meet somebody and you walk a little while in their shoes and see what their life is like. And then what does it mean to you? . . . Just saying what somebody had to say and not making too big a deal out of it."
>
> **BRUCE SPRINGSTEEN TO *MUSICIAN*, 1985**

> To think up a unique subject is not enough. You have to still put it in some relevant human context."
>
> **DAVID BYRNE TO *MELODY MAKER***

> I've always said that 'El Paso' was the song that made me want to write songs, it was the perfect meshing of melody and storyline, and I thought that here was something that married rhythms and the written word perfectly."
>
> **BERNIE TAUPIN, LINER NOTES TO ELTON JOHN'S *TUMBLEWEED***

Not all your lyrics have to be about you. Telling a story about another person, or through the eyes of someone else, can be liberating.

One of the most freeing stages in a songwriter's development is the realization that a lyric does not have to be confessional. Most songwriters initially write lyrics about their own experiences, in autobiographical first person. The breakthrough comes when you write a lyric from another point of view than "I," or narrate someone else's story.

Narrative lyrics offer a means to disguise your own experience and emotions, or to get away from yourself entirely. A confessional lyric can also be a narrative; you could be telling the story of something that happened to you. But when you write a lyric from someone else's perspective, new areas of life are available for your lyrics. This breakthrough in itself can open new sources of inspiration.

The narrative lyric is one of the most powerful lyric forms. It is probably the oldest type there is, found in folk music the world over. Long before people sang about how they personally felt, they sang songs that told stories about others. Narrative songs recorded and replayed the collective experience of the tribe, including historical events. In folk music, the designation "The Ballad of . . ." usually indicates a narrative lyric.

In a narrative song, the lyric is often more of a focus than the music. This is true of many folk songs, as well as the early Bob Dylan and the acoustic Bruce Springsteen (as on *Nebraska* and *The Ghost of Tom Joad*, right up to 2019's *Western Stars*), where chord progressions and melody may not be memorable in themselves.

Well-written narrative songs get our attention by describing a situation and teasing us for a few minutes with details, so that we care enough to want to know what happens. A series of narrative songs can tell a larger story—which of course can lead to the concept album.

How to structure a story

To write a narrative lyric, decide on five key structural elements:

- What is the end event? To what point is the lyric moving? This is usually something dramatic, unless you want an anticlimax or no resolution.
- How many characters are essential? As this is a lyric and not a novel, there isn't room for lots of them.
- Who are the main actors? What is their relationship to each other, and to the final event? What is their motivation? Why do they do what they do?
- What is the theme or point of this story? This arises from the relationship between the central characters and the final event.
- When did this story happen? The distant past, the recent past, or the present?

With these things in place, you can fill in the details needed to round out a story. For example, where is this story happening—in what sort of society and landscape? (This may have an important bearing on the content.) How much "backstory" is needed, and what is the first event in the lyric? Do you give away the ending in verse 1 or hold it in reserve to keep the suspense? Or, is it a mystery where there is no final explanation, as in the case of one of the greatest of all modern story songs, Bobbie Gentry's "Ode to Billie Joe"? Did Billie Joe jump, or was he pushed? What was the relationship between him and the young female narrator who can't eat her dinner? What was it that was thrown off the Tallahatchie Bridge? That's a lyric that repays careful analysis.

How to select a narrator

Another important decision is: who is going to be the narrator—the one who tells the story? If you write from a detached, third-person point of view, the narrator is not a part of the story but an invisible presence in which the listener may have no interest. Another approach is to tell the story in the first person, from the central character's point of view. A third possibility is to write it in the first person, but to give your first-person narrator an insight into the other characters' points of view. Each of these is valid. The sequence of events can stay the same, but the meaning of the story might differ.

A narrative lyric can also be divided so that it is multi-perspective, with more than one of the characters speaking. They could be given consecutive verses. This can be technically challenging to keep clear for the listener, but if the song is a duet by two singers (as in some of Meat Loaf's songs, or Elton John and Kiki Dee's "Don't Go Breaking My Heart"), it becomes clear enough.

The narrative story has no time to be introspective and dwell on moods. The emotion of a character (and the atmosphere as a whole) must be sketched in a couple of lines, perhaps with imagery. Moods and implications are conveyed in many ways—sometimes through descriptive details, sometimes by choice of words. If a story lyric begins "He strolled down to the shining lake / Of calm and dappled blue," the imagery establishes a positive mood; if the same line were "He crept down to the sullen lake / Of cloudy gun-metal gray," there is a sense of foreboding.

This is not simply because in one the lake is "shining" and in the other it's "gray." The verbs "strolled" and "crept" are important. "Strolled" suggests a carefree, relaxed movement; "crept" suggests something furtive, seeking concealment. Many lyricists seek to convey mood through adjectives, their descriptive words, and underestimate the power of verbs to do this. Take a line like this: "The windy dark night blew your hair." Compare it with the more dynamic "Darkness drums and pulls your hair," where the verbs work harder.

This is where a thesaurus is as handy as a rhyming dictionary. A thesaurus provides synonyms for words to make this kind of fine adjustment in later drafts, replacing adjectives with verbs. Controlling verbs in a narrative lyric is doubly important because verbs are words of action—and a story is usually about actions. So, choosing the correct verb is telling part of the story in itself.

Verses, choruses, and stories

So, how does a narrative lyric fit the common verse / chorus / bridge song structure? There is a slight mismatch here, because a story doesn't repeat sections, but a chorus often has the same words on each repeat. The traditional folk ballad avoided this problem by:

- Using a simple form with no choruses or bridges, only a sequence of verses.
- Attaching a short refrain—a single line—to the end of each verse. This refrain is sometimes formed by nonsense syllables with which people can join in, or a phrase or image that alludes to the song title or central event, and may comment on its mood. For example, "The lake was dark that day, that day / The lake was dark that day" is rhythmic, and could be a symbolic running commentary on each verse as the story advances.
- Add interest by changing a single word of the refrain from verse to verse—in this case, "the lake was" could be replaced by "the sky was," or even "his face was" or "her thoughts were."

A refrain on the end of a verse provides one solution to writing a narrative lyric in verse / chorus form. The chorus doesn't advance the story, it comments on it, indicating the theme; the verses convey the events. The bridge (if there is one) can handle either the critical moment in the story, in which case the last verse (if there is a verse after the bridge) describes the fallout and consequences; or the change of heart that pushes the events to their climax.

Imagine a story lyric where a young man is offered the prospect of fame and fortune but has to leave his hometown and girlfriend behind. She is not happy, so she issues an ultimatum: it's her or the road. Verse 1 could describe their relationship and usual life; verse 2 his career ambitions and his first opportunity which he turns down, then a chorus. In verse 3, he gets another opportunity, and this time he feels he should take it. In the bridge, his woman lays down the law;

he changes his mind for an instant, then realizes it's no good. In the final chorus, the words can then be altered to indicate he has made up his mind.

The love triangle

The narrative lyric can relate many different stories. One of the classic storylines in popular song involves a murder stemming from a love triangle: the motive is jealousy, and it leads to revenge, death, imprisonment, or escape.

In the lyric of "Hey Joe," a song made famous by Jimi Hendrix, there's a dialogue. It isn't narrated by the murderer, Joe. The events are:

- A friend asks where the narrator is going with a gun in his hand.
- Joe replies that he's going to shoot his woman, because she's been "messing round town" with another man.
- In a later verse, Joe tells his friend that he's done it.
- The friend asks where he's going to go now to escape the authorities, and the answer is Mexico (useful thing, Mexico, if you've just shot someone).
- There, he can escape punishment and live a free man.

Similarly, in Tom Jones's 1960s melodrama "Delilah," a jealous man kills his lover before the police break down the door; he even asks for her forgiveness as he does it. Dido's "Mary's in India" is a narrative about a love triangle with a happy ending:

- One half of a couple, Mary, goes off to India, leaving her partner behind.
- As she is having a good time there, she decides to end the relationship. Dido's refrain has the sun setting on the young man and rising metaphorically on Mary.
- The narrator takes pity on the poor chap and consoles him.
- Eventually, the narrator and the jilted young man form a new relationship. Now the sun is rising on him and setting on Mary.

The nice twist here on this traditional parallel between the motion of the sun and the waxing and waning of love is that the international time difference (albeit exaggerated) allows us to pretend that it could be literally as well as figuratively true. In Kate Bush's "Babooshka," the triangle is occupied by two people and a fantasy figure. The wife decides she wants to enliven her marriage, so she invents a Russian *femme fatale* character and sends letters to her husband to elicit from him the emotional response he once gave her. The irony is that in responding eagerly to this fantasy figure, he is actually responding to his wife.

The Eagles' "Lyin' Eyes" is interesting in the way it inserts the chorus into the storyline. The story concerns a woman who seeks out an affair because of the emotional austerity in which she finds herself. The chorus comments on this, through the image of the "lyin' eyes" that can't be hidden. Since she is addressed as "you," it is difficult to see who is saying this. Is it the man she lives with? Is it the voice of her conscience? Is it an accusation, or is there some sympathy in it?

Dire Straits' "Romeo and Juliet" takes characters from an existing narrative (Shakespeare's play by way of *West Side Story*) that is so famous that we know they represent doomed young love. Elvis Costello's "Watching the Detectives" takes imagery from detective *film noir* but doesn't quite provide enough information for us to know exactly what is going on; instead, we get a superbly wrought cinematic style packed with unforgettable images, but the song lacks the information to let us put it into a logical sequence. That lyric uses a filmmaker's vocabulary, with phrases like "long-shot," "cut to," and "close-up," as if the story is being recounted like a movie.

Not all love triangles need be unhappy. A great example of the relationship between a lyric's emotion and its perspective is the Beatles' "She Loves You," whose joy and energy partly depend on the fact that it's selfless. The song is spoken by a third-person go-between whose intention is to patch up a lovers' quarrel. It cast the Beatles as true peacemakers long before the less specific "All You Need Is Love" or Lennon's "Give Peace a Chance."

Stories of a rise and fall

A well-known narrative lyric form describes a rise to stardom. The archetype of this is Chuck Berry's "Johnny B. Goode," which tells of a country boy, illiterate but a gifted guitar player, who sits by the railroad making up rhythms that match the trains. The chorus simply exhorts Johnny to "go"—to play for all his worth and shoot for the big time. His mother foresees that one day he will have his name in lights. Although this doesn't happen in the song, we never doubt that it will.

David Bowie's "Ziggy Stardust" is part of a five-song sequence on the *Ziggy Stardust* album, but in itself it relates how a rock 'n' roll star is destroyed by success. Similarly, the Jam's "To Be Someone" tells of the rise and fall of a rock band from the point of view of one of the band members:

- He dreams of how great it would be to be famous, like a soccer player, a rock singer, or a movie star.
- He dreams of having lots of fans and lots of girls, proving his manhood, and getting rich.
- He achieves these things but starts taking drugs.
- He recklessly spends his money.
- His money and fame shrink.
- He loses his guitar-shaped pool, the media lose interest in him, he can't afford drugs; and, instead of taking taxis, he now has to walk everywhere.

The lyric ends with the ironic and sad return of the idea that to be someone "must be a wonderful thing." It is left ambiguous whether this means he is once more dreaming of climbing the ladder of success, or whether the whole thing was a daydream in which he (correctly) imagined both the positives and negatives of fame.

Julianne Regan's "Miss World" (recorded by the band Mice) does the same thing with a young woman who decides to enter a beauty contest. It follows the same curve from poverty and obscurity to success and then back to anonymity. It's a lyric that shows exquisite and economic handling of telling details.

Sometimes, stories don't have endings. It could be you don't know what the ending will be, or the characters leave in the middle of something. We never know what becomes of the lovers in Bruce Springsteen's "Incident on 57th Street," where there is a family, two young lovers, and a death, all mixed up.

A lyric like Bob Dylan's "All Along the Watchtower" is filled with dramatic events on a big scale, cryptic images, and buried connections. It ends with the two riders approaching the city. We never know what happens next. Handled well, the incomplete lyric invites the imagination of the listener to write what is left unwritten.

I can't have every song, not necessarily just about me, but from my point of view—I always say, you must be a very big-headed person to write about yourself, or only from your own point of view. Why should you want to?"

JOAN ARMATRADING TO *MELODY MAKER*

I feel like I write so people can think of it as theirs. If my song is exactly about your life right now, then it is—I don't even want to say that it's mine, because it's yours."

BILLIE EILISH

There's a lot of personal stuff that can go into songwriting, but there's also a lot of dramatization and fictionalization. You have to do that to make a good song."

NORAH JONES

On every album I adopt a different sort of character, and the character on this album [An Innocent Man] is sort of a sweet person who is in love and feeling good."

BILLY JOEL TO HANK BORDOWITZ

Point of view and voice

Whether a lyric is a story or not, it does not have to be written from the first person. "I looked out this morning" could be "He / she / they looked out this morning." Think about who could speak your lyric. If you feel too exposed writing in the first person, get a new perspective on personal themes by addressing yourself as "you." Most listeners will think you are talking to someone else. But be careful not to mix this with addressing someone else as "you" elsewhere in the same lyric.

Shifting point of view can change the emotion of a song. I once sketched a lyric based on the phrase "closing down sale," which I'd seen in the window of a junkshop. The many secondhand objects in the shop were taken from many lives. This made me think of endings, and then, metaphorically, of the end of a relationship as a closing-down sale. I sketched the idea from the point of view of a couple breaking up. Then I considered how the imagery would work if it was the initiator of the split using it. The song would become a cruel put-down, selling off the other's affections ("You thought you were out of the woods / But now you're just secondhand goods").

Going on from that, I imagined a third person coming on the scene and falling in love with the rejected individual. For him or her, the closing-down sale brings incomparable good fortune. The person who was rejected is swept up by this new love. The closing-down sale imagery turns into a song about happiness. It all depends on the perspective.

A different perspective could come from someone a different age to yourself. In his lyric book *Songs*, Bruce Springsteen writes of *Nebraska*, "I often wrote from a child's point of view: 'Mansion on the Hill,' 'Used Cars,' 'My Father's House'—these were all stories that came directly out of my experience with my family."

> *I didn't want any more confessional songs, and I wanted to put myself in other scenarios. I can do that, I'm a craftsman. I don't have to just do one thing. It was a good release for me."*
>
> **STING TO *MOJO* ON *TEN SUMMONER'S TALES*, DECEMBER 1993**

Dramatic monologue

Halfway between narrative and point-of-view, the dramatic monologue gives the chance to speak in someone else's voice. In essence, it requires you to:

- Choose an interesting character to be the "I" who speaks.
- Find their tone of voice, manner of speaking, and typical vocabulary.
- Let them describe their time, place, situation in life, and disposition.
- Start at a critical moment in their life, when something vital is about to happen to them, or when they are on the brink of an action or decision.
- Or, describe the immediate aftermath of such an event or action.
- The more critical this moment, the more drama the monologue has.
- This is a moment of self-revelation—the primary emphasis is on their state of mind, rather than on a sequence of events. The drama is an inner one.

A dramatic monologue can tell a story, but it can also imply what has happened, and instead concentrate on creating an intriguing mood.

An excellent example of this type of lyric is Jimmy Webb's "Wichita Lineman," which has the neatest of introductions, the first two lines telling us what the narrator does for a living. From that point on, Webb's lineman becomes a romantic, "everyman" figure, pictured poised between the land and sky in all weathers. His solitude is both a pleasure and a curse; it is his job and a symbol for the solitude of being human. He is an existential symbol, yet so concretely realized that you never consciously think of this, even as you are moved by it. Somewhere at the back of his dilemma, which is the drama, is a woman. He has realized now how important this woman is to him. But we don't know what will happen or needs to happen. The song retains its fascination. In 2005, Webb told Rob Chapman of the *Times*:

> A song like "Wichita Lineman" suggests the plains, the receding horizon, the loneliness of the lineman who's up this pole in the middle of nowhere. That's an actual image that I saw one day. I was driving along and saw this guy high up on a telegraph pole and I wondered to myself, "Gee I wonder who he's talking to and what he's talking about." There's a kind of tenacity, a blue-collar nobility to what he was doing ... [Billy Joel] said what that song says is that inside any normal Joe you might see on the street there could be great thoughts and aspirations and just because a guy is working at some menial job it doesn't mean that inside of him there's not some great passion or great dream.

It is a response worthy of the great American playwright Arthur Miller.

Another fine example, more obviously dramatic than "Wichita Lineman," is Springsteen's "Meeting Across the River" (from *Born to Run*). Producer Chuck Plotkin once said, "Bruce's gift is to locate the heart in some character's dilemma." The central character delivers a dramatic monologue talking not to us but to another character who is also part of the story. The result is an overheard conversation of unintended self-revelation. The "I" is attempting to put across a certain image to Eddie, but we form a different opinion.

In this scenario, a smalltime crook talks to his friend about a "job," for which he needs to borrow money and get a lift through the tunnel to the other side of the city. He has a troubled relationship with a woman called Cherry, who is angry and threatening to leave him for selling her radio to a pawn shop. We never know what the "job" is, whether it worked, or if they got away with it. But the song leaves us feeling we know these people and something of their past and present, and we sympathize with them. That in itself is a profoundly broadening experience.

The dramatic element can be given an ironic content if the character is placed in a situation on the cusp of events where we know what will unfold but they do not. An example would be a sailor volunteering to serve on a new ship: he tells his family about his good fortune, only for the end of the lyric to signal he has signed up for the Titanic's maiden voyage. We know what is coming; he doesn't. Anything the lyric mentions about safety or what he'll do when they arrive in New York becomes tragically ironic.

Another example would be a lyric where a young musician describes leaving a club after his band has played a terrible gig and they have split up. His dreams of success and fame appear to be dashed, but then the lyric reveals that this musician happens to be Jimi Hendrix.

Example lyric: "On Weymouth Sands"

Let's close the section with a detailed look at a dramatic monologue lyric. The speaker tells a story, with a dramatic element arising from the moment of the telling—in other words, the story is not yet finished, and the character is in a dilemma. This aspect differentiates the dramatic monologue from a simpler first-person character narrative.

"On Weymouth Sands" has a British context and a literary pedigree. The title was borrowed from a 1935 novel by John Cowper Powys (1872–1963). Weymouth is a large once fashionable town on the south coast of England, near to the Isle of Wight. It is close to Chesil Beach, which features in a novel and film of that name by Ian McEwan.

In terms of style, I imagined this as a Bernie Taupin lyric for an early Elton John album. It centers on a man who works as a provincial antiques dealer and who does house clearances. He leads a freewheeling life but gets emotionally involved with one of his customers. The portrait is psychologically complex because he admits that he sometimes deceives his customers and may not have as much feeling for the woman as his love letters imply. We cannot therefore simply identify with him. Instead, we feel sympathy for both characters, neither of whom is entirely in control of their actions.

Here first is the sketch, which lacks any settled rhythm or rhyme scheme.

"On Weymouth Sands" (sketch)

A salty breeze blows on Weymouth sands[1]

Standing alone in this foreign land[2]

Nothing seems to have been in that

As I travel from town to town

I deal in antiques, that's my trade[3]

The residue of lives gone by[4]

Mahogany and oak and walnut[5]

The dressing table mirror

Your father had just died[6]

When I called to clear the home

You were only carrying out instructions

Your father was a traveler frequently away

He left his daughter with a kindly aunt and maid[7]

You let me enter in as you wiped away a tear[8]

The colors from the stain glass window

Put color on your face[9]

The Rossetti prints were not your style, you

    said[10]

A box of paperback novels with a water mark

An ivory-handled paper knife to open my love

    letter[11]

1   The opening line takes us straight into the location.

2   "Foreign" will turn out to have a psychological (not literal) meaning.

3   The central character's job is his main identity.

4   One theme will be sadness at the possessions passing away from their owners.

5   Furniture from the 19th and 20th centuries would often be made with these woods.

6   A second character appears, and a reason why he has come into contact with this person: a death in the family.

7   This female with an aunt and a maid is probably unmarried. She seems slightly upper-class—i.e., above the dealer. Her father's traveling could mean she has suffered from a parent being absent. There is no mention of a mother.

8   The meeting of the two is hinted at. The woman is grieving and therefore vulnerable.

9   The repetition of color needs to be changed.

10   D. G. Rossetti (1828–82), the Pre-Raphaelite artist and poet.

11   The love letter reveals that the dealer has fallen for the woman after visiting on business. The sketch has the bare bones of a story to fill out.

1 Line 1 creates a tough, melancholy atmosphere.

2 The dealer's dilemma is placed very early, in lines 3-4. He contemplates what this relationship might be like.

3 The verse now has a settled rhythm (4+3 in a single line) and an AABB rhyme scheme.

4 In verse 2, the dealer explains how he makes his living.

5 Bow windows are common in British seaside towns and date back to the Georgian or Victorian eras.

6 To have "gone away for good" might be a euphemism for death.

7 The psychological portrait deepens when he confesses to sometimes deceiving customers by buying at a lower price than is fair. This complicates our feelings about him as the central character.

8 The phrase "next of kin" suggests that he is often called in after someone has died.

9 Another reference to the melancholy of his work.

"On Weymouth Sands" (final draft)

Verse 1

A salt wind blows cold and hard on Weymouth

    sands,[1]

Alone I walk to the waves as if in a foreign land.

Thrilled by your beauty, thinking about my life,[2]

Weighing the chances of harmony and strife.[3]

Verse 2

Just a travelling dealer, antiques are my trade[4]

One bow window to my name on an old seaside

    parade.[5]

I empty people's houses when they've gone away

    for good.[6]

Don't always give a fair price like I know I

    should.[7]

Bridge

I follow the direction to the next of kin[8]

To parcel up the past when all is safe at last.[9]

Verse 3

It is only three nights since you proposed to me,

And now we're on a knife-edge of possibility.[1]

You know your family will disapprove, so very

    much my better.[2]

Maybe I got carried away writing those love

    letters.[3]

Bridge 2

I follow my inclination, I love everywhere I go.

When all is said and done I always get my fun.[4]

Bridge 3

I sorted through the books with many a stolen

    look.[5]

We talked about the rain.[6]

The dusty smell of finished lives was more than I

    could take.[7]

Ash-blonde hair in a leather chair, can't always

    tell real from fake.[8]

You asked me to clear the house, I measured out

    your bed

With the inventory of a life,

And now I can't get you out of my head.[9]

1 This is the drama: he isn't sure what to reply.

2 The class theme: her family will disapprove.

3 He wonders whether he hasn't overstated his feelings and got in deeper than he wants to be.

4 The idea of committing is worrying—he enjoys his bachelor lifestyle.

5 The word "stolen" has two meanings—he steals looks at her, but he may also be stealing some of the property he is supposed to be buying.

6 This section is crucial for bringing out the drama. It recounts how they met.

7 The death theme is sometimes too much for him, and it is this that has precipitated his feelings for her.

8 The phrase "real from fake" refers to furniture, possibly her hair, and also his own feelings.

9 The irony is that his feelings have overwhelmed him.

1 Verse 4 gives details of the woman's life. As an ambassador, her father was often absent from her life—a "subtle wrong" when she was a child.

2 The father used his job to distract from the pain of losing his wife, her mother.

3 The dealer sees her vulnerability to him. He sees himself, also a traveler and therefore liable to set off emotional wounds in her, taking love—taking advantage. He feels guilt, and yet he is also vulnerable himself.

4 The song ends with a repeat of the first line. We are left to imagine what happens next.

Verse 4

The daughter of an ambassador, a childhood's

subtle wrongs,[1]

Who hardly knew a father, he never stayed for

long

'Cos he was running from a wife who died when

you were two,[2]

And here I am a traveler taking love from you,[3]

Taking love from you.

Coda

A salt wind blows cold and hard

On Weymouth sands.[4]

writing lyrics today

> *You see I'm always going for the sound of things. I have a hard time just writing things out, I have to hear them first. Sometimes I put it on a tape recorder, but then I transcribe it and it's lost its music."*

TOM WAITS TO THE *DAILY TELEGRAPH*, JANUARY 2006

Writing for today's commercial market, and for other singers, new challenges are inevitable. So, it's time to work out your basic approach—and what you want to achieve from your writing.

Are lyrics the same as they've always been?

Surveying popular music since the 1920s, it is possible to identify some general shifts in lyric writing. In the 1930s and 1940s, mainstream lyrics were mostly conservative in their overt topics and technique. There were formulas for imagery and phrasing, some tied to musical structures like the 32-bar form. Wit, elegance, and refinement were prized. Conscious artistry was held in high esteem, and extreme statements were held in bad taste. Naughtier meanings were veiled behind imagery and archly implied. Subject matter was more limited but executed with greater clarity. Audiences did not expect to puzzle over the meaning of a lyric, and they were not required to. If a lyric was obscure enough to mean whatever you wanted it to mean, it would have been considered that the lyricist had not done their job.

This continued in pop music through the 1950s, though it was challenged from the rock 'n' roll field and the blues, where nonsense or thinly veiled sexual double entendres were common, and slang brought a crude linguistic energy. A significant change came with the protest movement of the early 1960s (from Woody Guthrie to Joan Baez and Bob Dylan), which introduced lyrics with social themes and observations, and a wider range of imagery to express them. This style of lyric was taken into the mainstream by Simon and Garfunkel and other singer/songwriters, and also by Bob Dylan when he went electric.

What Dylan did (and Leonard Cohen, too) was to raise the possibilities of what the popular song lyric could talk about. Much greater wordplay and freewheeling imagery came to the fore in Dylan's mid-1960s work—which in turn influenced the Beatles to be more adventurous with their lyrics; for example, Dylan influenced John Lennon's narrative "Norwegian Wood." Pressures from the counterculture meant that lyrics diversified even more in the second half of the 1960s. Subject matter embraced greater eccentricity.

Rock music aspired to become a form of art, and lyricists like Jim Morrison and Laura Nyro regarded the lyric as a form of poetry. The lyric became more ambitious in its style and its subjects, but a lack of craftsmanship (not to mention the influence of mind-altering substances) meant such ambitions were not always executed well. This was the period when it became acceptable to be ambiguous to the edge of meaninglessness, because being clear about your meaning was regarded as inauthentic and old-fashioned. Only "straights" were bothered with precise meanings; the dominant attitude was that words could mean whatever the listener wanted them to mean. Mike Love of the Beach Boys was swimming against the cultural tide when criticizing Van Dyke Parks's lyrics for the *Smile* sessions as "over-acidized."

Lyrics became sexually explicit, more poetic (imitating literary models), and at the same time more obscure. In the early 1970s, progressive-rock bands continued to write in a self-consciously poetic manner. Singer/songwriters such as Neil Young, Joni Mitchell, Cat Stevens, and Nick Drake used the poetic style to probe feelings and relationships in greater depth. By the 1980s, "artier" bands had lyrics that could be inexplicable, as in the case of the early R.E.M. songs. More and more lyrics could be written and left as raw material for the listener to interpret.

The ultimate development of the lyric along one line was the global success of rap and hip-hop in the 1980s and 1990s, where the lyric broke free from the constraints of melody, harmony, and musical rhythm. Its linguistic rhythm is forcefully assertive and sets words to minimal musical accompaniment. Rap lyrics are often much longer than typical song lyrics and contain more verbal fireworks, such as multiple rhymes on the same sound. But there is a sense in which rap lyrics are really a form of performance poetry set over and against music, rather than being song lyrics.

It is hard to find another time in popular music history when words alone took so much of the focus. To its critics, rap's claim to be poetry rather than doggerel is contested, owing partly to stylistic crudities, and there is a view that severing the link between melody and words may prove to be historically limiting.

It is probably true to say that in the 21st century, song lyric styles have become more diverse than at any other time, though many of these styles are not necessarily found in chart songs. Overall, lyric writers are freer now to be obscure and less focused than in earlier periods. More lyrics suggest meaning rather than clarifying or defining it.

> *I slowly began to cut the words down. Most poets do, you'll find. After a couple of years of writing flowery poetry—and I don't down that, but it's not really suited to rock 'n' roll particularly—things I write now are just street poems."*
> **MARC BOLAN OF T.REX TO *MELODY MAKER***

Lyrics and poems

Having raised the issue of poetry, let's turn to one concern that bears significantly on style: is there a difference between song lyrics and poems?

If writing lyrics involves being sensitive to words, does this make it basically the same as writing poems? This is a common but mistaken assumption, and for those who write poetry as well as lyrics it can cause problems. A far greater number of people write poetry than read it, as any poetry publisher or editor will tell you, and this is especially true when it comes to *modern* poetry. The average person's concept of poetry is based upon 19th-century poetics and language. If you write poems or song lyrics from that example, they will be stylistically out of date. So, it is helpful to grasp the differences between writing poems and lyrics, because, for the songwriter, it's the differences that matter most.

Lyrics are words whose full effect depends upon music. A lyric is a set of words intended to be sung, and to be supported by music. A lyric happens in time, so a listener cannot on first hearing ask the singer to stop and go back a line; reading a poem you could. Poems communicate ideas and feelings by word alone, straight off the page. This is crucial. Music is so potent it can lend banal and clichéd words an expressiveness they could never have in a poem. Delivered by Aretha

Franklin, Levi Stubbs, Sam Cooke, or Jeff Buckley, the most pedestrian phrases can still "work." The music can compensate for the lack of style and substance in the lyric. Poetry has nothing to rescue it in the same way. The music can compensate for whatever profundity or style is missing from the words. Music can excuse or even temporarily revive clichéd words and images.

Music is so powerful it can also work against a lyric's content, instead of with it. Generally, we expect words and music to be congruent—i.e., pointing in the same expressive direction. The assumption is that a happy song needs a happy lyric; a sad song needs a sad lyric. But this doesn't have to be so. Such are the subtle shades of meaning which music itself creates, the relationship between words and music can be more complex. A knowledgeable songwriter knows a lyric that appears to be a happy love story could be set in a minor key so that the song does not sound happy at all, and leaves us feeling that this happiness is a sham.

The mournful music of 10cc's "I'm Not in Love" guarantees that we do not believe what the singer is saying. He spends the lyric asserting that he isn't in love, yet we get the clear impression that he *is*, and, contrary to what he says, that it *does* all mean that much to him. Likewise, Elvis Costello's "I'm Not Angry" is delivered with such musical punch and vocal venom that we know the singer is very angry indeed. A similar effect results if a lyric of political satire is matched to a jolly up-tempo pop song, as with Costello's "Oliver's Army." Likewise, the breezy, radio-friendly sound of Blue Öyster Cult's "Don't Fear the Reaper" is at variance with its chilling death-wish lyrics.

Bobbie Gentry's "Ode to Billie Joe" is haunting because the troubling story of apparent suicide is related in a relaxed, laconic country style. All the disturbance is under the surface. The Police's "Every Breath You Take" has been sentimentalized as an elegy despite the fact that it is a confection of horrible possessiveness, and in Bob Dylan's "Just Like a Woman," the music seems to be rebelling against the disdain of the lyric. Another special property of the song is that, with backing vocals and countermelodies, music allows for more than one line of words to be delivered simultaneously, which is impossible on the linear printed page.

So, a lyric and a poem are truly different artistic entities. But some lyrics read well without their music, and they can have a "poetic" quality in terms of imagery or phrasing—for instance, "Across the Universe," which was one of John Lennon's favorites, or Joanna Newsom's "Inflammatory Writ." But even poetic qualities don't of themselves turn a lyric into a poem. The language of poetry is often too complex to set to music. Good poetry has less tolerance of cliché than song lyrics. There are images you can get away with in a lyric that could not be used in serious poetry. Poetry requires higher standards of grammar, control of syntax, and precision of language than lyrics as they are currently written, not to mention sensibility and intellectual content.

In practical terms, the good news for songwriters is that you can get away with a lot in a song lyric—things that would sink a poem without trace—and still have a hit record. I am not saying that the quality of a lyric doesn't matter, and it doesn't mean that there aren't real differences of merit between lyrics. A song lyric can achieve a quality of language and expression that deserves the adjective "poetic"—yet it is still not a poem. But a song can be commercially successful even with a lyric that is formulaic and clichéd. In fact, a realist would opine that many are successful precisely because they *are* formulaic and clichéd.

Successful lyrics have to streamline their ideas in ways poems do not. They must simplify their language and imagery to avoid things getting too complicated to follow. But if you write poetry, you can insert lines from your poems into lyrics, or rewrite a poem as a lyric. Kurt Cobain used to put lyrics together by choosing lines from notebooks of his poems. The Lovin' Spoonful's "Summer in the City," a US #1 hit in 1966, began life as a poem by John Sebastian's brother, Mark.

Sometimes, a poem by someone else might inspire you, as happened with Sheryl Crow when she read a poem called "Fun" in *The Country of Here Below* by writer Wyn Cooper. Its first two lines run *"All I want to do is have a little fun / Before I die, says the man next to me."* She took that as the basis for a song, adding and deleting to make the words her own, but decided in the end that she could not match the spontaneity of the original. So, she called the poet and agreed terms to use his work. The resultant song became "All I Wanna Do," a global hit.

On rare occasions, songwriters have incorporated poetic forms into their songs. The Verve's "Sonnet" was not a sonnet, but Frank Black of the Pixies tacked a formally correct sonnet onto the end of "The Happening." He also used the Japanese *haiku* form, which has lines of five, seven, and five syllables, for the verses of "Hang Wire." Occasionally, songwriters put the word "ode" in a title to give a song an air of sophistication.

Another theme that underpins the relationship between poetry and lyrics is the assumption that lyrics matter anyway. Not all songwriters care equally about the words, and even those who do care are aware that part of the audience may not be bothered about the lyric. When Blur's album *13* was released, vocalist Damon Albarn commented to *Mojo* magazine, "I don't put my lyrics [on the inner sleeves] anymore. I think you'll find that most people don't know what you're singing about until they look at the lyric sheet anyway. As long as the feeling is right, I don't care."

> In 'Caroline, No,' [Brian Wilson] talked about a young girl who has lost her innocence, but the specific words both in terms of rhyme and being less obvious—that's what I saw as my job. If there was a word he didn't like, I would change it. Or I would say, 'How does this sing?' So he would sing it. Words that have long vowel sounds are much easier to sing, so if it wasn't a word that you could 'hold out' we would try to find an alternative."

LYRICIST TONY ASHER, COWRITER OF "CAROLINE, NO,"
AS QUOTED IN "THE MAKING OF *PET SOUNDS*"

> Sometimes I would write a word that fit my conception of the phrase, and Burt would point out that it actually added a note. Or that there was a pick-up note where there shouldn't be, or some little detail like that, which would require me to find different words to say the same thing."

ELVIS COSTELLO TO *MOJO* ON HIS COLLABORATIONS
WITH BURT BACHARACH, OCTOBER 1998

Words as sound

Meanings are one thing, but the words of a lyric are for singing. You may have the right words for what you want to express, but you must consider how good they sound when sung. Some combinations of sounds are hard to vocalize clearly (because of the relation of vowels and consonants), some phrases might be grammatically correct but unrhythmic, and some styles of lyric don't go with a particular musical genre.

A song lyric results in one type of rhythm (the words) being fitted to another (music). The words of a lyric have a rhythm before you put a melody to them. The English language naturally gives some words greater stress than others.

In the past, students of poetry were required to mark ("scan") which syllables were stressed and which less stressed. One common "meter," meaning a pattern of stresses, is "ballad meter." This has four stressed syllables in the first line, followed by three in the second, and so on. It is the meter of many folk songs and hymns, for instance "Amazing Grace" (stressed syllables underlined):

A<u>ma</u>zing <u>grace</u>! How <u>sweet</u> the <u>sound</u>
That <u>saved</u> a <u>wretch</u> like <u>me</u>!
I <u>once</u> was <u>lost</u>, but <u>now</u> am <u>found</u>,
Was <u>blind</u>, but <u>now</u> I <u>see</u>.

Whatever the pattern of stressed and unstressed syllables, it needs to fit the beat of the music and the melody, so that unstressed syllables do not fall on points in the music which carry emphasis. This is too complex an issue to discuss fully here, but here's a simple example.

If the first line of a lyric scans as "The <u>sun</u> comes <u>up</u> on a <u>bright</u> new <u>day</u>," "the" should not fall on the first beat of the bar when you sing it. That would place too much emphasis on what is an unstressed word. "Sun" belongs on the first beat, and the melody will probably start with "the" as the last beat of the previous bar. It would also sound wrong if "the sun" was on beats three and four of a bar, so that "comes" falls on the strong first beat of the next bar. Most people avoid this problem by instinct, because it feels wrong, rather than by conscious intervention. As a general rule, if words like "the," "of," "a," "at," "to" are on a strong beat, your setting of the lyric to a melody needs adjusting.

The effect of not matching syllabic rhythm to musical rhythm is clumsy, but in certain contexts intentionally playful, comic, even endearing. In the Darkness's song "Friday Night," singer Justin Hawkins sings "badminton" as bad-<u>min</u>-ton, instead of the usual stress of "<u>bad</u>-min-ton."

Some singers even give words extra syllables for reasons of rhythm. In Catatonia's "Londinium," singer Cerys Matthews amusingly turns the three-syllable "endlessly" into the four-syllable (and much easier to sing) "en-der-less-ly."

> *I don't have a record of writing hit after hit, the way Billy Joel or Paul Simon has, or Stevie Wonder had—which I wish I had, but it isn't what I do. Even when I set out to try, it doesn't turn out that way . . . my taste does not correlate with the taste of the general public, for the most part."*
>
> **RANDY NEWMAN TO *MOJO*, AUGUST 1998**

> *When the song was over, I said, 'Great, Norman—it was really great. But the words, you gotta change them. They just don't work. We can't put this record out. Not because it isn't a good song but because it sounds like you're promoting drugs.' 'No,' Norman protested, 'It's not drug-related. It's art.'"*
>
> **BERRY GORDY TO PRODUCER NORMAN WHITFIELD**
> **ABOUT THE TEMPTATIONS' "CLOUD 9"**

> *Language consists almost entirely of fashionable slang these days; therefore when somebody says something very blunt lyrically it's the height of modern revolution."*
>
> **MORRISSEY TO *MELODY MAKER*, 1984**

The songwriter, the lyric, and the marketplace

One basic question for a songwriter is: What do you want to write about? This is not merely a matter of self-expression. What you write affects whether you win an audience, how big that audience might be, who might cover your songs, and what commercial success your music might have. The default subject matter for most people's lyrics is their own experience, especially the universal experiences that move people most when they are young: searching for love, falling in love, winning it, holding onto it, losing it, finding it again. Most songwriters write love songs, which is no bad thing, since the majority of commercially successful songs fall in this territory—and that's because those lyric themes are what the greatest number of people can relate to.

In terms of artistic freedom, the good news is that almost anything can be (and has been) a subject for lyrics. You can write about any subject in the world, within the legal limits of copyright and assorted laws of libel, obscenity, incitement to commit crimes, depending on the law of the land or religious oppression under which you live.

If your songwriting remains a private concern between you, your guitar or piano, and your favorite technology for making demos, there isn't anything else to consider. You can be as naïve, as silly, as clever, as opinionated, as arch, as allusive, as low-brow, as high-brow, as complex, as simple, as obscure, or as clichéd, as you wish. Songwriting is a hugely enjoyable pursuit even if you never intend to make a career out of it. Your music-making may not be your profession, but it offers a fulfilment beyond the range of many hobbies.

However, when you seek an audience, the game changes. Singing for other people is an act of communication. It entails awareness of who makes up your audience and who you would like in it. "Audience" here includes the people who hear you busk in the street, the band members you want to play your songs, the audience who come to your gigs, the promoter you want to get bookings with, the manager you want to impress enough to take you on, the record company who might sign you, the DJs who play your music, and the wider public who stream it and buy CDs, downloads, and concert tickets.

Lyrics are a crucial part of the interface between your music and the audience. Music may have meanings of its own, but a lyric colors and channels those meanings. What a song means is almost always defined in the terms of what its lyric appears to be about. So, how will the audience relate to your subject matter? Will they understand it? What can they find in it for themselves?

As some of the quotes here show, commercial issues can affect lyrical content. The most obvious instance of this is when singers and bands put profanity or obscene images in their lyrics. This used to cause songs to be banned. The amount of bad language in mainstream pop has certainly increased. Sometimes there are conflicts between band and record label or producer about political or religious content. Sometimes songwriters pitching at an artist take into consideration how well-known the artist is. Here is songwriter Tony Macaulay:

> I spent hours sweating over the psychology of how the songs were put together. For example, if it was an unknown artist, we felt that if we started with a long, engaging verse, by the time they got to the chorus, the disc jockey would take it off and play another one, so if it was an unknown artist, we'd start with a bit of the chorus just to tell them how good it was going to be. If it was a name artist, we could afford to start with a verse and then get that nice lift into the chorus so that you lulled them into the mood of the song, so when the chorus came it was a sort of big thrill.

But commercial songs did not always have to suffer in quality. The artistry of Bacharach and David's classic 1960s hits is acknowledged everywhere. For example, k. d. lang contrasted the lyric style of "groove-oriented pop" with a song like "Walk on By," telling *Mojo*, "It can be the most moving song and the most ambient song. The detail of those songs catches up with you later on. You can be as involved as you want because it's less intrusive. You lean towards it and the more you lean towards it the more vast it is inside."

Finding your themes: lyrics as identity

A songwriter who is also a performer forges an identity. This identity is comprised of many things, from haircut and clothes to the size of your band (or whether you have one), the guitar you play, the way you sing, the style of your music. Some genres of music have a limited number of themes and it is difficult to go outside them. The content of your lyrics is another element, as is how significant the lyrics are in relation to the music. In some cases, musical content is second best to lyric content. With a band like Led Zeppelin, the lyrics are less important to their reputation than lyrics are to the reputations of Bob Dylan, Bruce Springsteen, Leonard Cohen, Randy Newman, Joni Mitchell, Elvis Costello, Joanna Newsom, P. J. Harvey, Ron Sexsmith, and Stephen Merritt.

Among songwriters for whom lyrics are central, there are those who write more or less from experience and about themselves in the "confessional" manner. In 1993, Loudon Wainwright III told *Mojo* magazine, "I'm interested in me: I'm interested in what's happened to me and what went wrong with my folks' marriage and my erotic thing about my mother, all that interests me terribly. And I like to explore myself in song."

For others, the art is in how you start with a personal experience or feeling but develop it. For Kristin Hersh, there is the idea of not being completely self-centered. "For me, the only time I can write is when I see really clearly—and I'm so unselfconscious for that reason I can hear what the songs are saying, and I let them say whatever they want regardless of how much it has to do with my situation," she told *Melody Maker*. "Not that you should make things up—it should resonate with you. You shouldn't pretend. But if it's just about you, who the hell would want to buy that? That's when egos come into the equation."

The notion of confessional lyrics leads to the assumption that what makes the song authentic is its being rooted in a personal experience. But songwriters know that the meaning of a song changes as time passes, even for the writer, as Joni Mitchell once shrewdly observed to *Mojo*:

> I know a song falls differently against your life many times. To keep it alive it has to—you're bringing new experience to it all the time, and it's not the experience you wrote it with, so it's open to interpretations. . . . The songs shift around—either it means something to you or it doesn't. And that's one reason why I resent the "who is it about?" fixing it in time, "It's about that over there." No it isn't, it's a mirror—and it reflects you if you take the time to look as you pass it by.

With natural curiosity, many feel that if they know the origins of a song—its roots in the writer's personal experience—they will get closer to its meaning. This is one of the great misunderstandings about art, and it is partly the consequence of a metaphor. Ever looked at a flower's roots and compared them to its petals in bloom? Which would you rather have on display in a vase on your table? Tom Waits provided an important insight when he said, "The stories behind most songs are less interesting than the songs themselves. So you say, 'Hey, this is about Jackie Kennedy.' And it's, 'Oh, wow.' Then you say, 'No, I was just kidding, it's about Nancy Reagan.' It's a different song now."

Moving from writing about self to a wider frame of reference is something that has exercised Bruce Springsteen since the 1980s. It is obvious that when a songwriter wants to expand out from personal experience, their lyrics can seem thinner and less convincing.

In 2002, Springsteen told *Uncut*, "The secret of the songwriting was to get personal first, then you sort of shade in universal feelings. That's what balances the songs. All experience is personal so you have to start there, and then if you can connect in what's happening with everyone, the universality of an experience, then you're creating that alchemy where your audience is listening to it, they're hearing what they're feeling inside and they're also feeling "I'm not alone.'"

Songwriters also go through phases as to how they feel about this issue, because it is so fundamental. In 1984, Paul Weller declared that he had stopped writing about characters and situations and that his songs were becoming more direct. But by 1995 he felt differently, stating he was wary of autobiographical songs, and that while they might start from personal experience, he would develop the lyric away from it.

The British group Siouxsie and the Banshees were notorious for avoiding anything that could be construed as a mainstream lyric theme. Instead, they ploughed a gothic furrow of songs about split personality, voodoo, darkness, suffering, perversity, S&M imagery, and so on. For bass player Steve Severin, it was a case of taking apart traditional rock lyrics and putting them back together differently. This was one factor that prevented the band reaching a bigger audience (not everyone wants a big audience, or the compromises that go with it). Likewise, the Cramps centered many of their lyrics around imagery drawn from sci-fi and horror B-movies, '50s Americana, and fetishistic sexual imagery.

Nothing could be further from the subject matter of Roy Harper, Richard Thompson, or John Martyn, singer/songwriters influenced by the late-1960s counterculture, or Springsteen's meditations on blue-collar life in America. In 1985, the latter explained to *Rolling Stone*, "When I sit down to write, I try to write something that feels real to me. Like, what does it feel like to be thirty-five or something right now, at this point in time, living in America? It's not much more conscious than that. I generally try to write songs that are about real life, not fantasy material. I try to reflect people's lives back to them in some fashion."

Some key questions about lyric intention

- Should people understand your songs on first hearing?
- Is it desirable for them to reread the lyrics and discuss the meanings?
- How far is it okay for them to construct their own meanings?
- Do you want to be ambiguous or plain-speaking?
- Will you sing about your own experiences and provide unguarded autobiography?
- Will you write about your experiences but veil them to some extent?
- Do you want to write about other people or general situations?
- Do you want to invent characters and tell stories?
- Will your themes be everyday things that feature in most lives, or fantasy lyrics which are the door to an imaginary world (which might be truth by an alternative route)?
- Do you want to be playfully serious or seriously playful?

- Will you be direct and outspoken, funny, satirical, ironic, witty?
- Do you want to suggest you're everyman or everywoman, muddling along, writing songs about what "we" all feel?
- Will you be a *prophet* with a *message*—someone who wishes to expose complacency and corruption?

These choices affect the kind of lyrics you want or need to write. It is a big factor in commercial success, especially in the realm of the hit pop single, where the range of subject matter and its treatment is often conformist and shallow. The commercial viability of a song can be reduced by lyrics that, by style or content, do not fit some very prescriptive limitations. The challenge is to be original within the formulae.

Writing songs for other singers

If you pitch songs to acts who do not write their own, the lyric has to be one that the artist in question can sing. What is deeply meaningful to you may be a closed book to them. You may have to discipline your lyric style to be transparent and direct. Obscurity, merely hinting at meanings, is often mistaken for profundity. It is often symptomatic of fear, or not being sure what it is you're saying. Depending on your habits, there may be a need to avoid obscurity, and to restrain the imagery, to write less of what Randy Newman amusingly called "crystal explosions in the eventide" lyrics.

Subject matter is also a significant factor in who might cover your song. The melody and music could be great, but unfortunately the lyric might break the deal. Emmylou Harris once said, "It's always the lyric that I look to first. It's always about the emotions. I've always been drawn to songs that deal with our vulnerability but also our undercurrent of strength."

This is a major aspect of the discipline of writing songs for other people. Some themes will be inappropriate. Middle-of-the-road balladeers are not going to cover songs about the CIA, politics, torture, or corrupt business deals. Conversely, can you imagine Arianna Grande or Taylor Swift singing a death-metal lyric? Or Nirvana singing a lyric about the joys of disco dancing? Or Norah Jones singing a witty but miserable Morrissey lyric? Or Travis doing a Rolling Stones–style ode to debauchery?

English rocker Marc Bolan of T.Rex was one of rock's most original lyricists.

He thought other people were unlikely to cover his songs because of the words. In 1972, he told *Melody Maker*, "It's like nobody really covered the Stones' songs... I feel the lyrics are maybe too artistically camp for, say, [fictional stereotypical pop act] Twitch Younger and the Rockabeads to get away with, even though the melody might get them, but they'd look weird saying some of the words. I don't see people, apart from friends, covering my songs."

In fact, since Bolan's early death in 1977, there have been many covers of T.Rex songs by bands on the margins of pop history, but not by mainstream artists, unless you count the Power Station's "Get It On." This only changed very recently, with the release in 2020 of the Bolan covers album *Angelheaded Hipster*. It is hard to cover "Children of the Revolution," for example, without seeming to be acting out Bolan's part, because only he could put across its camp lyrics about driving a Rolls-Royce. The world of his songs is *lyrically* idiosyncratic, despite the continuing appeal of his riffs.

To take a different example, you can imagine a soul singer covering U2's "One" with a gospel slant and genuinely making the song their own. It wouldn't sound like someone pointing at U2. That's because the lyric doesn't put up any impediments. Likewise, the Jimi Hendrix Experience's "All Along the Watchtower" does not sound like someone pretending to be Bob Dylan, even though Hendrix's vocal has a Dylan-esque slur, but most covers of "Purple Haze" or "Voodoo Chile" sound like homages to Hendrix because no one else can convincingly inhabit those lyrics. We suffer from working weeks, tired limbs, broken hearts, and relationship disputes, but not purple hazes—nor do we tend to chop down mountains with the edge of our hand.

Do you need to know what you mean?

How much control can you exert over what your songs mean? Regardless of how good you are as a lyricist, if you perform or release songs, the audience may find things in your lyrics which you either didn't know were there, or didn't intend. Some writers are content with this—they even encourage it. But listeners can willfully misinterpret a lyric by not paying enough attention. People who call radio stations to request R.E.M.'s bitter put-down "The One I Love," in the mistaken belief that it is a passionate love song, have failed to respond to the song's lyric beyond the first line. I have also heard people interpret "Everybody Hurts" as a good song to commit self-harm or suicide to! This despite the fact that the lyric's whole point is to *dissuade* people from feeling that way, by saying everybody has those moments and you have to hold on and keep going.

Another point is that a song does not necessarily mean what the author *thinks* it means, and sometimes the author doesn't even have a conscious, worked-out meaning. Kate Bush has said that "Love and Anger" "was an incredibly difficult song for me to write, and when people ask me what it's about, I have to say I don't know because it's not really a thought-out thing." Hendrix once confessed to changing his explanation of what his lyrics meant, when interviewed, because he wasn't sure of their meaning either. For Gavin Rossdale of Bush, it's a case of, "I just try to be as natural as possible. Sometimes I know what I'm going on about and other times I don't."

> *I can't necessarily interpret 'American Pie' any better than you can."*
> **DON MCLEAN TO *LIFE*, 1972**

> *The amateur songwriter's greatest single failing, and one that is immediately obvious to the listener, is that the writer does not know exactly where the song is going."*
> **JIMMY WEBB**

Sometimes the meaning of a song only comes to a songwriter much later. Working in the dark can be part of the process, and exciting in its way. The more personal the material, the more likely this is to happen, because the unconscious may play a larger part. Skin of Skunk Anansie has said, "I think sometimes it doesn't hit you until later on what the song really means because you were probably hiding something from yourself—a couple of weeks later, you're a bit more honest and you realize what the lyric is about." Paul McCartney told *Mojo* in 2001, "I think 'Yesterday' was about the death of my mother . . . but it was only 20 years later when somebody made that suggestion, that I went, 'Yeah.'" Pete Townshend of the Who once observed, "The interesting thing is how a person's mind, my mind, becomes very one track at certain times. When I decided to put *Tommy* together as an 'opera,' I simply amassed all the songs I had, and remarkably, about 80 per cent of them fit in somewhere. I seemed to have been unconsciously writing on a theme for almost a year without realizing it."

Songwriters don't always have a clear intention concerning the song they want to write. Canadian singer/songwriter Bruce Cockburn claims almost never to write a song about a particular subject. Instead, his songs come from imagery or odd lines and are built from there.

Some songwriters are happy not to seek to define meanings. Neil Finn of Crowded House told *Mojo*, "The writing of a good song is enough of a mystery to me that I'm prepared to let things be unexplained and abstract even to me. If the words sound right, if they convey a certain depth or extremity of emotion, it doesn't matter if they don't relate to the line before, particularly."

Time and events in the world can alter the meaning of some of your songs, whether you like it or not. On a personal level, this is the result of natural changes in your life, but on rare occasions it can also happen when the imagery of a song accidentally refracts a national event.

In May 2005, I wrote a song that referred two London Underground tube stations. It started, "I traveled far on the black Northern line" and had Edgware in the title. The second chorus began, "City nights—they try to warn you." It was a love song, deliberately English in its imagery. Two months later, four bombs exploded in London, three of them in the underground, one at Edgware and one on the Northern line. Suddenly, and unintentionally, the lyric had gained another level of meaning, whether I liked it or not. My love song had become an elegy. To eliminate this new association, I would have to change the tube stations. Which goes to show that the notion of what a song is "about" and *how* songs can be "about" things is complex and mysterious. And that is one thing which keeps us writing lyrics and composing songs.

Several of my songwriting books give hundreds of chord progressions that could be the basis for songs. The same can't be done with lyrics; it isn't possible to provide readymade verses, because that would involve decisions about meanings and themes, which only you can do. A guide to writing lyrics can't tell you *what* to write; that you must decide. It can't choose your images, characters, or stories. It must be *your* words on the page. But with this book close by, the words and lines will come easier than they did before.

a gallery of lyrics

> *I think the dimension of lyric writing has gotten kind of slim and I think there's been many reasons for it. You see videos where there are all kinds of images going on while a guy is singing. When you have images going on you don't really need the images provoked by words, and a tendency to let down your guard and go easy on the lyric writing is there. It's not there musically, 'cos you need the music but you're really not dependent that much on the word, and I think the tendency in today's songwriting is to go with this almost ulterior, subliminal flow of what is needed and what isn't, and that all the kids that are writing songs know that the stuff is eventually headed for the screen . . ."*

JERRY LEIBER TO SEAN EGAN

> *The world of music is way huger and more life-giving and permanent than the music business will ever be. The real world of music. And that gives me comfort."*

JEFF BUCKLEY TO *MOJO*, AUGUST 1994

> *They are more than tunes. They are little houses in which our hearts once lived. When we hear them, we go visiting."*

PLAYWRIGHT BEN HECHT ON COLE PORTER'S SONGS

Here are some example lyrics to illustrate various techniques and contrasted approaches to writing words for songs. Several belong to a songwriting project where the challenge was to write songs in the style of famous bands or singers. In these, I deliberately wrote in the language and themes their respective songs often exhibit.

There are of course a huge range of lyric styles, so these necessarily provide a personal angle. In my own songs, I aim for a certain amount of wordplay and metaphor, a literate sensibility, cultural allusion, and evocative titles.

"Where Lovers Walk"

This is an observational lyric, meditating on infidelity between people who used to be lovers. Through restless feelings and an all-too human weakness, they slip into an affair that has unintended destructive results. Exactly what these are is not spelt out. The narrative is compressed and often implied through images, as in verse 2. The chorus recognizes the element of the unintentional when things get out of hand. The song is a meditation on their impulse, understanding why they did it and sadly reflecting back in the chorus what went wrong. The chorus occurs first in a shorter form but is extended in the final instance.

Verse 1

A promenade where lovers walk,[1]

They only met for a drink and a talk.[2]

For old times' sake, innocent desire,

Thinking it was safe to meet and play with fire.[3]

Chorus

You only meant a backward look,

Not to open that old book.

Change descends [just like] dark as a hawk[4]

If you go where lovers walk.

Verse 2

They grab the keys and briefly kiss[5]

Those who believe nothing's amiss.[6]

A secret room, a distant train,

A torn-up letter where affection runs[7]

In the rain.

1 A "promenade" can be a verb or a noun, an action or a place. It also implies relaxation.

2 Notice the key word "only," an early warning that this situation is going to develop unexpectedly.

3 To "play with fire" is proverbial for risky behaviour. The conventional rhyme of "desire" / "fire" is refreshed because of the overall emotional complexity.

4 "Just like" is weaker than "dark as," which evokes the bird and reinforces the falling sun of the previous line.

5 "Grab" is an urgent verb. Notice the alliteration of "keys" and "kiss."

6 A less common rhyme for "kiss." Here, a narrative of infidelity is compressed into a few images.

7 The phrase "affection runs" could refer to the ink of the letter but also to the lovers themselves running.

Bridge

Two birds in flight through crimson light[1]

Lives that twist and won't go right.

Dreams now raided, put to the sword[2]

As maps are redrawn.[3]

Verse 3

Seekers of the fire and flood,[4]

Restless as a stormy night or fever

In the blood.[5]

Last Chorus

You only meant a backward look[6]

Not to open that old book.

You only meant to walk on by[7]

Not to tear the sun from the sky.[8]

Change descends [just like] dark as a hawk

If you go where lovers walk.

Coda

They run to higher ground[9]

Till their turn comes round.

1 The flight metaphor suggests the hope of escaping the mundane through the affair. Crimson is associated with passion. There is also an internal rhyme here.

2 The "raided" dreams could be exhausted by action or released.

3 Maps are redrawn because life plans have changed. The sword image implies someone has suffered.

4 This half verse quickens the return to the final chorus.

5 An encompassing description of the restlessness which drives the lovers to act as they did.

6 The final chorus is extended. Notice the parallel phrasing of "You only meant."

7 This phrase evokes an ironic world of sorrow to anyone who knows the Bacharach song.

8 The violence of the verb "tear" evokes terrible unintended consequences.

9 The coda offers one bittersweet observation: the unfaithful lovers feel they are on "higher ground." But they may one day take their turn on the opposite side of infidelity.

"Trouble"

This lyric is written in the frenetic new-wave style of an early Elvis Costello song. It works a single metaphor by utilizing many phrases and images associated with it. In this case, the primary metaphor is clothing, and the wordplay is pushed to an extreme. Notice that this clothing metaphor fills the song by addition but does not function as deeply as the primary Alaska metaphor in "White as Alaska." The basic situation is a love triangle seething with envy and desire. It uses alternate rhyming. Many of the lines are quite long, so many syllables have to be sung quickly. This is appropriate for an up-tempo song, as it gives the vocal urgency and extra rhythm. The speaker has a lot to say in three minutes!

Verse 1

So they say you're tailor-made:[1]

Very well-suited and dressed up to the nines.[2]

Silver linings are my trade,[3]

I step into the party and feel a tender crime[4]

Creeping up on me when I look at you.

My heart is a patchwork shade of blue.[5]

I've measured his words and they're not true.[6]

You've got me seeing double

And double often means trouble.[7]

1   They are "tailor-made" for each other. The person he loves is part of a couple at present.

2   "Well-suited" is a pun; to be dressed "to the nines" means to be dressed perfection.

3   As in the proverb, "Every cloud has a silver lining"—the speaker claims to make the best out of bad situations.

4   A "tender crime" is almost paradoxical. It most likely refers to him stealing her away.

5   Blue is the traditional color of melancholy in pop lyrics.

6   "Measured" as a tailor might.

7   There is no separate chorus— the hook is reinforced by an internal rhyme.

Verse 2

Cut your cloth to circumstance,[1]

You can slip and you can tie but it's on your

sleeve.[2]

He's collared you for a dance,[3]

I'm not a pincushion and you'd better believe

He thinks that you'll be with him tonight.

But off the cuff it can't be right.[4]

You'd make a tailor's dummy ignite[5]

Because you've got me seeing double

And double often means trouble.

Bridge

My inner child wants to scrabble with your lives,

My inner child wants to dabble with fate's

knives.[6]

They say the child is father to the man,[7]

He's got his playpen—it's such a sham—

But a little later a car door slams.

1　This is close to the proverbial "cut your coat to suit your cloth."

2　Hearts are proverbially worn on the sleeve when people are open about their feelings. "Slip" and "tie" are verbs and nouns.

3　Another play on words.

4　Something that is "off the cuff" is a spontaneous action.

5　This is an example of a hyperbole—an exaggeration.

6　There are two rhymes in these lines. Parallel phrases mark off the bridge.

7　This quote goes back to the Romantic poet Wordsworth but is also used in the Beach Boys song "Surf's Up."

Verse 3

1 Inversion gives this, instead of a Rosetta stone—the multilingual artefact used in Egyptian studies. Proverbially, it is something that provides the key to understanding something hidden.

2 To be "off the peg" is to be ready-made. The singer claims that he and the woman are made for each other.

3 This is a darkly humorous allusion to criminal punishment, indicating that the speaker has a revenge fantasy.

Oh that dress whirls through my mind—

A stone Rosetta sticking to the letter.[1]

He can look but he won't find,

'Cos I want you and there's no better.

We're off the peg just as I knew.[2]

Think of the lips that were never true.

He's out there being fitted for concrete shoes.[3]

Because you've got me seeing double

And double often means trouble.

"The Rising Sun"

This is a narrative song written for a Dire Straits–sounding track that, unlike "Where Lovers Walk," explicitly details the events rather than implying them through imagery. The story is the cost of success and the gap between generations at certain times in history. It evokes the archetypal rock myth ("Johnny B. Goode") of the boy in the late 1950s or early 1960s who dreams of being a famous guitarist. By the end of the first verse, he has already impressed a girl at school enough for her to get romantically attached. The second verse takes him through recording studio to hit record to touring, and the pain of being separated from Jeannie. Left alone too long, she marries someone else. He meets and falls in love with a Japanese woman. This relationship is difficult for both sets of parents to accept because of the legacy of the Pacific theatre in World War II. The song leaves the story unfinished. It provides an example of how a title image can have different meanings attached to it and also when a chorus can have variant forms.

Verse 1

He grew up in a Midwest town where you could

    walk the streets at night.[1]

On summer evenings he'd look at the stars and

    dream of his name in lights.[2]

He got a guitar and practiced hard, singing all

    the hits in the old schoolyard,[3]

Jeannie loved to hang on his arm, his very own

    lucky charm.

[1] This implies that they are safe.

[2] Stars naturally suggest the bright lights of stardom.

[3] The rhyme pattern switches here, so the main rhyme is within the line, not at the end. "Guitar" / "hard" is a close rhyme, as is "yard" / "charm."

1 The rhymes here are internal.

2 Already freshly successful, he looks back to the past. This prepares us for the emotion revealed in the last line of verse 2.

3 The chorus is more compressed than the verse. The third line implies that his life is now limited by legal obligations. Here is the title image.

4 The young lovers are separated by circumstances.

5 On one level they walked until the early hours, but on another "into" is unusual.

Verse 2

They cut a record, got it played, his mind went

  back to those far-off days[1]

When stars were diamonds on velvet black, life

  was simple, nothing lacked.[2]

It struck a chord in a million hearts, soon the

  tune was high in the charts.

In a lost hotel he wrote the words: Missing you

  my hometown girl.

Chorus

He formed a band and the band got good,

Played the clubs in the neighborhood.

But a contract signed is more than fun,

Golden as the rising sun.[3]

Verse 3

Jeannie married a hometown boy, while in

  Japan the chords rang loud.[4]

After the gig, with a backstage glance, he saw

  someone through the crowd—

She was the head of press for Tokyo, he'd never

  seen a face so pretty before.

They walked into the early hours, and in a few

  days he felt sure.[5]

Bridge

She liked the group but she loved this man.[1]

Such sweet kisses and the touch of her hand

Was electric in a Kyoto house

Where they stole some time from the band.[2]

End of the tour it was time to leave[3]

In each other's arms they grieve.

Now he sleeps alone in his bed.

And she is somewhere else, a day ahead.[4]

Verse 4

Back in the States he went home to say, "Dad,

    with this woman I will live."[5]

But Joe served long in the Pacific war, there are

    some things a man can't forgive.

And when she told her parents turned away,

    haunted by the pain of their own dead.

Some shadows stretch too dark and wide, where

    maybe no love can reach inside.

Chorus

He formed a band and wrote each hit,

But never could stop thinking 'bout it—

Shining gold in his imagination:

Was it a setting or a rising sun?[6]

1   A change of rhythm for a bridge that sketches the Japanese setting for new love.

2   Lines 1–4 of the bridge are separated from lines 5–8 by an instrumental passage.

3   This part is quieter, with a sparse arrangement, and has fewer words.

4   Touring separates the new relationship with the complication of time zones.

5   There is resistance from their parents, the older generation. The song becomes about a generation gap.

6   The final chorus is not a strict repeat of the earlier one. But it does reuse the golden sun image, this time asking whether the sun is rising or setting on the lovers. The image of the sun is associated with Japan.

"Repossession"

This lyric holds theme and situation at a considerable level of abstraction. If the theme is a relationship situation, that orients the title word, and the last line refers to lovers. Perhaps someone is being repossessed. Repossession is a term commonly encountered in the buying, selling, and renting of property. People sometimes treat other people as property. Here, possession implies being in the grip of an invisible force. Where there are verbs denoting actions, we do not know clearly who is doing them. The lyric suppresses pronouns—there is no "I," "he," "she," or "they"—which hides the nature of the relationships. This is obvious in the chorus, which poses unanswered questions: "Who can guess?" "Who meets?" What the lyric doesn't make clear, the music can make up for by suggesting the dominant emotion.

Verse 1

All these days are in arrears[1]

Mixed up with unspoken fears:

Bridges burning, tables turning,[2]

Spirit-rapping, hearts are mapping.[3]

Verse 2

All these days are poker-faced,

Gambling a state of grace.[4]

Life in clover, cards turn over.[5]

No explaining, summer raining.

1 When something is "in arrears," it means payment is owed.

2 To burn a bridge is to embark on a course of action from which there is no turning back. This suggests a high stake situation. To turn the table on someone is to reverse fortune.

3 The table image leads by association to spiritualist séance phenomena—unseen forces making sounds—which links to the song's title. A map links to a course of action.

4 Card game imagery: to be poker-faced is to hide your intentions. To gamble a state of metaphorical grace is a high-stakes game indeed. Is it gambling to win it or lose it?

5 To be "in clover" is to be in a happy condition. Perhaps this is what is at stake.

Chorus

Who can guess by words so token,

Magnetic lies, a compass broken?[1]

Who meets now in secret session

To discuss this repossession?

Verse 3

All these days are empty till[2]

The journey ends, the truth will spill.

Distant looks can't judge a book,[3]

Bless the lovers who run for cover.[4]

1 Words are found insufficient ("token") and could be untrue. The lies are magnetic because they are attractive. It is hard to judge direction if a compass is broken.

2 Each verse starts with the phrase "All these days."

3 Proverbial: you can't judge by appearances—but if there is secrecy and distance, that is all you may have to go on.

4 The lyric ends with a blessing on the unnamed characters caught in this problem. To run for cover is to seek shelter (from the rain of verse 2?), but they are also running to the book cover of the previous line.

"Mucha's Girl"

Sometimes, a lyric can be inspired by an artwork of some kind—a picture, poster, photograph, film, novel, poem, or play. The inspiration for "Mucha's Girl" is a famous Art Nouveau poster by Czech artist Alphonse Mucha (1860–1939) called "Zodiac" from 1896. The poster depicts the head of a young woman fabulously adorned with jewelry, encircled by the 12 signs of astrology. The music for this lyric was broadly glam-rock (imagine T.Rex recording with composer John Barry).

1 Verse 1 is descriptive, but it does state that art confers a kind of immortality to transient beauty.

2 "Inca" is used in an imprecise way to suggest the exotic quality of her appearance.

3 The lyric has no chorus but repeats the title at the conclusion of the verse.

4 Verse 2 evokes the world of Paris art and its loves, dreams and desires. The imagery—especially the leopard—is typical of Symbolist art and poetry in the era. Mucha's Art Nouveau period was a defining feature of 1890s Paris.

Verse 1

Mucha's girl—she lives on[1]

Image of beauty decades gone

An Inca queen of old Paris[2]

Caught in profile the years to see.

Her looks are peaceful, so serene—

Mucha's girl.[3]

Verse 2

In robes among the salon set

Who dream of Julie and Antoinette.

White hands of passion, eager to know

Secret as a leopard in the snow.[4]

Her looks are peaceful, so serene—

Mucha's girl.

Bridge

Oh, she's so fine.

Oh, she blows my mind.[1]

Oh, she's so fine.

Verse 3

With curls of red and jewelry bright[2]

Slim as a dancer, hot as the night.

A head encircled, perfume of south,

He drops the brush to taste her mouth.[3]

Her looks are peaceful, so serene—

Mucha's girl.

[1] The use of a 1960s slang term like "blows my mind" provides an entertaining juxtaposition with the 1890s subject matter. Art Nouveau and Mucha's posters were revived in the 1960s.

[2] These details come straight from the poster.

[3] The artist is taken with the beauty of his model.

"Turning the Other Cheek"

This lyric is something of a put-down song, but it is even-handed enough to suggest the speaker may be exaggerating to convince himself (and the person addressed in the chorus) that he is more free from the situation than he claims. The speaker also ridicules himself at points. The long lines create the need for words to be sung rapidly in short duration notes, giving a splenetic effect. Sarcasm is evident from the opening line.

Verse 1

Here is a newsflash! See what you have done—[1]

Put the tears in frontiers, a kingdom undone.[2]

Our special correspondent with the bit between

    his teeth[3]

Wanted it said with flowers but you threw a wreath.[4]

Chorus

I'm not thinking about you,[5]

I'm not losing sleep, Miss Beautiful;

I'm not thinking about you,

I'm turning the other cheek.[6]

Verse 2

Three pence none the wiser standing in the rain,[7]

Break negotiations though it goes against the grain.[8]

War and peace and battles gone, who would be so

    bold[9]

To talk of mining riches like the kings of old?

1 A dramatic first statement.

2 A topographical metaphor—the failed love affair as geography. There is also a play on words here with "tears" and "tiers."

3 The phrase "special correspondent" is familiar from news media, and is here used sarcastically by the speaker.

4 Usually, people express love through flowers. The speaker gets a "wreath" instead— something associated with loss.

5 Three parallel phrases, all negatives, assert that he is not focused on the ex-lover.

6 To refuse to answer an injury with a strike of your own.

7 Pence, like cents, is small change. The speaker is again self-satirizing.

8 "Negotiations" combines the world of relationships with the world of politics.

9 This image is an example of hyperbole. "Mining riches" implies belief in the relationship.

"Trojan Like November"

This lyric is in the style of *Blonde on Blonde*–era Bob Dylan. Its meaning is not at all clear, but there is an undertone of sarcasm which breaks out, making the refrain at the end of each verse read as though ironic: the speaker says it can't hurt that bad . . . but maybe it does. Since there is a "you" and "his," it could be an embittered address to an ex-lover, or the bitterness could even be directed at the speaker in a self-accusatory way.

The approach is poetic, not particularly disciplined, playful and allusive in its cultural and historical references. The classical world is evoked through words like Spartan, Roman, Carthaginian, Venus, Menelaus, and the Trojan of the title. The lyric also mentions the painter Cezanne, and Marie Antoinette. Using "Trojan" as a simile for a calendar month, and connecting Spartan with February, are examples of unusual yoking of words.

Verse 1

Spartan were the streets of February thought[1]

Gone they were forgetful and would not be

    caught.

The past was like a tenement, with no one left

    inside[2]

With a diamond heartbeat and a Roman pride.

With his jigsaw mind and your hope, it seemed a

    piece of cake.[3]

You thought you had the pieces all together but

    the promises were fake.[4]

Don't be sad—it can't hurt you that bad.[5]

1 February could be "spartan" because it is late winter. But these streets are also a state of mind.

2 The simile suggests a haunted empty and run-down building.

3 A "jigsaw mind" might be made up of little pieces, not giving the picture as a whole. It could also mean a jigsaw the speaker could put together. Here, "your" could the be the speaker or the speaker's lover—this opens two different interpretations.

4 The repetition of "pieces" is possibly acceptable as it links the jigsaw and cake images.

5 After six lines rhymed in couplets, two short rhymed phrases act as a refrain for each verse, replacing any chorus.

Verse 2

Carthaginian summers' mosaic of blue and

   green[1]

The hand of Antoinette comes electric,

   unforeseen [unseen][2]

Whose Cezanne eyes are wide-awake, reflect the

   alleyways.[3]

The fortune-teller's glance is quick to vanish in

   the haze.[4]

Once upon a promise the fields were brimming

   with the wheat.[5]

So what now with no past led by a clown up a

   one-way street.[6]

Don't be sad—it can't hurt you that bad.

Bridge

And spare a thought for Venus[7]

Drinking coffee on the outskirts of the day.

She gave the lovers pictures of heaven

But they have gone astray.

They were warned but all the same

It's such a shame to watch it slip away.

1   Verse 2 moves away from winter to summer. "Mosaic" echoes the earlier jigsaw. Blue and green are linked with summer and the sea.

2   Marie Antoinette is an archetype of beauty, exclusivity, riches, indifference, and downfall. The word "electric" pulls her into the modern era. She famously said, "Let them eat cake," which links to verse 1.

3   To have eyes like Cezanne the French painter.

4   The fortune-teller is an archetypal figure—one who knows the future.

5   "Once upon a promise" plays on the phrase "once upon a time." The word "brimming" is fresh here because it is normally applied to liquid.

6   An insult. The woman has been led astray.

7   A possibly sarcastic reference to another woman involved in the scene. It is startling to imagine a goddess drinking coffee.

Verse 3

Trojan like November, a thousand false alarms,[1]

Neglected are the candleflames, all your lucky

charms.

Trojan like November to steal away the sun[2]

The blame of yesteryear and a tattooed

accusation.[3]

Evidently all the rains, the rattling trains, pass

on through the night.[4]

The ones who should be here are like a bruise

that won't heal in this light.[5]

So personal I wouldn't be, except like Menelaus

in his spite.[6]

Don't be sad—it can't hurt you that bad.

1 Verse 3 asserts the song title twice. There is a sense here of romantic frustration and disappointment.

2 November steals the sun as the days shorten.

3 Polysyllabic words come into their own in songs that are attacks or satirical.

4 An extra internal rhyme: "rains" / "trains."

5 The pain of the speaker is clear in this line. The lyric becomes more direct as it approaches the end.

6 "So personal I wouldn't be" is a Dylan-like inversion.

"She Paints the Picture"

This love lyric comes from a set of songs intended to resemble *Pet Sounds*–era Beach Boys. The primary metaphor is drawn from the world of art and painting. The associations with color and perception are appropriate for the psychedelic mid-1960s. The lyric belongs to a sub-genre of songs which pay homage to a young woman with a transcendent power for the speaker, as in "Good Vibrations."

1 A cliché lyric opening, given a twist by the paradox that follows.

2 Notice the variation "I walk" / "I talk," and the repetition of line 2.

3 Perhaps this woman only exists in his mind. Or, she exists but is not physically present at this moment.

4 The song title occurs in the chorus.

5 The repetition of this word is justified by the way the music handles it.

Verse 1

I walk with her along a crowded street[1]

And no one can see her—

There's no one to meet.

I talk with her as if in another zone[2]

And no one can see her—

I'm talking on my own.[3]

Chorus

She fills my eyes, she paints the picture.[4]

She fills my eyes and she's gone,

Gone, gone, gone.[5]

Verse 2

I see with her gaze[1]

A world that's green and bright,

And when she leaves there's ordinary light.[2]

I smile with her and breathe such joy like air,

And then she leaves King Canute[3]

With a sea of cares.

Bridge

Who's gonna be in the frame?[4]

Verse 3

I see her brush on the canvas of a heart.[5]

She colors days a thousand ways[6]

So far apart.[7]

1 "I see" picks up the pattern of verse 1.

2 This is an unusual use of the word "ordinary."

3 King Canute famously tried to stem an incoming tide. He signifies an impossible effort.

4 The bridge adds a further painting reference. To be "in the frame" is to be in the know.

5 Here are two more painting images: "brush" as a verb, and "canvas."

6 Note the extra internal rhyme.

7 This indicates the separation implied in verse 1.

"Last Is the Lasting"

This love song is written in the style of classic Motown singer and songwriter Smokey Robinson. In songs such as "Tears of a Clown" and "Tracks of My Tears," recorded with the Miracles, Smokey's protagonist is something of a mournful outsider hiding his true feelings. The lyric recreates that scenario, drawing also on time-honored scenes from pop songs such as the "party room." Parties are meant to be happy events but in songs they sometimes provide a setting for hidden sadness and tragic emotions. As Lesley Gore sang, it's her party and she'll cry if she wants to. The chorus is a good example of how that section of a song benefits from a more highly patterned approach than the verse.

Verse 1

People say of me

He's never alone but they don't see.[1]

In the midst of a crowd

I want to call your name out loud.[2]

Laughter in the party room,

Watch the night's lonely gloom.[3]

Chorus

First love looks back a long time.[4]

Second love looks for a rhyme.

Third love's doubt is slow passing.

But in the end last is the lasting.[5]

1   This lyric opens with a proposition that the speaker immediately questions.

2   The self in the crowd is a common trope in popular music.

3   The six-line verse is rhymed in couplets.

4   The chorus is strongly symmetrical, using a list and variation technique.

5   The song title is an example of play on different forms of a single word, as with "Love of the Loved" or "Please Please Me."

Verse 2

People think I'm a clown—[1]

They come round here whenever they're down.[2]

In a heart winter calls:

Shake the toy—snow will fall.[3]

Like a map without a route,

Like a prayer with no substitute.[4]

Bridge

I write your name and mine on a wall

On a street where no one goes at all.[5]

1 A specific Smokey allusion.

2 Another Smokey hit was "Come Round Here."

3 The heart is compared to a child's toy snow scene inside a glass.

4 This is an allusion to Smokey's "Tracks of My Tears," and is sung "sub-sti-toot."

5 An image of love, anonymity, and the urban, as in "Walk Away, Renee."

"Rainy Day Market"

This lyric about love and longing uses an ABABCC rhyme scheme and a six-line stanza rather than the more common four or eight. Lines 5–6 would lend themselves to be set as a short pre-chorus. Part of the theme concerns the way early love transforms a mundane everyday location—the rainy-day market of the title. The rain image and the market offer possibilities for developing metaphor.

Verse 2 shows how a song might use a metaphor to unify one verse without dominating the whole lyric. The lyric shows a number of emotions in the speaker which are entwined, giving a bittersweet effect. It begins with the speaker observing others.

Verse 1

Lovers are jumping in rainy taxis,[1]

Heading home to bed by four.[2]

How I envy their steamy window—

It's curtains for the one they adore.[3]

How can I walk these streets

Seeing the places where we'd meet?[4]

Chorus

What am I going to do at your side?

Rainy day market.[5]

What am I going to do holding hands?

Rainy day market.

1   Jumping because they are eager. Taxi because of the weather.

2   For afternoon lovemaking.

3   "Curtains" is a play on words— literally drawn across the window, but carrying the erotic death connotation.

4   The past tense of "we'd" suggests not all is well.

5   The chorus is structured around two questions, both answered by the title. The compression here is typical of a chorus.

Verse 2

Who burned down the playhouse?[1]

Watched the props go up in smoke.[2]

Who tore up the censored script?[3]

If this is funny, I don't get the joke.

What is there left to try?

What turn of mine is left unstoned?[4]

Bridge

Our path should be through roses

But the thorns are mine.[5]

Verse 3

You in the rain: tangled dark hair—

How will I ever forget this?

The look of love is in your eyes.[6]

This is the hope I cannot dismiss.

Whenever we part, I see

Your eyes saying, "Hold me, hold me."

1 Verse 2 is constructed on a single metaphor of the theater, acting, and plays. The playhouse was their relationship.

2 The word "props" expresses disillusionment by the speaker. Props are not real in themselves; they are used to create an illusion.

3 Psychologists talk about relationship "scripts." This one has been censored and torn up. This does not bode well.

4 The proverbial "leave no stone unturned" is inverted. In the theater, a "turn" is an act or a performer.

5 The bridge presents a traditional romantic image—the rose garden—with the speaker lamenting he has been left only with the thorns (the worse part). The thorns line was sung four times in the buildup to the return of the verse.

6 "The look of love" is a ready-made phrase from love songs of the past. The speaker's longing comes out more in this verse, contrasting with the second. It seems there is still hope.

1 This song ends with chorus 1, and then a second chorus whose words are different. The market image supplies the idea of a "heart for sale." "Shop Around" is an allusion to the Smokey Robinson song.

2 The coda delivers a variation on the time-honoured equation of tears and rain.

Chorus 2

A heart for sale—only one left?[1]

Rainy day market.

If you shop around you'll find no better.

Rainy day market.

Coda

My face is washed with rain,

So you'll never know if I've been crying.[2]

"Strange Fine Religion"

This lyric belongs to a subgenre of love song that imagines a love not yet met and expresses longing for this ideal. (Dire Straits' "On Every Street" is a great example, partly using the metaphor of hiring a private detective.) Here, the hope of the meeting is described through the primary metaphor of religious faith. The subject of the hope and love is invisible, and other people may doubt its existence. There is a long tradition of romantic songs taking religious imagery for a secular purpose. The title combines two emotions. The speaker recognizes that this longing is like a faith; it is "strange" to feel it thus because there is no apparent cause, but also beautiful ("fine"). The speaker is not only expressing this hope but also subjecting it to some degree of scrutiny, and is not sure how long he can continue. The note of desperation adds drama.

Verse 1

If you're going to meet me[1]

You'd better make it soon.[2]

The mason cuts and shapes the stone,[3]

The moon is turning full.[4]

All the ships at anchor[5]

Are riding ready to leave:[6]

It's a strange fine religion,

A strange fine religion in which to believe.[7]

1   This line begins with a preposition. How much longing rests upon that one "if"?

2   A sign of impatience.

3   The imagery is plain and archetypally simple. The mason's stone may be a gravestone. Perhaps the speaker is about to give up on this belief.

4   The full moon suggests mysterious forces and also something maturing in a cycle. Things get darker after this point of maximum light.

5   The ships are ready to sail— there is a proverbial phrase "that boat has already sailed."

6   The verb "riding" evokes the motion of the sea.

7   This lyric has no chorus. The hook is the repetition of the title at the end of each verse.

1 This replicates the syntax of line 1 in verse 1. "Meet" is replaced by the more desperate "reach."

2 The speaker is hoping for a miracle.

3 This alludes to "getting blood from a stone"—i.e., something really difficult.

4 The archetypal image is placed in an everyday urban setting.

5 The verb "tug" is unexpected and poetic because its physicality gives immediacy and form to the beloved.

6 "You're" makes a small variation to the refrain.

7 These are the voices of doubt.

8 The meeting may depend on unknown choices by a fallible person.

9 The speaker's ideal seems impossibly distant.

10 This plaintive image leads directly to the last verse.

11 Line 1 is repeated here.

12 The idea of a magical spell to summon spirits.

13 The speaker is getting "deafer" as hope or faith fades.

14 These are the tides that will carry away the ships of verse 2.

15 The final refrain uses "you're" and the more distanced "it's."

Verse 2

If you're going to reach me[1]

It's time to part the sea.[2]

Take this stone and draw out blood—[3]

All the joy there can be.

Any windy city corner[4]

Tug my soul, my sleeve.[5]

You're a strange fine religion,[6]

A strange fine religion in which to believe.

Bridge

Whispers come: "It can take an age."[7]

It's a mortal hand that turns the page.[8]

Whoever held a distant star?[9]

They say it's heaven where you are but . . .[10]

Verse 3

If you're going to meet me[11]

Chant the ancient song.[12]

I'm getting deafer by the day,[13]

The ocean tides are strong.[14]

Are the traces hidden

In the stories that we weave?

You're a strange fine religion,

It's a strange fine religion in which to believe.[15]

"Waiting for a Car"

This is a playful glam-rock lyric that draws on two areas of historical imagery: the American cars of the rock 'n' roll era, and the space-age adventures of the Apollo moon missions. Both these types of image can be found in many glam-rock songs of the early 1970s, as songwriters such as Marc Bolan, David Bowie, and Bryan Ferry sought to revive certain aspects of rock's earliest periods. The title of the song is reiterated throughout the verse, which is musically a variant on a 12-bar progression.

Verse 1

I was standing new moon landing

Waiting for a car.

In the cosmic dust like Chris Columbus[1]

Waiting for a car.

Pretty sleek, headlamps shine,

Moves like a jaguar[2]

I clocked the day in a special way[3]

Waiting for a car.

Chorus

It's the kind of car that will take you far

Bullion bar, it'll make you a star.[4]

It's the kind of car that will take you far

Knows who you are, it'll make you a star.[5]

1   The informality of "Chris" produces an amused and flippant tone.

2   Glam-rock songs often reference big cats. The "Jaguar" / "car" rhyme also features in T.Rex's "Jeepster."

3   Cars have clocks, but here "clocked" is a verb.

4   Notice the simplicity of the obvious "far" / "star" rhyme— star having two meanings in this space-age context.

5   Bowie used the theme of becoming famous in the "Ziggy Stardust" song suite.

1   A classic 1950s car detail,
    when tail fins were influenced
    by rocket shapes.

2   "Clutch" has a double
    meaning—it's the car's clutch,
    but also a verb. Cars were once
    places where teenagers could
    explore sex.

3   Perhaps this is a memory of
    Elvis?

4   The bridge lyric is short
    because the phrase is repeated
    many times.

5   An amusing personification
    of two abstractions imagined
    sitting in the back.

6   A bit of hip slang.

Verse 2

I was dreaming, new sun beaming

Waiting for a car.

In the cosmic wind, cherry-red tail fins[1]

Waiting for a car.

Hubcap mama with a silver clutch[2]

On a nebula.

With a curl of the lip I said, "Get a grip"[3]

Waiting for a car.

Bridge

Gotta get my hands on the wheel,

Hands on the wheel.[4]

Verse 3

I was sliding, new earth gliding

Waiting for a car.

Follow the track and watch your back,

Waiting for a car.

Time and space, backstreet drivers[5]

With a shooting star.

In a seat so lush it was such a rush—[6]

Waiting for a car.

"Blackweir"

This acoustic love ballad invokes an archetypal encounter with water, in the image of going down to a river for reflection and rebirth (as with Bruce Springsteen's "The River"). A weir is a manmade barrier, a low dam raising the level of water upstream. The title combines this with a feeling of darkness ("black"), and the lyric is set at night, so it might be described as a nocturne. There is no separate chorus; the last four lines of each verse are variations on each other. The lyric also has a sting in its tail—something brought in as a dramatic twist.

Verse 1

Tonight I'm going down to Blackweir,

Going down to the grassy slope.

Tonight I'm going down to the river[1]

That's full of night and broken hope.[2]

But just to see you smile.[3]

And I'll cast my cares to the water,

Maybe sing a blues or two;

Watch the shadows in the park,

Find some quiet but no peace without you.[4]

[1] Notice the repetition and parallel phrasing of lines 1 and 3.

[2] The waters are dark, hence "full of night."

[3] This line is a disconnected desire, set aside from the previous lines and those that come after. It occurs in the middle of each stanza.

[4] The song is revealed at this point to be something of a lament for an absent lover.

1 The full moon makes it possible for there to be shadows. It also symbolises events having reached some sort of maximum or turning point.

2 These two lines are the same as in the previous verse.

3 This reinforces the title.

4 The speaker is trying to talk himself into reassurance and distraction.

5 Now the situation changes—a third person is introduced, almost as a threat.

6 Yet the speaker still seems in a negative mood.

7 This third person is revealed to be another possible lover.

8 The word "fond" is telling in its relative weakness. The lyric ends with a kind of confession signalled by "but."

9 Self-criticism.

10 The lyric ends with a moment of honest and realization: the speaker admits that his involvement with this other person is only a distraction and running away from the truth of where his feelings actually lie. This in turn pays homage to the true beloved.

Verse 2

Tonight I'm going down to Blackweir,

And I'll sit and watch the moon:[1]

Tonight it's silver to the full,

Tomorrow can't come too soon.

But just to see you smile.

I'll cast my cares to the water,

Maybe sing a blues or two;[2]

Reflections in black water[3]

May hypnotize me from thinking about you.[4]

Verse 3

Tonight I'm going down to Blackweir,

And maybe not alone;[5]

Tonight I'm going down to the river

With a mind as dull as stone.[6]

But just to see you smile.

And perhaps I'll take her there[7]

But though I'm fond of her it's true,[8]

It's only a way of running from the fact that[9]

I'm in love with, I'm in love with you.[10]

PART 2

further exploration, words of wisdom

a sourcebook of themes

> *Knowledge of and respect for the work of others is the first essential ingredient in the development of a truly effective technique.*"
>
> **JIMMY WEBB**

In the long history of popular songwriting, a vast number of subjects, themes, and issues have been explored in lyrics. Here are just a few of them. This final section of *How to Write Lyrics* is a sourcebook of themes, created by categorizing thousands of song titles into basic subjects. Many of the songs are famous, though the inventive titles of some less well-known songs demanded inclusion too. If you do not know the song or have a recording of it, there are many internet sources. Copyright restrictions make it difficult to reproduce lyrics, or even sections of lyrics, in a book of this nature. Besides, this is a manual about *how* to write lyrics, not an analytic discussion of the merits and meanings of other people's.

Dip into this sourcebook if you can't think of anything to write; have a look at what others have done, and the catalogue of themes will get you going. This book has already quoted many songwriters, spelling out how important they find titles. If you see an intriguing title, search out the lyric and see how it handles the theme. The extent to which these titles engage with their apparent subjects varies, and in some cases (such as the crime section) the groupings are intended to be not without humor. If there is more than one title using the same word or phrase, you have an opportunity to compare the lyrics.

This sourcebook has the following categories covering the main themes of lyrics: love; sex and desire; names A–Z; clothing; rejection and put-downs; communication; media; dances and parties; living in the city; work; money; country and escape; amusement park and circus; geography: places in the USA; places in the UK; places in the rest of the world; journeys; homeward bound; transport—cars, trains, boats and planes; crime and punishment; time past; children and childhood; time present; divisions of the day; divisions of the week;

months and seasons; time future; smart answers; songs inspired by the arts; songs inspired by history; songs about music; politics and protest; fantasy; the supernatural; spirituality. Songs can belong in more than one category, so don't think of them as exclusive. And if you get interested in one of these categories, internet searches will locate hundreds more related lyrics on the same theme.

Every so often, a songwriter composes some music, and then has to come up with lyrics because none have immediately occurred to him or her. Thus looms the question, what to write about? In this situation, you might choose to sketch from what has been happening or is currently on your mind, though not everyone wants to write "confessional" lyrics. Instead, find a new subject. The challenge is to make a connection between it and your feelings and interests. An element of identification or imaginative possession helps what you write ring true. This sourcebook has many avenues to explore.

Happy songs and sad songs

On the whole, sad is easier than cruel, as both cruel and happy are close to vain and foolish. They require qualification or totally unbridled joy (or relish in the case of cruel) . . . There is just more sadness in the world."

ELVIS COSTELLO TO *THE WORD*, FEBRUARY 2005

The sad lyrics make the funny lyrics funnier and the funny lyrics make the sad lyrics sadder. If you spend a whole song in just one half, then there's kinda nothing special about it."

PHOEBE BRIDGERS TO *AMERICAN SONGWRITER*, NOVEMBER 2020

What if, in a song like this ['When You're Smiling and Astride Me'], that's sort of engineered for big grand sentiments, what if you included sentiments about vulnerability and nakedness that are kind of in total conflict with the song itself?"

FATHER JOHN MISTY TO *LOUD AND QUIET*, MAY 2015

Consider the most basic emotional element of a lyric: is it (broadly speaking) happy or sad? If you have been writing songs for a while, I wager there are more sad songs in your catalogue than happy ones. If this is true, you are in good company—it's probably true of most songwriters. Why? Simply put, from an inspirational point of view, when you're happy you feel full of life—filled full (the literal meaning of "fulfilment"). When you're unhappy, there is a sense of emptiness, of something missing. At its most concrete, this is the feeling expressed in thousands of songs about love unrequited or love lost. The songwriter hopes to remedy that lack of fulfilment and emptiness by creating something . . . i.e., the song.

Chris Collingwood of Fountains of Wayne once said, "I don't do happy. I do sad or angry or frustrated. My songs are obviously written with characters, but typically they are not happy characters. Happy songs are hard." For Stevie Nicks of Fleetwood Mac, whose mega-selling *Rumours* was born from emotional conflict in the personal lives of band members, it's a case of "they say great art comes out of tragedy and, unfortunately, I think it does. I like sad songs." For Stephen Merritt of the Magnetic Fields, the problem can be put thus: "What is there to say about a happy relationship? It's only interesting if it's a happy relationship in conflict with something else." This sheds a light on why so many love songs involve the conceit of an unnamed, unspecified group of people who in some way frown upon the lovers or put obstacles in their way. Their presence is registered in clichés like "no matter what they say."

This may also explain why the Who's "Happy Jack" is an unusually and genuinely happy song. Seen as something of a throwaway single, "Happy Jack" is an eccentric lyric about a character who lives at the beach on the Isle of Man, set to music that features typical mad Keith Moon drumming, Townshend power-chording, and abrupt switches in volume. He is teased relentlessly by kids, who drop things on him and treat him as a donkey. Despite this ill-treatment, the kids cannot stop the waves, nor can they (as if there is some parallel between the two) stop Jack being happy. In the end, lyrically, the effect is convincing because of one key word: "prevent." His tormentors were unable to *prevent* Jack being happy. It implies that his happiness is as unstoppable as the ocean. This is funny and mysterious at the same time.

Genuinely happy songs are harder to write and make convincing. A sad song readily draws our sympathy (we've all been there); a happy song might draw our envy (because we don't spend as much time being happy as we'd like). "Bully for you," we feel, listening to someone telling the world of their blistering new-found happiness which will last forever and ever. "Now get out of my face!"

For a happy song to be sympathetic, it must avoid provoking a skeptical envy. Dance records achieve it better than most via their rhythmic energy. But finding happy songs that aren't driven by the lyric platitudes of the dance floor is a challenge.

Whatever the emotion of your lyric, the music's emotion is going to have a big effect on the final result—which is the most significant difference between writing lyrics and poetry (as was discussed in section 9).

Love

> *We were always writing about the same subject, and it's just a new way to say, 'I love you.'"*
>
> **JEFF BARRY TO SEAN EGAN**

> *When I was ten, I was into ABBA. I was impressed by how adult they were. They had songs about divorce, people with kids breaking up."*
>
> **STEPHEN MERRITT OF THE MAGNETIC FIELDS TO** *MOJO*

> *When you're accepting that you're maybe not the best and easiest person to love back, you have to have a sense of humor about it. Otherwise, the songs would be way too closed-off. If you're honestly going to analyze your own shortcomings as someone in a relationship, you have to have a laugh at yourself."*
>
> **LEWIS CAPALDI TO** *ROLLING STONE***, MAY 2020**

Love is overwhelmingly the most popular topic for song lyrics. There are innumerable angles and situations from which you can write as people go through all the stages of falling in and out, and back in love. Here, the need is to strike a balance between the general and the specific, the personal and the universal. This central experience comes across more powerfully when the lyric evokes a specific time and place, as Dylan did to bittersweet effect with the Polaroid snapshot imagery of the lyric to "Sara," and as Al Stewart did in "Year of the Cat." Of this balance between the personal and the universal, Phoebe Bridgers has said, "For the most part, I have no idea when I'm making something universal. I heard something in a movie I watched recently that talked about the 'accidental universal in the specificity' of something. What it comes down to is: the most influential music, to me, is always what's most personal to the artist."

Every story tells a picture

Love songs often express an emotion or set of emotions around a conflict or crisis. The lyric may not tell us how this came about. One way to move away from always writing about feelings is to consciously tell a love story with a beginning, middle and end. This can grab the listener's attention through narrative interest—they want to know what is going to happen. There are songs like the Hollies' "Bus Stop," Manfred Mann's "Do Wah Diddy Diddy," or Squeeze's "Up the Junction" that tell the whole story of a love affair.

Love songs tend to be defined as romantic. In the lyric chapter of my book *How to Write Songs on Guitar*, several pages map the existential positions people can take up towards one another in love lyrics. But love also manifests itself between friends, between siblings, between parents and children, and so on. Spiritual love is dealt with under "spirituality" at the end of this section. First, here are some archetypal "love lyric" situations:

Searching for love
This is about chasing love and dreaming of an ideal.

» *The Eagles, "One of These Nights"; Bruce Springsteen, "Dancing in the Dark," "Night"; Dire Straits, "On Every Street"; Neil Young, "Heart of Gold"; the 1975, "Love Me."*

Love at first sight
This can happen across a crowded room, at a party, on the street, in a café. There is an additional poignancy when it is someone in a crowd who you know you won't see again.

» *Leona Lewis, "Bleeding Love"; James Blunt, "You're Beautiful"; Roberta Flack, "The First Time Ever I Saw Your Face"; the Monkees, "I'm a Believer"; the La's, "There She Goes"; Elvis Presley, "All Shook Up"; Tommy James, "Dizzy"; the Supremes, "The Happening."*

Love requited, or that's had time to intensify
» *Faith Hill, "The Way You Love Me"; Fleetwood Mac, "You Make Loving Fun"; Moody Blues, "Nights in White Satin"; Eurythmics, "There Must Be an Angel"; the Searchers, "Every Time You Walk in the Room"; Stevie Wonder, "I Was Made to Love Her"; Dusty Springfield, "The Look of Love"; the Beatles, "Eight Days a Week"; the Temptations, "My Girl"; Mary Wells, "My Guy."*

Love in pursuit

An intention is formed to pursue and to get noticed. This is a lyric where romantic heroism is emphasized. There may be an obstacle to be overcome.

» *The Temptations and the Supremes, "I'm Gonna Make You Love Me"; the Pretenders, "Brass in Pocket," "Talk of the Town"; Bruce Springsteen, "She's the One"; Bob Dylan, "I Want You"; Elton John, "Your Song"; Spencer Davis Group, "Keep on Running"; Roy Orbison, "Pretty Woman"; the Ronettes, "Be My Baby"; the Beach Boys, "Wouldn't It Be Nice"; Madonna, "Cherish."*

Promising to be there

Emotions are sublimated through a degree of selflessness. This also includes songs of friendship.

» *The Beatles, "From Me to You"; the Jackson 5, "I'll Be There"; the Four Tops, "(Reach Out) I'll Be There"; Cyndi Lauper, "Time After Time"; Queen, "You're My Best Friend"; (friendship) James Taylor, "You've Got a Friend"; Simon and Garfunkel, "Bridge Over Troubled Water"; Bill Withers, "Lean on Me."*

Finding out your feelings are unrequited

» *Buzzcocks, "Ever Fallen in Love with Someone You Shouldn't've"; the Temptations, "Just My Imagination"; Elton John, "Sorry Seems to Be the Hardest Word."*

Denying your feelings

» *10cc, "I'm Not in Love"; Thin Lizzy, "Don't Believe a Word"; Elvis Presley, "The Girl of My Best Friend."*

Togetherness

These songs are difficult to pull off because they arouse envy in the listener.

» *Ed Sheeran, "Thinking Out Loud"; Bruno Mars, "Just the Way You Are"; the Carpenters, "We've Only Just Begun"; Paul McCartney, "Maybe I'm Amazed"; Bruce Springsteen, "If I Should Fall Behind"; the Turtles, "Happy Together"; Mama Cass, "Dream a Little Dream of Me"; Dave Clark Five, "Glad All Over"; the*

Four Tops, "I'm in a Different World"; the Casuals, "Never My Love"; the Beach Boys, "God Only Knows"; Herb Alpert, "This Guy's in Love with You"; the Beatles, "Something."

Existential need

The "I can't live without you" lyric. Deeply unfashionable since the 1990s, at least.

» Foo Fighters, "Walking After You"; Duncan Sheik, "Half-Life"; Maria Carey, "We Belong Together"; Snow Patrol, "Chasing Cars"; Christine and the Queens, "People, I've Been Sad"; the Four Tops, "I Can't Help Myself," "Bernadette"; Harry Nilsson, "Without You"; Bob Dylan, "If Not for You."

Conflict inside a relationship

» My Chemical Romance, "I'm Not Okay (I Promise)"; Avril Lavigne, "Complicated"; Kate Bush, "Running Up That Hill"; U2, "With or Without You," "One"; Elvis Presley, "Always on My Mind," "Suspicious Minds"; the Beatles, "Ticket to Ride," "We Can Work It Out"; the Supremes, "You Keep Me Hanging On"; Stevie Nicks and Tom Petty, "Stop Draggin' My Heart Around"; the National, "Oblivions."

Love rivals, love triangles

This increases the emotional *ante*. The emotion and rivalry might be openly expressed or not.

» Shaun Mendes, "Treat You Better"; Tame Impala, "The Less I Know the Better"; Sam Smith, "Leave Your Lover"; Lemar, "If There's Any Justice"; Jet, "Are You Gonna Be My Girl"; Billy Paul, "Me and Mrs. Jones"; Mary MacGregor, "Torn Between Two Lovers"; Elvis Presley, "The Girl of My Best Friend"; Spin Doctors, "Two Princes."

Parting when you don't really want to

» Adele, "All I Ask"; Emeli Sandé, "Suitcase"; Coldplay, "Another's Arms," "Christmas Lights"; Moody Blues, "Go Now"; the Rolling Stones, "Angie"; the Walker Brothers, "Make It Easy on Yourself"; Diana Ross, "Remember Me"; Blur,

"Tender"; Roy Orbison, "It's Over"; the Righteous Brothers, "You've Lost That Lovin' Feeling"; Carole King, "It's Too Late"; Fleetwood Mac, "Dreams," "Songbird"; Abba, "The Winner Takes It All"; Paul Simon, "Graceland"; the Libertines, "Can't Stand Me Now"; Thelma Houston, "Don't Leave Me This Way."

Parting when you do want to

A popular lyric subject because it demonstrates emotional independence.

» Maroon 5, "This Love"; Adele, "Rolling in the Deep"; Carole King, "It's Too Late"; Bob Dylan, "It's All Over Now, Baby Blue," "Sooner or Later One of Us Must Know"; Dido, "Hunter"; Paul Simon, "50 Ways to Leave Your Lover"; Soft Cell, "Say Hello, Wave Goodbye"; Fleetwood Mac, "Go Your Own Way"; Blondie, "Heart of Glass."

Getting back together again

» Kid Rock feat. Sheryl Crow, "Picture"; Peaches and Herb, "Reunited"; the Supremes, "Back in My Arms Again"; the Jackson 5, "I Want You Back"; John Lennon, "(Just Like) Starting Over."

Post-split

Few events are more likely to cause an eruption of songwriting than the relationship breakdown, especially if it wasn't you who initiated it. These events make songwriters so productive it is now a commonplace to talk about the "breakup album." Odes to unrestrained grief tend still to outnumber celebrations of independence and self-determination.

» Lorde, "Green Light"; the Magnetic Fields, "Busby Berkeley Dreams"; Smokey Robinson, "Tracks of My Tears"; Taylor Swift, "My Tears Ricochet," "Cardigan"; Dionne Warwick, "Walk on By"; Gloria Gaynor, "I Will Survive"; the Four Tops, "Ask the Lonely"; Dido, "White Flag"; Sinead O'Connor, "Nothing Compares 2 U"; the Zombies, "She's Not There"; the Everly Brothers, "Cathy's Clown"; the Police, "Every Breath You Take"; R.E.M., "The One I Love"; the Supremes, "Reflections"; the Who, "A Legal Matter."

Refusing to give up after the split

» *Coldplay, "The Scientist"; Adele, "Hello," "Someone Like You"; Diana Ross, "I'm Still Waiting"; the Police, "I Can't Stand Losing You"; Elvis Presley, "A Fool Such as I"; Dusty Springfield, "I Just Don't Know What to Do with Myself"; the Supremes, "Someday We'll Be Together"; Phil Collins, "Take a Look at Me Now."*

Jealousy and infidelity

» *Rihanna, "Unfaithful"; Elvis Costello, "I Want You"; Pilot, "How Long"; Roxy Music, "Jealous Guy"; Dire Straits, "You and Your Friend"; Marvin Gaye, "I Heard It Through the Grapevine"; Stephen Stills, "Love the One You're With"; the Velvet Underground, "Pale Blue Eyes"; Rod Stewart, "Reason to Believe"; the Tremoloes, "Silence Is Golden"; Bryan Adams, "Run to You."*

Sex and desire

This theme is one of the most basic in popular music because of its connection with people going out and having a good time. The issue here is how explicit or subtle you want to be. In many lyrics, what appears to be a love song is, consciously or unconsciously, really about sex. There are a vast number of songs about sexual encounters, covering all shades of innocence and explicitness.

Imagery, metaphor, and wordplay have a role here in disguising the true subject, often because that is the only way around the censor. Popular music has been courageous and daring at times in challenging oppressive social attitudes, and at other times merely smutty or vulgar.

How such a song is put across depends on your persona. Before attempting any explicit lyrics, take an objective look at your performing style. The subject matter and double entendres (or even single entendres) that Prince sold in the 1980s might sound tawdry down at your local bar or club on a midweek evening in front of 50 people. Know what you can convincingly put across.

Genre also has an influence on how explicit lyrics can be. In some genres, being explicit is a no-no. Blues, 1970s hard rock (see Led Zeppelin and Aerosmith), 1980s heavy metal, and rap and hip-hop are genres where rude and often misogynistic lyrics are endemic. This can be disguised by slang or innuendo, some of which can be amusing, or the sheer speed with which lyrics are delivered. There's a difference between the innuendo of an AC/DC track like "Dirty Deeds Done Dirt Cheap" and that of the Darkness's "Holding My

Own" because of the effect of the music. The Darkness track is brash but slightly mournful, which softens the double entendre of the title, making it intriguingly half-funny, half-sad.

It is striking just how indecent some well-known songs are, especially considering they were released many decades ago. Common metaphors for sexual activity include dancing, driving cars, and activities in kitchens involving cooking and food. Heat, melting, and fire are another group of images with physiological origins. There are fine lines to tread between intelligibility and obscurity, and between ingenuity and the unintentionally comic. Medicine and healing references in this context can come across as unctuous and hypocritical—as though the singer is in some profound suffering when all they want to do is get laid. There's also quasi-Freudian stuff about riding horses and ponies, fish, cats, and snakes, and what might be termed "human geography"—all those references to "going down" or "going south."

Along with this imagery goes a long-standing tradition of sexual boasting—both to the object of the seduction and to the listener. One of the great sexual lyric clichés involves the phrase "all night long." Lovers in popular song seem never seem to get tired or have mornings feeling crushed by lack of sleep. Spare a thought for the character Lincoln Duncan in Paul Simon's song of that name, trapped in a motel room next to a couple who noisily make love all night.

A similar lack of realism is demonstrated by the fact that there are far fewer songs that deal with the *consequences* of sexual activity. This is why the Shirelles' "Will You Still Love Me Tomorrow" was so powerful in voicing a common worry for young women living in a society that exposed them to a sexual double standard. There aren't that many songs about abortions and miscarriages; Graham Parker's "You Can't Be Too Strong" is a rare example of a lyric dealing with the former. The coded reference to menstruation as a "losing streak" in the Rolling Stones' "Satisfaction" was daring for its time, and it remains so (two other songs that refer to it are Alice Cooper's "Only Women Bleed" and Tori Amos's "Silent All These Years").

Sexual identity itself is an important lyric theme for teenagers exploring and defining their sexual roles. Relevant songs include the Who's "I'm a Boy," Johnny Cash's "A Boy Named Sue," the Kinks' "Lola," Lou Reed's "Walk on the Wild Side," the Velvet Underground's "Venus in Furs," Billy Bragg's "Sexuality," Madness's "House of Fun," the Undertones' "Teenage Kicks," Blur's "Girls and

Boys," Garbage's "Androgyny," and Aerosmith's "Dude Looks Like a Lady."

An interesting story lies behind one of the most candid of sexual songs, the Who's "Pictures of Lily," about which Pete Townshend told *NME*, "The idea was inspired by a picture my girlfriend had on her wall of an old Vaudeville star—Lily Bayliss. It was an old 1920s postcard, and someone had written on it 'Here's another picture of Lily—hope you haven't got this one.' It made me think that everyone has a pin-up period."

Once, writing lyrics about sex was genuinely rebellious. In a time as permissive as the present, where pornographic images are part of the mainstream, true rebellion may lie in doing something else.

The song titles you may like to investigate are separated out into songs written or sung by men as opposed to women to get a sense of the difference. With some notable exceptions, the latter tend to be less explicit and crudely assertive, less apt to push emotion out of the picture.

Sung by men

» *Marvin Gaye, "Sexual Healing"; Led Zeppelin, "Whole Lotta Love"; Buzzcocks, "Orgasm Addict"; Bad Company, "Feel Like Makin' Love"; the Rolling Stones, "Let's Spend the Night Together," "Beast of Burden," "Start Me Up"; Wings, "Hi Hi Hi"; Pulp, "This Is Hardcore"; Frankie Goes to Hollywood, "Relax"; Sam and Dave, "Hold On! I'm Comin'"; the Kinks, "All Day and All of the Night"; the Cure, "Let's Go to Bed"; George Michael, "I Want Your Sex"; Squeeze, "Pulling Mussels from a Shell"; Ed Sheeran, "Shape of You."*

Sung by women

» *Tori Amos, "Professional Widow"; Aretha Franklin, "Natural Woman"; Madonna, "Erotica," "Justify My Love"; Siouxsie and the Banshees, "Slowdive"; Maria Muldaur, "Midnight at the Oasis"; Jane Birkin and Serge Gainsbourg, "Je t'aime . . . moi non plus)"; the Shirelles, "Will You Still Love Me Tomorrow?"; Dusty Springfield, "Some of Your Lovin'"; Rita Coolidge, "Help Me Make It Through the Night"; Peggy Lee, "Fever"; Kate Bush, "Feel It"; Lady Gaga, "Bad Romance"; Mariah Carey, "Touch My Body"; Rihanna, "S&M"; Norah Jones, "Turn Me On."*

Names

*Emma is not a person; Emma is a place that you get stuck in; Emma is a pain
that you cannot erase.*"

JUSTIN VERNON (BON IVER) ON THE TITLE OF HIS

2007 ALBUM *FOR EMMA, FOREVER AGO*

Since so many popular songs are about love, it's unsurprising there are many whose
titles include, or are, a woman's name (there are fewer with male names). Love is
the great inspirer of songs. A song is conjured to fill (temporarily or permanently)
the beloved's absence. There is a long tradition of singers attempting to win the
affections of the person they desire by writing a song for that person. What better
way to personalize the song than to name it after them? And, if you have *more*
than one beloved, why not put them all in, as Lou Bega did with "Mambo No. 5,"
whose lyric pays homage to Angela, Pamela, Monica, Erica, Rita, Tina, Sandra,
Mary, and Jessica. Likewise, Paul Simon used Gus, Lee, Roy, Stand, and Jack and
their respective rhymes in the chorus of "50 Ways to Leave Your Lover."

A name in itself is not going to give you a story or a theme, although some
lyrics (like the B52's' "52 Girls") list them. But names stir the imagination, and
if you find a rhyme for the name, that might set off a lyric sketch. The origin of
this is probably that when you're in love the name of your beloved is one of the
most magical words in the language. Favorite names in lyrics are Carol, Caroline,
Mary, Sue, and Jimmy.

As an example of a lyric named after a woman, take Leonard Cohen's "Suzanne"
(1967). The song is partly a portrait of a bohemian young woman who lives near
a river, her exotic appeal captured in a wealth of colorful detail, like the tea she
gives him, and oranges from China. She attempts to draw him into a relationship,
though he is ambivalent about this. The second verse digresses into Christian
myth, talking about Jesus as a sailor who walked on the water. The third implies
there is something redemptive about Suzanne. It is a song that evokes sensuality
and a retreat far from the madding crowd.

A name doesn't have to stand alone as a title. You can attach a phrase to it
to make it more interesting. The weakest tactic is to attach the word "song" (as
in a title like "Annie's Song"). It's great for the dedicatee but less engaging for
everyone else (or at least, that section of the population which isn't going out
with Annie or Bill or whichever name you've put). So, as a title "Mandy," is not as

interesting as "Mandy in the Morning" (which also has the virtue of alliteration) or "Mandy's Dreaming," or "Mandy, How Could You Do It?," which intrigues us: how could she do *what*? Any addition to the name can hint at a theme. For example, "Mandy and Christine Go Out to Play" suggests to anyone aware of 1960s British history that this lyric could be about Mandy Rice-Davis, Christine Keeler, and the famous Profumo Affair.

A name title can originate in wordplay. David Bowie's character Jean Genie was derived from the French writer Jean Genet. Many albums have one song whose title is a name but, unusually, on the Cocteau Twins' *Treasure* (1984) every track is so titled: "Ivo," "Lorelei," "Beatrix," "Persephone," "Pandora (for Cindy)," et cetera.

Another way to use a name for a song title is to think of a famous person who embodies a particular quality, good or bad, and make that a title for a song whose lyric is about the quality but not specifically the person. Tori Amos did this with "Jackie's Strength," where the Jackie is question is Jackie Kennedy, and the "strength" is the fortitude she showed after the president's assassination in 1963.

Here is an A-Z of name titles. I've excluded names of famous people (located in another part of this section). This list shows which names have been used and the variety of modifiers put with them. By checking the lyrics of names or titles of interest, you can see the ways songwriters have built lyrics round a name. Female names occur first, male names second.

A

» *The Magnetic Fields, "Abigail, Bell of Kilronan"; Elvis Costello, "Alison"; Boston, "Amanda"; Joni Mitchell, "Amelia"; the Rolling Stones, "Angie"; John Denver, "Annie's Song"; the Beatles, "Anna (Go to Him)"; Long John Baldry, "Annabella"; Leonard Cohen, "Alexandra Leaving"; Arctic Monkeys, "Arabella."*
» *Paul Simon, "You Can Call Me Al"; Jackson Browne, "Song for Adam"; the Killers, "Andy, You're a Star"; Christopher Cross, "Arthur's Theme"; Cilla Black, Lily Allen, "Alfie"; Paul McCartney, "Uncle Albert"; Pink Floyd, "Arnold Layne."*

B

» *The Beach Boys, "Barbara Ann"; Michael Jackson, "Billie Jean"; the Four Tops, "Bernadette"; KISS, "Beth"; the Ram Jam Band, "Black Betty"; Scott English, "Brandy"; Taylor Swift, "Betty"; Julia Holter, "Betsy on the Roof."*

» *Janis Joplin, "Me and Bobby McGhee"; Bobbie Gentry, "Ode to Billie Joe"; the Marvellettes, "Don't Mess with Bill"; Pulp, "Seductive Barry"; the Jam, "Billy Hunt"; Kate Bush, "Bertie"; Elmore James, "Bobby's Rock."*

C

» *Elvis Costello, "Just Like Candy"; Joni Mitchell, "Carey"; Neil Sedaka, "Oh, Carol"; Europe, "Carrie"; Neil Diamond, "Sweet Caroline"; the Beach Boys, "Caroline, No"; the Hollies, "Carrie Ann"; the Everly Brothers, "Cathy's Clown," "Claudette"; Simon and Garfunkel, "Cecilia"; Siouxsie and the Banshees, "Christine"; the Jesus and Mary Chain, "Taste of Cindy"; Gilbert O'Sullivan, "Clair"; the Cure, "Charlotte Sometimes"; Bob Dylan, "Corinna, Corinna"; Little Richard, "Lawdy Miss Clawdy"; the National, "Carin at the Liquor Store."*
» *Rickie Lee Jones, "Chuck E's in Love"; Vinegar Joe, "Charley's Horse."*

D

» *America, "Daisy Jane"; Tyrannosaurus Rex, "Deborah"; Tom Jones, "Delilah"; Paul Anka, "Diana"; Fleetwood Mac, "Oh Diane"; Frankie Vaughan, "Dolly"; Jimi Hendrix, "Dolly Dagger"; 10cc, "Oh Donna"; Ritchie Valens, "Donna"; Stackridge, "Dora the Female Explorer"; Louis XIV, "A Letter to Dominique"; Vampire Weekend, "Diane Young"; Dave Matthews Band, "Dancing Nancies."*
» *Blondie, "Denis"; Kinks, "David Watts"; Elton John, "Daniel"; the Levellers, "Dirty Davey"; Modest Mouse, "Cowboy Dan."*

E–F

» *Joni Mitchell, "Edith and the Kingpin"; Dexys Midnight Runners, "Come on Eileen"; Roy Wood, "Dear Elaine"; the Turtles, "Eleanor"; Franz Ferdinand, "Eleanor Put Your Boots On"; the Beatles, "Eleanor Rigby"; the Stone Roses, "Elizabeth My Dear"; Barry Ryan, "Eloise"; Pink Floyd, "See Emily Play"; Laura Nyro, "Emmie"; Hot Chocolate, "Emma"; Bon Iver, "For Emma."*
» *Tom Waits, "Poor Edward"; the Small Faces, "Eddie's Dreaming"; Loudon Wainwright, "Edgar"; Roy Harper, "Francesca"; Abba, "Fernando"; Morrissey, "Our Frank"; Curtis Mayfield, "Freddie's Dead"; the Who, "Uncle Ernie"; Sandie Shaw, "Frederick."*

G–H–I

» *Clifford T. Ward, "Gaye"; Them, "Gloria"; Supergrass, "Grace"; Van Morrison, "Madame George"; the Alex Harvey Band, "Isabel Goudie"; Ian Dury and the Blockheads, "Geraldine"; Mika, "Grace Kelly"; Huddie Ledbetter, "Goodnight Irene"; Jimi Hendrix, "Izabella"; Björk, "Isobel."*

» *The Violent Femmes, "Gordon's Message"; Rod Stewart, "The Killing of Georgie"; Sham 69, "Hurry Up Harry"; ELO, "The Diary of Horace Wimp"; Ian Dury and the Blockheads, "Mash It Up Harry"; Madonna, "Isaac."*

J

» *Tori Amos, "Jackie's Strength"; Franz Ferdinand, "Jacqueline"; R. Dean Taylor, "Gotta See Jane"; Eddie Cochran, "Jeanie Jeanie Jeanie"; the Casuals, "Jesamine"; the Hollies, "Jennifer Eccles"; Donovan, "Jennifer Juniper"; Mitch Ryder and the Detroit Wheels, "Jenny Take a Ride"; Hole, "Jennifer's Body"; Madonna, "Dear Jessie"; Bob Dylan, "Visions of Johanna"; Dolly Parton, "Jolene"; John Lennon, "Julia"; Pink Floyd, "Julia Dream"; the Levellers, "Julie"; Shania Twain, "Juanita"; Van Halen, "Jamie's Crying"; John Fred and the Playboys, "Judy in Disguise"; Cockney Rebel, "Judy Teen"; Fats Domino, "My Girl Josephine"; the Band, "Jemima Surrender"; Lady Gaga, "Joanne."*

» *The Beatles, "Hey Jude"; the Undertones, "Jimmy Jimmy"; Manfred Mann, "My Name Is Jack"; Ray Charles, "Hit the Road, Jack"; the Rolling Stones, "Jumpin' Jack Flash"; David Bowie, "John, I'm Only Dancing"; Martha Reeves and the Vandellas, "Jimmy Mack"; Pearl Jam, "Jeremy"; Chuck Berry, "Johnny B. Goode"; the Who, "Happy Jack"; Bryan Ferry, "Tokyo Joe"; Jimmy Dean, "Big Bad John"; Grandaddy, "Jed the Humanoid"; the Killers, "Joel the Lump of Coal."*

K

» *The National, "Karen"; Ben Folds Five, "Kate"; Johnny Cash, "Katy Too"; Marillion, "Kayleigh"; Bruce Springsteen, "Kitty's Back"; Josh Ritter, "Kathleen"; Simon and Garfunkel, "Kathy's Song."*

» *Manic Street Preachers, "Kevin Carter"; the Who, "Cousin Kevin."*

L

» *Cat Stevens, "Sad Lisa"; Derek and the Dominoes, "Layla"; the Who, "Pictures of Lily"; Wings, "The Lovely Linda"; Scott Walker, "Big Louise"; Little Richard,*

"Lucille"; the Beatles, "Lucy in the Sky with Diamonds"; the Hunches, "Lisa Told Me"; the Jam, "Liza Radley"; Scissor Sisters, "Laura"; Al Stewart, "Lori Don't Go Right Now"; Smashing Pumpkins, "Lily (My One and Only)."

» The Kingsmen, "Louie Louie"; Family, "Leroy"; Bat for Lashes, "Laura."

M

» Rod Stewart, "Maggie May"; 10cc, "I'm Mandy Fly Me"; Tom Waits, "Martha"; Jacques Brel, "Mathilde"; the Association, "Along Comes Mary"; Alice Cooper, Marshall Crenshaw, "Mary Ann"; Donald Fagen, "Maxine"; Joe Cocker, "Marjorie"; the Monkees, "Mary Mary"; Rick Nelson, "Hello Mary Lou"; the Beatles, "Michelle," "Martha My Dear"; Marianne Faithfull, "Lady Madeleine"; Procol Harum, "Magdalene (My Regal Zonophone)"; Jackson C. Frank, "Marlene"; Lloyd Cole, "Margo's Waltz"; Leonard Cohen, "So Long, Marianne"; Nick Drake, "The Thoughts of Mary Jane"; Little Richard, "Good Golly Miss Molly"; the Cosmic Rough Riders, "Melanie"; Al Stewart, "Waiting for Margaux"; Scissor Sisters, "Mary."

» Franz Ferdinand, "Michael"; Toni Basil, "Mickey"; Cat Stevens, "Matthew and Son"; Bobby Darin, "Mack the Knife."

N–O

» Prefab Sprout, "Nancy (Let Your Hair Down for Me)"; Elton John, "Nikita"; Prince, "Darling Nikki"; Rufus, "Natasha"; the Killers, "Believe Me Natalie"; Ed Sheeran, "Nina"; Ronnie Hawkins, "Odessa"; Don Nix, "Oloena"; Reba McEntire, "Moving Oleta"; Stella Parton, "Ode to Olivia"; Brother George, "Olivia Oh Yeah"; Bryan Ferry, "BF Bass (Ode to Olympia)"; the Lumineers, "Ophelia"; the Band, "Ophelia"; Peter Hammill, "Ophelia"; Tori Amos, "Ophelia"; One Direction, "Olivia."

» XTC, "Making Plans for Nigel"; the Supremes, "Nathan Jones"; Elvis Costello, "Oliver's Army"; Fleet Foxes, "Oliver James."

P–Q

» Wayne Fontana, "Pamela"; the Beatles, "Polythene Pam," "Dear Prudence"; Paul and Paula, "Hey Paula"; No Doubt, "Paulina"; Bob Dylan, "Peggy Day"; Buddy Holly, "Peggy Sue"; Nirvana, "Polly."

» The Monkees, "For Pete's Sake"; XTC, "The Ballad of Peter Pumpkinhead"; Bob Dylan, "Quinn the Eskimo."

R

» Kevin Ayers, "The Lady Rachel"; Chuck Berry, "Ramona, Say Yes"; the Small Faces, "Rene"; the Beach Boys, "Help Me, Rhonda"; the Beatles, "Lovely Rita"; Bob Seger, "Rosalie"; Bruce Springsteen, "Rosalita"; Mungo Jerry, "Hey Rosalyn"; the Police, "Roxanne"; Tom Waits, "Ruby's Arms"; the Four Tops, "Walk Away Renee"; Stackridge, "Ruth, Did You Read My Mind"; Dr. Feelgood, "Roxette"; Grateful Dead, "Rosemary"; Neil Diamond, "Cracklin' Rosie"; Toto, "Rosanna"; Kenny Rogers and the First Edition, "Ruby, Don't Take Your Love to Town"; Kaiser Chiefs, "Ruby"; Foo Fighters, "Dear Rosemary."

» The National, "Rylan"; Steely Dan, "Rikki Don't Lose That Number"; Joni Mitchell, "The Last Time I Saw Richard"; the Beatles, "Doctor Robert"; Simon and Garfunkel, "Richard Cory"; Lemonheads, "It's a Shame About Ray."

S

» The Beatles, "Sexy Sadie"; Bruce Springsteen, "Sandy"; Fleetwood Mac, "Sara"; the Knack, "My Sharona"; the Smiths, "Sheila, Take a Bow"; Frankie Valli and the Four Seasons, "Sherry"; Leonard Cohen, "Suzanne"; Ramones, "Suzie Is a Headbanger"; the Everly Brothers, "Wake Up Little Suzie"; Dr. Hook, "Sylvia's Mother"; the Stone Roses, "Sally Cinnamon"; Pulp, "Sylvia"; Love, "Stephanie Knows Who"; Dion, "Runaround Sue"; Eels, "Susan's House"; Fountains of Wayne, "Stacy's Mom."

» Eminem, "Stan"; the Small Faces, "Happiness Stan"; Eddie Cochran, "Cut Across Shorty"; Everything But the Girl, "Sean"; Al Stewart, "Samuel, Oh How You've Changed"; Randy Newman, "Simon Smith and His Amazing Dancing Bear"; Steve Harley and Cockney Rebel, "Sebastian"; the Killers, "Sam's Town"; Kasabian, "Stevie."

T–U–V–X–Y–Z

» Debbie Reynolds, "Tammy"; the Cufflinks, "Tracy"; Barclay James Harvest, "Ursula"; Steve Winwood, "Valerie"; Pink Floyd, "Vera"; Elvis Costello, "Veronica"; Roxy Music, "Virginia Plain"; the Beach Boys, "Wendy"; the Association, "Windy"; Joni Mitchell, "Yvette in English."

» The Hollies, "Lullaby to Tim"; the Smiths, "William, It Was Really Nothing"; Blondie, "Victor"; Manic Street Preachers, "William's Last Words."

Clothing

> *There's a button at the top of my navy peacoat, and it's the hardest button to button. I thought that was a great metaphor for the odd man out in the family."*

JACK WHITE OF THE WHITE STRIPES TO *MOJO* ON THE

ORIGINS OF "THE HARDEST BUTTON TO BUTTON"

An article of clothing can be the focus for a lyric. It could be something you have seen in a shop, or that a friend has, or that a celebrity is pictured or filmed wearing. Build it into a title and write a lyric about the person who wears it, why they wear it, and what might happen when they wear it:

- Consider its color, its texture; how common or rare, how cheap or expensive it is.
- What do they want it to say about them? Is there a gap between the two?
- How does it make you feel?
- How do they look wearing it?
- What aspects of their personality might it express?
- What social situations does it suggest (you don't wear a coat indoors, nor a ballgown on the street).

Song lyrics about clothing often revolve around how attractive the character looks in them. This is usually a woman who becomes lodged in a man's mind by her dress. As far as materials go, silk and velvet have always had a special cachet in the popular song, standing as they do for luxury, sensuality, and something out of the ordinary.

» *The Hollies, "Long Legged Woman in a Black Dress"; Mitch Ryder and the Detroit Wheels, "Devil with the Blue Dress"; Kings of Leon, "Taper Jean Girl"; Gene Vincent, "Bluejean Bop"; U2, "If You Wear That Velvet Dress"; Lori McKenna, "Pink Sweater"; Laurie Anderson, "Beautiful Red Dress"; Depeche Mode, "Blue Dress"; Neil Diamond, "Forever in Blue Jeans"; Eddie Cochran, "Pink Pegged Slacks"; Pulp, "Pink Glove," "Pencil Skirt"; the Cramps, "Miniskirt Blues"; Taylor Swift, "Cardigan."*

People express individuality and rebellion through clothes—hence the significance of songs about blue jeans in the 1950s–1960s when they were frowned on by many adults, and the persistently impressive effect of wearing colored shoes. Even when a song is not organized around an image of clothing, lyrics often make passing descriptive mention to evoke a character or a situation. In love songs that deal with how people meet, it can often be a style of dress that catches the eye of the protagonist. The phrase "blue collar" is associated with a certain economic class and the life that goes with it. Black clothes denote power, mystery and sexuality.

» *Ian Dury and the Blockheads, "New Boots and Panties"; ZZ Top, "Sharp Dressed Man"; Adam and the Ants, "Dirk Wears White Sox"; Bachman Turner Overdrive, "Blue Collar"; David Bowie, "Black Tie, White Noise"; the Tremeloes, "Blue Suede Tie"; Everclear, "White Men in Black Suits"; Johnny Cash, "The Man in Black"; Irving Berlin, "Top Hat White Tie and Tails"; Madness, "Baggy Trousers"; the Who, "Zoot Suit"; Paul Weller, "Peacock Suit"; Justin Timberlake, "Suit and Tie."*

Nightwear

Sexuality is also expressed through clothes that reveal as much as they conceal, most notably underwear and swimwear.

» *Paul Weller, "Moon on Your Pyjamas"; Bryan Adams, "Your Underwear"; Pulp, "Underwear"; ZZ Top, "A Fool for Your Stockings"; Babybird, "Man's Tight Vest"; Tori Amos, "The Power of Orange Knickers"; Edie Brickell and the New Bohemians, "Oak Cliff Bra"; Brian Hyland, "Itsy-Bitsy Teeny-Weeny Yellow Polka Dot Bikini"; the Cramps, "Bikini Girls with Machine-Guns."*

Footwear

Shoes are also significant because of their association with dancing, dressing up and going out, attracting a partner, being on the move. Boots tend to carry associations of dominance and a lack of elegance. Shoe colors tend to be conservative, so colored shoes (especially for men) are quite radical.

» *Carl Perkins, "Blue Suede Shoes"; Elvis Costello, "Red Shoes"; Tommy Tucker, "High Heel Sneakers"; Jane Siberry, "Red High Heels"; Nancy Sinatra, "These Boots Are Made for Walking"; the Velvet Underground, "Venus in Furs" (the most famous*

shiny boots of leather in rock); Jeff Beck, "Rock My Plimsoll"; Billy Joel, "Stiletto";
Traffic, "Hole in My Shoe"; Run DMC, "My Adidas"; the Beatles, "Old Brown
Shoe"; Stereophonics, "Step on My Old Size Nines"; Jimmy Nail, "Crocodile Shoes";
Arctic Monkeys, "Dancing Shoes."

Hats

At one time, hats were expressive of character, and characters in songs who travelled described hanging their hats somewhere temporarily. Hat-wearing might characterize a dandy in a society where that is not the norm. Berets have a special allure, the natural headgear of the political radical (see Che Guevara) or the French sophisticate.

» *Bob Dylan, "Leopard-skin Pillbox Hat"; Prince, "Raspberry Beret"; Procol*
Harum, "Homburg"; Marvin Gaye, "Wherever I Lay My Hat"; Steeleye Span,
"All Around My Hat"; Randy Newman, "You Can Leave Your Hat On"; the Go-
Betweens, "Ghost and the Black Hat"; Kevin Ayers, "Hat Song."

Outdoor wear

Since the weather is often rainy on Planet Pop, characters need a striking coat as they walk down rain-soaked boulevards of misery.

» *Leonard Cohen, "Famous Blue Raincoat"; Marty Robbins, "A White Sport Coat*
(and a Pink Carnation)"; Bob Dylan, "Man in the Long Black Coat"; Ice Cube,
"Dirty Mac"; Bonzo Dog Doo Dah Band, "Button Up Your Overcoat"; XTC,
"1000 Umbrellas"; Tori Amos, "Parasol"; Frank Zappa, "Little Umbrella."

Jewelry, et cetera

A piece of jewelry or an accessory gets you noticed. It's also true that clothes need repair. Elton John wrote "Tiny Dancer" about a young woman—the "blue jean baby"—who worked with his band to keep their clothes and stage gear in shape and repaired. The song reached a bigger audience on the soundtrack of the movie *Almost Famous.*

» *Guy Mitchell, "She Wears Red Feathers"; Buzzcocks, "Lipstick"; the White*
Stripes, "The Hardest Button to Button"; R.E.M., "Crush with Eyeliner"; Patti

Page, "Scarlet Ribbons"; Steely Dan, "Green Earrings"; Carl Perkins, "Lend Me Your Comb"; Glen Campbell, "Rhinestone Cowboy"; Shirley Bassey, "Diamonds Are Forever"; Marilyn Monroe, "Diamonds Are a Girl's Best Friend"; the Raspberries, "Rose-Coloured Glasses"; the Cramps, "Sunglasses After Dark"; Rihanna, "Diamonds."

Secondhand clothing

If new is unaffordable, sometimes you have to make do with "pre-used" and the social stigma that goes with it.

» *Rod Stewart, "Handbags and Gladrags"; the Faces, "Three Button Hand Me Down"; Elvis Costello, "Big Sister's Clothes."*

Put-down songs

We have already covered songs about being rejected in love. This is the section for satire, envy, and more general put-downs.

This is the type of lyric that appeals to your darker side. Imagine a person who seems to have it all, then write a lyric either describing how great it would be to be them, or your resentment that you are not in that position. For a rejection song, say goodbye to someone in bitter tones. A subtler put-down song is where the "you" of the lyric is actually yourself, in a self-critical mocking piece. Lucinda Williams's "Lonely Girls" starts out as an observational lyric about others but by the end has turned the spotlight ruefully on herself. Ed Sheeran's lyric for "Galway Girl" is clever not only in its concrete detail and scene-building but the way the "I" is disguised as "the Englishman."

The power of this type of lyric is governed by how technically sharp it is. Put-down songs are better witty than abusive, otherwise you raise suspicions against yourself. Multiple rhyme can be more effective here than in most lyrics. The invective in Blur's "Beetlebum" is managed through repeated rhymes on the same sound: "gun," "done," "numb," "come," "young," "thumb," "bum." The repetitions of a refrain can be powerful in this context, and other wordplay.

There is a sub-genre of songs about teenage envy, in which a young person sees another who is better advantaged or gifted, possibly a few years older, as in the Kinks' "David Watts" and the Undertones' "My Perfect Cousin." This friction could be between siblings. There is also the self-loathing song, typified by Nirvana's "Negative Creep," the Sex Pistols' "Seventeen" and "Pretty Vacant," and Radiohead's "Creep."

» *Bob Dylan, "Like a Rolling Stone," "Positively Fourth St." (and many others!); Dido, "See You When You're Forty"; Carly Simon, "You're So Vain"; R.E.M., "The One I Love"; Leonard Cohen, "Everybody Knows"; the Darkness, "Get Your Hands Off My Woman"; Radiohead, "Karma Police"; the O'Jays, "The Backstabbers"; the Sex Pistols, "Liar"; Hole, "Celebrity Skin."*

Stereotypes

In rock lyrics there is a tradition of mocking suburbia, or the people the hippies scorned as "straights"—people who go to work and do boring jobs (thereby catering for hippies and punks when they get toothache or need a plumber). Married people, bureaucrats, politicians, and the clergy are also frequent targets. When this feeling runs rampant, the satire is directed at seemingly the whole of humankind in a torrent of misanthropic invective (see songs by both Pink Floyd and Radiohead).

» *Manfred Mann, "Semi Detached Suburban Mr. James"; the Kinks, "Dedicated Follower of Fashion"; the Jam, "Mr. Clean"; Blur, "Charmless Man," "Mr. Robinson's Quango"; Mungo Jerry, "Memoirs of a Stockbroker"; the Beatles, "The Continuing Story of Bungalow Bill"; the Jimi Hendrix Experience, "If 6 Were 9"; Paul Kantner and Grace Slick, "White Boy"; Pink Floyd, "Another Brick in the Wall"; Elvis Costello, "This Year's Girl."*

Music business satires

The music business is the target of songs from bands who have been mistreated by their managers and agents, critics, or other band members. Money and artistic freedom are the usual bones of contention.

» *Queen, "Death on Two Legs"; Stereophonics, "Mr. Writer"; the Jam, "All Mod Cons"; the Sex Pistols, "EMI"; Blur, "Beetlebum"; Siouxsie and the Banshees, "Drop Dead"; John Lennon, "Serve Yourself," "How Do You Sleep?"; Free, "Mr. Big"; Graham Parker and the Rumour, "Mercury Poisoning"; Robert Plant, "Tin Pan Alley"; the Who, "They're All in Love"; the Beatles, "Only a Northern Song."*

Telephones

To paraphrase Chuck Berry, this subject is about long-distance information. Imagine a situation where you have to communicate—by phone, mobile, email, letter, text, or even a video call. For the moment, let's confine it to the phone:

- Who are you contacting or waiting for?
- Why do you need to contact them?
- Why is this urgent?
- What happens if you don't make the call?
- Who are you waiting for?
- Why can't you call them first?
- How long have you been waiting?
- How long are you prepared to wait?
- What happens if they don't make the call?

Answer these questions, create a scenario and write a lyric. In both cases pose the question: why can't you go and physically meet the person? Perhaps they are away in another town or country. Why is that? By asking the questions, you can generate the scenario; when you have the scenario, there's something to write about.

Despite changes in technology, the exchange of a phone number remains a milestone moment in relationships, as is the universal anxiety that the person might lose it. Most communications in popular songs are made by lovers with a problem. Desire, fear, rejection; make it necessary to make the call urgently. These communications are therefore dramatic. Some older songs now quaintly record changes in social life because their lyrics depend on what is now antiquated technology. People no longer have to routinely talk to an operator on the phone system; the difficulty of placing long-distance calls or getting a number has diminished. There were songs where the distraught lover phones and pours out their story to the operator. It is also said that many people tried calling "Beechwood 4-5789" after that record was a hit.

Cellphones have changed things, too. Calls used to be made on payphones in hotel lobbies or on the street in a callbox. That picturesque old movie scene where someone waits in a callbox for a phone to ring has gone. It was Marc Bolan who sang on T.Rex's "Metal Guru" that God was all alone and without a telephone... maybe He now has a cellphone, too. These days a songwriter might be using a phone to record ideas on rather than to talk to someone, as is the case for Phoebe Bridgers, who told *World Cafe* in 2018, "I have an ongoing note on my phone of weird stuff that I feel like would make it into a song. Basically, I tweet at myself all day, [or] I'll have a melody in my head and the words will just come naturally."

» Maroon 5, "Payphone"; the Undertones, "You've Got My Number (Why Don't You Use It)"; Blondie, "Hanging on the Telephone"; ELO, "Telephone Line"; the Four Tops, "Just Seven Numbers (Can Straighten Out My Life)"; the Marvellettes, "Beechwood 4-5789"; Chuck Berry, "Memphis Tennessee"; Mercury Rev, "Pick Up if You're There"; R.E.M., "At My Most Beautiful"; Phil Collins, "Don't Lose My Number"; the Drifters, "You're More Than a Number in My Little Red Book"; Stevie Wonder, "I Just Called to Say I Love You"; Lady Gaga, "Telephone"; Carly Rae Jepson, "Call Me Maybe."

Letters

The letter offers a ready-made way to lay out a story or a change of mood in a lyric. You begin, "Dear [name]," and take it from there. Gene Pitney's "24 Hours from Tulsa" remains a brilliant example of how the "letter lyric" can relate a story in vivid detail. In it, a man who travels for work is returning home and is only a day away. He stops at a motel, meets a woman, falls in love, and decides he can't go home and resume his old life. For extra drama have your character write the letter in a life-or-death situation. To see how much can be done with this style of lyric, look at *The Juliet Letters* by Elvis Costello and the Brodsky Quartet, where every track is a letter.

For a more dramatic form of communication, telegrams and telegraphs were used by lyricists, as in Abba's "S.O.S." or Edwin Starr's "Stop Her on Sight (S.O.S.)," which plays with the meaning of the acronym. Cash on delivery (C.O.D.) is a comparable old postal abbreviation.

One interesting religious slant on this approach was the letter form used by Stevie B. for the song "Because I Love You (The Postman Song)," a US #1 in 1990. He turned a religious song into a pop song by pretending that the letter was written between lovers. This is an example of smuggling into a lyric what you want to say to avoid popular prejudice.

» David Bowie, "Letter to Hermione"; Joe Cocker, "The Letter"; Roxy Music, "Strictly Confidential"; Stevie Wonder, "Signed Sealed Delivered"; the

Marvellettes "Please Mr. Postman"; Elvis Presley, "Return to Sender"; the Box Tops, "The Letter"; the Beatles, "P.S. I Love You"; the Bee Gees, "I've Gotta Get a Message to You"; Blondie, "Fan Mail"; Buddy Holly, "Mailman, Bring Me No More Blues"; Kristin Hersh, "The Letter"; Louis XIV, "A Letter to Dominique"; Wilco, "Box Full of Letters."

Media songs

" *I was writing the song with the Daily Mail propped up in front of me on the piano, I had it open at their "News in Brief," or "Far or Near," whatever they call it. There was a paragraph about 4,000 holes in Blackburn, Lancashire, being discovered . . ."*

JOHN LENNON ON WRITING "A DAY IN THE LIFE"

An excellent way to get ideas for lyrics is to scan the newspaper, magazine, or the internet and look for stories, images, or phrases.

Newspapers, magazines, and comics

The newspaper and the idea of a headline can in themselves become the start of a lyric. Imagine picking up a newspaper and a face or a story catches your eye. Maybe someone you once knew is unexpectedly in the paper. Why? Is the news good or bad? Is this how you find out about the new life they've made since they parted with you?

» Edwin Starr, "Headline News"; the Beatles, "A Day in the Life," "Paperback Writer"; the Jam, "News of the World"; Joe Jackson, "Sunday Papers"; Billy Bragg, "Tatler"; Madonna, "Vogue"; the J. Geils Band, "Centrefold"; Dire Straits, "Lady Writer"; Elvis Costello, "Everyday I Write the Book"; Carter the Unstoppable Sex Machine, "Good Grief Charlie Brown"; the Royal Guardsmen, "Snoopy v. the Red Baron"; Tori Amos, "Not the Red Baron"; the Spin Doctors, "Jimmy Olsen's Blues"; XTC, "That's Really Super, Supergirl."

Radio

Songwriters have been concerned with the radio as the main channel by which their songs are heard. The effect of hearing someone else's song on the radio can be a powerful subject.

Songwriters have also attacked the radio for too-narrow playlists and conservatism. DJs can be figures of gratitude or dislike.

» *R.E.M., "Radio Free Europe"; Rush, "Spirit of Radio"; the Smiths, "Panic"; Queen, "Radio Ga Ga"; Joni Mitchell, "You Turn Me On (I'm a Radio)"; Roxy Music, "Oh Yeah (On the Radio)"; Stereophonics, "I Wouldn't Believe Your Radio"; Elvis Costello, "Radio Radio"; the Libertines, "Radio America"; Robbie Williams, "Radio"; the Ramones, "Do You Remember Rock 'n' Roll Radio"; Patti Smith, "Radio Baghdad"; the Wedding Present, "Don't Touch That Dial"; the Sports, "Who Listens to the Radio"; Queens of the Stone Age, "God Is in the Radio."*

Television

Popular songs are almost invariably scathing about television, seeing it as a means of control of "the masses"—which usually meant everyone not in the band or on the tour bus. Individual singers and bands never consider themselves consumers, even as they try to persuade you to buy their CD. In future, there may be more songs about the internet and chat rooms, like Blink 182's "Online Songs." Laptops and gaming consoles have already inspired Swans' "Screen Shot" and Lana Del Rey's "Video Games."

» *Pulp, "TV Movie"; David Bowie, "TVC15"; Bruce Springsteen, "57 Channels"; Vast, "My TV and You"; ZZ Top, "TV Dinners"; Billy Joel, "Sleeping with the Television On"; John Fogerty, "I Saw It on TV"; Talking Heads, "Television Man"; Dead Kennedys, "MTV—Get Off the Air"; Blink-182, "TV"; AC/DC, "Blow Up Your Video"; Violent Femmes, "I Hate the TV"; Martha Wainwright, "TV Show"; St. Vincent, "Digital Witness"; Gym Class Heroes, "New Friend request"; Girli, "Girl I Met on the Internet"; Nick Borgen, "World Wide Web"; Chixdiggit, "Geocities Kitty"; Britney Spears, "Email My Heart"; Todd Rundgren, "I Hate My Frickin' ISP"; Fun 100, "Computer"; Prozzak, "www.nevergetoveryou."*

Aside from the generic idea of television, specific shows have influenced songwriters, as in the case of Portishead's "Mysterons" (from puppet series *Captain Scarlet*), Radiohead's "Paranoid Android" (a character in the BBC radio series *The Hitch-Hiker's Guide to the Galaxy*), Squeeze's "Cool for Cats" (which namechecks British TV cop series *The Sweeney*), 10,000 Maniacs' "Daktari,"

Oasis's "Wonderwall" (named for a film with music by George Harrison), and the Police's "Man in a Suitcase" (a British detective series).

Cinemas and drive-ins (see Eddie Cochran's "Drive-In Show") were once significant in lyrics because they were places where teens could go to enjoy limited physical contact with the other sex. This significance has been eroded by home video and DVDs, not to mention the growth in television channels and online viewing. Two famous songs about courting at the cinema as it was are the Drifters' "Saturday Night at the Movies" and "Kissin' in the Back Row of the Movies."

In terms of specific films, some songwriters are inspired by the imagery or mood of a film, or at the least borrow the title because it will have connotations for the audience even before they have heard the song. The 1975's "Robbers," about a robbery that goes wrong, was inspired by the film *True Romance* (1993) which has one of singer Matty Healy's favorite movie characters. "I suppose you can read it as a metaphor, and a girl who's obsessed with her professional killer boyfriend," he told *Clash* magazine. "It's a romantic ideal."

» *The National, "Roman Holiday"; Dave Edmunds, "The Creature from the Black Lagoon"; Los Lobos, "Angels with Dirty Faces"; Bruce Springsteen, "Thunder Road" (named after a Robert Mitchum film); Siouxsie and the Banshees, "Bring Me the Head of the Preacher Man" (Bring Me the Head of Alfredo Garcia); Elton John, "Goodbye Yellow Brick Road" (alludes to The Wizard of Oz); Kate Bush, "Hounds of Love" (inspired by Night of the Demon); Catatonia, "International Velvet"; Pulp, "Wickerman" (The Wicker Man); Gorillaz, "Dirty Harry."*

Dances and parties

Popular music has always been bound up with dancing. What happened from the late 1950s on is that the distance between a lyric about a dance and the song being the dance narrowed. Popular songs of the 1920s and 1930s might be *about* a waltz, but you couldn't necessarily waltz to them. But Chubby Checker's "Twist" songs were meant for twisting. There are many songs which feature a dance reference in the title like bop, boogie, mambo, without being about those dances.

Boogie, bop, jive, twist, mambo, tango

» *Bill Haley, "Rock a Beatin' Boogie"; Earth, Wind, and Fire, "Boogie Wonderland"; Heatwave, "Boogie Nights"; the Ramones, "Blitzkreig Bop"; T.Rex, "Jitterbug Love";*

Gene Vincent, "Be-Bop-A-Lula"; Wizzard, "See My Baby Jive"; the Bee Gees, "Jive Talkin'"; Bill Haley, "Shake, Rattle and Roll"; Sam Cooke, "Twisting the Night Away"; Chubby Checker, "Let's Twist Again"; Elton John, "Your Sister Can't Twist (But She Can Rock 'n' Roll)"; Bill Haley, "Mambo Rock"; Lou Bega, "Mambo #5."

Some dance lyrics give instructions on how to perform their dance. If you want your lyric to encourage people to dance set it in a venue where this might happen, like a club or a party.

Bespoke dances

» *Bobby Pickett and the Crypt Kickers, "Monster Mash"; Little Eva, "Do the Locomotion"; Ashton Gardner and Dyke, "Resurrection Shuffle"; Roxy Music, "Do the Strand"; the Swinging Blue Jeans, "The Hippy Hippy Shake"; Duran Duran, "The Reflex"; Stackridge, "Do the Stanley"; the Table, "Do the Standing Still"; Smokey Robinson and the Miracles, "Mickey's Monkey"; Major Lance, "Come On Do the Jerk"; Rufus Thomas, "Do the Funky Chicken."*

Parties, clubs, and dance floors are places where people congregate to have fun, forget their troubles, enjoy the music, and find a partner to dance with. One associated lyric theme is being where the "in-crowd" are—however you define them. Dance floors witness ego-driven competitions of display, as immortalized in the image of a white-suited John Travolta strutting in *Saturday Night Fever*. Abba's "Dancing Queen" and James Brown's "Sex Machine" are other well-known lyrics in which one particular dancer becomes the center of attention.

Disco fever

» *Trammps, "Disco Inferno"; the Bee Gees, "Night Fever"; Pulp, "Disco 2000"; Michael Jackson, "Burn This Disco Out"; Arctic Monkeys, "I Bet You Look Good on the Dancefloor"; M/A/R/R/S, "Pump Up the Volume"; U2, "Discotheque"; KC and the Sunshine Band, "Queen of Clubs"; Funkadelic, "One Nation Under a Groove"; Madonna, "Into the Groove"; Sam Smith, "Dancing with a Stranger"; Bruce Springsteen, "Dancing in the Dark."*

A variation on this is the lyric of brazen self-assertion as a seduction tactic. Thin Lizzy's "The Rocker," Chuck Berry's "I'm a Rocker," the Black Crowes'

"Hard to Handle," Simple Minds' "Don't You Forget About Me," and the Spin Doctors' "Two Princes" are examples of the self-assertion song: *Look at me, I'm brilliant, I'm larger than life.* Dancing can also be a metaphor for sex—a parallel Elvis Costello exploited to good effect (and more wittily than most) in "Mystery Dance."

» *Sly and the Family Stone, "Dance to the Music"; the Jackson 5, "Dancing Machine"; Martha Reeves and the Vandellas, "Dancing in the Street"; Edwin Starr, "Funky Music Sho' Nuff Turns Me On"; Smokey Robinson and the Miracles, "Going to a Go-Go"; Stevie Ray Vaughan, "The House Is Knockin'"; Irene Cara, "Flashdance . . . What a Feeling"; the Drifters, "Save the Last Dance for Me"; Robbie Williams, "Rock DJ"; Danny and the Juniors, "At the Hop"; Wanda Jackson, "Let's Have a Party"; the Beastie Boys, "(You Gotta) Fight for Your Right (to Party)"; LMFAO, "Party Rock Anthem."*

A more introverted party lyric evokes the emotional undercurrents of such gatherings. This can express the shock of seeing someone you love with someone else, or going off with someone else; the thrill of seeing someone to whom you're attracted dressed up for the first time (think of the power of the reference to a "party dress" in Costello's "Alison"); and, when it's over, the game of who is leaving with whom. This is captured in Costello's "Party Girl" and Leslie Gore's "It's My Party (and I'll Cry if I Want To)," and in the form of general alienation in Three Dog Night's "Mama Told Me Not to Come."

Living in the city

Millions of people live and work in cities. Some would like to get away, dreaming of a better life somewhere else, but can't. This was the theme of Gerry Rafferty's million-selling "Baker Street" and Stevie Wonder's "Living in the City."

A dislike of city life is readily expressed through the clichéd metaphor of the "urban jungle." On the other hand, some people like the city, as in Hefner's "We Love the City." So, write lyrics about the dramas of life in a modern city: the buzz, the speed of life, the unpredictability. Write about wanting to be there or wanting to get away. If you take as your starting point what daily city life is like for millions, you have a potential audience of millions.

For example, there is a specific city love song about the common experience of urban life—seeing a beautiful stranger in a crowd, or on the opposite side of the stair, and not being able to do anything about it, as in James Blunt's "You're Beautiful." Another possible theme arises from cities having shops. There are many general songs about shopping or that use it as a metaphor, like the Miracles' "Shop Around," for finding a partner. Think about the variety of locations and buildings in a city, where people meet and relationships might start:

» *The Hollies, "Bus Stop"; Babybird, "Corner Shop"; Rory Gallagher, "Laundromat"; the Clash, "Lost in the Supermarket"; the Animals, "House of the Rising Sun"; Village People, "Y.M.C.A"; Sleepy John Estes, "Fire Department Blues"; Rose Royce, "Car Wash"; Muse, "Muscle Museum"; the Dixie Cups, "Chapel of Love"; Eels, "In the Yard, Behind the Church"; Laura Nyro, "Louise's Church."*

There are lyrics about landmarks, parks, and other city features:

» *The Small Faces, "Itchycoo Park"; the James Gang, "Ashton Park"; Richard Harris, "MacArthur Park"; Prince, "Paisley Park"; Blur, "Parklife"; Beach House, "Walk in the Park."*

Some lyrics survey whole areas of a city:

» *Petula Clark, "Downtown"; Dire Straits, "Wild West End"; the Pet Shop Boys, "Suburbia"; the Jam, "In the City"; Bruce Springsteen, "Backstreets."*

Though a city is full of people, paradoxically this can make people feel lonely and isolated—hence the saying that you're never as alone as you are when you're in a crowd. The complementary image for this is the individual isolated in a room or house. In lyrics, this can be a positive (the room or house as security) or a negative (the room or house as prison), depending on the individual's psychological state or state of romance. (The phrase "these four walls" is a related cliché.)

» *The Four Tops, "Seven Rooms of Gloom"; the Beach Boys, "In My Room"; Coldplay's "In My Place"; Dodgy, "In a Room"; Martha Reeves and the Vandellas, "In My Lonely Room"; Depeche Mode, "In Your Room"; LCD Soundsystem, "New York, I Love You but You're Bringing Me Down."*

» *Soft Cell, "Bedsitter"; Madness, CSNY, "Our House"; the Jimi Hendrix Experience, "Red House"; the B52's, "Love Shack"; Jefferson Airplane, "The House at Pooneil Corner"; Asleep at the Wheel, "House of Blue Lights"; Ryan Adams, "This House Is Not for Sale"; Badly Drawn Boy, "Rachel's Flat"; Mary J. Blige, "Mary's Joint."*

If you don't have a place of your own in the city, then you need somewhere to stay. Hotels are significant for characters in lyrics who are travelling or in-between different times in their lives. These lyrics are supplemented by those hubs of social activity: places where people eat.

» *Eagles, "Hotel California"; the White Stripes, "Hotel Yorba"; Elvis Presley, "Heartbreak Hotel"; Ryan Adams, "Hotel Chelsea Nights"; Graham Parker and the Rumour, "Hotel Chambermaid"; Pulp, "Bar Italia"; Carole King, "Hard Rock Café"; Suzanne Vega, "Tom's Diner"; Arlo Guthrie, "Alice's Restaurant"; Dire Straits, "Espresso Love"; Father John Misty, "Chateau Lobby #4 (in C for Two Virgins)."*

You can write songs about real streets and roads, or invented ones. Streets and roads are also spaces where people are seen by others. Often, songs about real streets and places mythologize them so that it is as if they exist in a separate, unchanging world. This is certainly true of the relationship between the real place and the song in Springsteen's "4th of July, Asbury Park," the Beatles' "Penny Lane," and Scott Mackenzie's "(If You're Going To) San Francisco."

» *Rod Stewart, "Gasoline Alley"; Nashville Teens, "Tobacco Road"; the Rolling Stones, "Exile on Main Street"; Bob Dylan, "Positively 4th St."; Bobby Darin, "On the Street Where You Live"; Van Morrison, "Cyprus Avenue"; Dire Straits, "Telegraph Rd."; the Mamas and the Papas, "Creeque Alley"; Paul Weller, "Stanley Road"; Lil' Nas X, "Old Town Road."*

The street can be a metaphor for a state of mind or a situation, as in the phrases "to go down a blind alley" and "that's right up my street." A dead-end street is any situation that goes nowhere. Once there was a colloquial usage in American English that put the suffix "-ville" after a word, denoting a mood or expression, as in "thrillsville." Asked what you thought of a party, you might reply, "Dullsville."

In the mid-1980s, it was easy to interpret R.E.M.'s "(Don't Go Back to) Rockville" as an indie band's rejection of all things rockist, rather than a reference to an actual place. In this connection, think also of clichés such as "don't even go there" and "let's not go down that road."

A one-way street is a metaphor for a situation where there's no going back. You cast a new light on metaphors when they're combined—so what about "one-way street over a burning bridge," which links two similar ideas? Streets can mix with dance and music references. In love songs, the most magical street is the one where the beloved lives, as in "On the Street Where You Live."

A love affair could itself be regarded as a street, perhaps named after the beloved, or a park. A street could carry a moral quality, as in a title like "Temperance Street." Here are some examples of streets with modifiers:

» *The Kinks, "Dead End St."; the Flying Burrito Brothers, "Dark End of the Street"; Morrissey, "Late Night, Maudlin Street"; Prince, "Alphabet St"; Super Furry Animals, "Vulcan St."; Aerosmith, "One Way Street"; the Bangles, "Walking Down Your Street"; Sisters of Mercy, "Destination Boulevard."*

Some songwriters are excited by the lyric detail of having a numbered street or road:

» *The Wallflowers, "6th Avenue Heartache"; Ryan Adams, "Shakedown on 9th Street"; Mick Ronson, "Slaughter on Tenth Avenue"; Rufus Wainwright, "14th Street"; Gil Scott-Heron, "17th Street"; Iron Maiden, "22 Acacia Avenue"; Janis Ian, "42nd St Psycho Blues"; the Ramones, "53 & 3rd"; Simon and Garfunkel, "The 59th Street Bridge Song (Feelin' Groovy)"; Bruce Springsteen, "Does This Bus Stop at 82nd?"*

If a city has a waterfront it evokes the magic of being by the ocean whilst retaining the energy of the urban environment. Water juxtaposed with urban life can bring a feeling of romance (as in the real-life instances of Venice, Paris, and Amsterdam).

» *Simple Minds, "Waterfront"; the Drifters, "Under the Boardwalk"; Blondie, "Love at the Pier"; Bruce Springsteen, "Seaside Bar Song"; Frankie Ford, "Sea Cruise"; All About Eve, "Martha's Harbour"; the Platters, "Harbour Lights"; Otis Redding, "(Sittin' on) the Dock of the Bay"; Mac DeMarco, "My House by the Water."*

Money and work

> *Everybody writes about love. I wanted to write about something different. But what? Then it popped into my head, the most obvious thing of all, the thing I needed most—money. . . . Some will be shocked, some will think it's cute, some will think it's funny. I think I'll make money."*

BERRY GORDY ON WRITING "MONEY (THAT'S WHAT I WANT)"

Naturally allied with the city is the work song. In this lyric, the speaker sings about whether they like or hate their job, whether it will lead anywhere, and if they want to escape it. A work lyric can describe the daily journey to and from work, friends and colleagues in the office, the morning coffee stand, the lunch hour, the commute home at the end of the day, and the contrast with the weekend.

In the folk and blues traditions there are many songs about being exploited, working in terrible conditions, and about the privations and hazards of various trades, such as "The Weaver and the Factory Maid," "The Blacksmith," "My Johnny Was a Shoemaker," "Fisherman's Wife," and "The Blackleg Miner." Jimmy Webb's "Wichita Lineman," about a man who repairs telegraph poles, has a potent tradition behind it. Alternatively, in Bacharach and David's "Say a Little Prayer," the monotony of the working day throws the speaker's romantic feelings into greater relief.

Employment

» *The Silhouettes, "Get a Job"; the Miracles, "Got a Job"; Talking Heads, "Found a Job"; Elvis Costello, "Welcome to the Working Week"; Jane Wiedlin, "Rush Hour"; Cat Stevens, "Matthew and Son"; Rose Royce, "Car Wash"; the Beach Boys, "I Get Around"; Paul McCartney, "Another Day"; R.E.M., "Finest Worksong"; the Jam, "Man in the Cornershop"; the Clash, "Career Opportunities"; Rihanna, "Work."*

Work and money are universal concerns. Millions know how it feels to have no money or to work for peanuts, hence lyrics about wanting to make more money. The granddaddy of all songs about money is "Buddy, Can You Spare a Dime."

Songs titled "Money" have been recorded by Pink Floyd, Badfinger, Lovin' Spoonful, and the Berry Gordy composition cited above, recorded in a no-nonsense manner by Barratt Strong in the early 1960s. Its lyric shocked people by challenging the proverbial wisdom that the best things in life are free—a view expressed successfully by the Beatles in "Can't Buy Me Love." The same cynicism apparent in Gordy's "Money" is felt in "Diamonds Are a Girl's Best Friend" and "Diamonds Are Forever." in the case of Pink Floyd's "Money," the theme is handled from the other end of the bank account, where people have too much money.

The vocabulary of finance is a mine of similes and metaphors with which to color a lyric—words like tender, account, and currency can have double meanings.

Money

» *Abba, "Money Money Money"; Chuck Berry, "No Money Down"; Simply Red, "Money's Too Tight to Mention"; the Pet Shop Boys, "Opportunities (Let's Make Lots of Money)"; the Contours, "First I Look at the Purse"; Annie Lennox, "Money Can't Buy It"; Wham!, "Credit Card Baby"; Funkadelic, "Funky Dollar Bill"; Alice Cooper, "Billion Dollar Babies"; the Pretenders, "Brass in Pocket"; ZZ Top, "Just Got Paid"; the Clash, "Working for the Yankee Dollar"; the Beatles, "Taxman"; Aloe Black, "I Need a Dollar."*

Rural life

In song lyrics, the country exists as the polar opposite of the city. Where the latter is dangerous, exciting, modern, the country stands for a romantic pastoral vision of rootedness, belonging, beauty, tranquility, safety, healthy living, and getting back to nature. In the USA, rural also stands for the old frontiers.

This symbolism was strengthened in the late 1960s by growing environmentalism, with its focus on self-sufficiency, communal living, and escaping capitalism. This contrasted with the aspiration of earlier generations employed in poorly paid jobs and often vulnerable to the unpredictable, destructive powers of nature. They could be glad to escape to the city, leaving behind small-town gossip and parochial attitudes. Now, city-dwellers dream of escape to the country.

In the country

» *Buddy Guy, "Country Man"; Elton John, "Goodbye Yellow Brick Road," "Country Comfort"; John Denver, "Take Me Home, Country Roads"; Canned Heat, "Going Up the Country"; Rory Gallagher, "Country Mile"; Red Hot Chili Peppers, "Backwoods"; Neil Young, "Are You Ready for the Country"; James Taylor, "Country*

Road"; America, "A Horse with No Name"; Hacienda Brothers, "Saguero"; Marty Stuart and His Fabulous Superlatives, "Lost On the Desert"; Calexico, "Ballad of Cable Hogue"; Johnny Cash, "I've Been Everywhere"; My Chemical Romance, "Desert Song"; Sting, "Desert Rose."

In lyrics, the country symbolically includes small-town (or village) life and farms—so there are songs about working on farms. No one should use a title with the word "farm" in it without being aware of Bob Dylan's "Maggie's Farm."

In country music, the countryside is seen as the place of traditional, conservative values, opposed to the decadent modernism of the city. For landscape features like rivers and woods, see the topography metaphors in section 6.

Farms, country houses, castles

» *The Faces, "Miss Judy's Farm"; Bob Dylan, "Maggie's Farm"; Mose Allison, "Parchman Farm"; Blur, "Country House"; Barenaked Ladies, "King of Bedside Manor"; Wings, "Big Barn Red"; Eels, "Ant Farm"; Yoshikawa and the Blue Comets, "Blue Chateau"; the Four Tops, "Keeper of the Castle"; the Jimi Hendrix Experience, "Spanish Castle Magic"; Little Feat, UK Subs, "Down on the Farm"; Ed Sheeran, "Castle on the Hill."*

Amusement parks and the circus

> *At the end of 'Relay,' I just started to say what was on my mind ... 'Going up to the Ferris wheel to throw your anger out the door'—that doesn't make sense, so I just stopped. But that line is true. Around the time of recording Extraordinary Machine, I used to get up every morning and walk to the Santa Monica Pier, which is like two and a half miles away, to be first in line on the Ferris wheel. When I got up to the top I'd try and take all the anger that I had about shit and just get rid of it."*

FIONA APPLE TO *PITCHFORK* ON HER SONG "RELAY," DECEMBER 2020

We know from Shakespeare that "all the world's a stage," and men and women the players thereon—a notion restated in modern guise in the musical *Cabaret*. This sense of life as a play in which people have roles can be felt wherever people gather for entertainment. Hence lyrics about amusement parks and rides, carnivals, and circuses. These places and activities provide rich material, whether literal or metaphorical. Everyone relates to the feeling of performing in social situations, sometimes enjoyably, sometimes not. For this reason, the line about being in the spotlight in R.E.M.'s "Losing My Religion" struck a chord with many.

Young people haunt amusement parks; lovers wander through the crowds. At night, they are noisy and colorful places, sometimes with fireworks. People gamble, win and lose. Each ride or attraction could individually be a metaphor, as in the case of Madness's "House of Fun," about a shy youth wanting to buy contraceptives in a chemist shop. The most often cited ride in lyrics is the tunnel of love, followed by the ghost train.

Amusement parks and rides

» *Madness, "House of Fun," "Ghost Train"; Dire Straits, "Tunnel of Love"; Bruce Springsteen, "4th of July; Asbury Park (Sandy)"; the Beach Boys, "Amusement Parks USA"; 13th Floor Elevators, "Roller Coaster"; the Beatles, "Helter Skelter"; Richard Thompson, "Wall of Death"; the Hollies, "On a Carousel."*

The circus is a romantic symbol. Here is a group—often eccentric or playing eccentric roles—who live outside the usual world of work and travel the country, apparently with a freedom the majority do not have. In role, they are almost a set of caricatures of what it is to be human, often with exaggerated powers or misshapen in some way. A circus also carries the derogatory meaning of an enterprise which is frivolous, unreal, and promises more than it delivers. The carnival is a closely related possible setting.

Circuses and carnivals

» *Bruce Springsteen, "Wild Billy's Circus Story"; the Beatles, "Being for the Benefit of Mr Kite"; Procol Harum, "'Twas Teatime at the Circus"; Junior's Eyes, "Circus Days"; Mountain, "The Animal Trainer and the Toad"; the Butthole Surfers, "Human Cannonball"; Tim Buckley, "Carnival Song"; the Seekers, "The Carnival Is Over"; the Coasters, "Little Egypt"; the Band, "The WS Walcott Medicine Show," "Life Is a Carnival"; Cher, "Gypsies, Tramps and Thieves"; Massive Attack, "Paradise Circus."*

The central figure of the circus is the clown who pretends to be funny and jovial, but who underneath it is solitary and alone. This image expresses the disappointed lover who wears a mask of pride to hide his or her hurt, the socially awkward, or the person made a fool of. The more literary version is the jester, an attractive figure to adolescents who feel clumsy and alienated. The clown is a tricky image to put in a lyric now because the happy outside, sad inside association has become a cliché.

Clowns

» *Smokey Robinson and the Miracles, "Tears of a Clown"; the Kinks, "Death of a Clown"; Ron Sexsmith, "Clown in Broad Daylight"; Judy Collins, "Send in the Clowns"; Turin Brakes, "Last Clown"; Neil Sedaka, "King of Clowns"; Emeli Sande, "Clown"; Goldfrapp, "Clowns."*

Society itself can be seen as a set of people who are wearing masks, not showing their true feelings, and thus a "masquerade." Life becomes like a theater performance.

» *The Band, "Stage Fright"; Graham Parker, "I'm Gonna Tear Your Playhouse Down"; Fish, "Black Masquerade"; Leo Sayer, "I Won't Let the Show Go On," "The Dancer"; Marilyn McCoo and Billy Davis Jr., "You Don't Have to Be a Star (to Be in My Show)"; Badly Drawn Boy, "Exit Stage Right"; Van Morrison, "Ballerina."*

Geography

Geography easily evokes pictures and suggests a story which can make a lyric. A geographical title is more interesting if a verb or adjective is attached to the placename, rather than it stand on its own. The additional word can lend drama and imply what the song is about. This technique is more important the better known the place. Let's face it, calling a song "New York" puts you up against some stiff competition.

Consider Leonard Cohen's "First We Take Manhattan." The title refers to a place, but it also conveys something else. The hyperbole is intriguing—what does he mean by "take"? Is he being literal? Is this a war song? And then he has the word "first," which begs the question, what happens second? (They take Berlin.)

Some placenames are intrinsically more evocative than others. A placename like Phoenix, for example, has poetic possibilities because of the association with the legendary bird that renews its immortality by burning in a pyre and rising from the ashes. With Jimmy Webb's "By the Time I Get to Phoenix," the title immediately makes us wonder, "By the time he gets to Phoenix . . . what?" Similarly, "Do You Know the Way to San Jose?" has us thinking, *Why is the speaker asking? Why does she want to get there?*

Places in the USA

The geography of North America, the notion of a wild frontier, the two oceans, and the idealism associated with its origins, lends itself to a projection of imagined values and dreams which would not be prevalent in a smaller country. A lyric like the Beach Boys' "Surfin' USA" is exhilarating as it crisscrosses the continent naming places.

There are many songs about the U.S.A. itself:

» *Chuck Berry, "Back in the USA"; the Ramones, "I'm So Bored with the USA"; the Steve Miller Band, "Living in the USA"; the MC5, "Back in the USA"; Bruce Springsteen, "Born in the USA"; Ray Charles, "America the Beautiful"; Simon and Garfunkel, "America"; Elvis Presley, "An American Trilogy"; Childish Gambino, "This Is America."*

Travel often expresses a desire to find a better life, from the time of the old blues songs, when African Americans freed from slavery in the South journeyed by whatever means they could toward the cities. This impulse to make a better life somewhere is also expressed in the early songs of Bruce Springsteen, which initially focused on travel as escape but matured to ask what happens when you arrive at your so-called "dream place." Another group of people liable to write songs about different places are musicians themselves, since they spend so much time touring.

In the early 2000s, singer/songwriter Sufjan Stevens recorded two albums dedicated to individual states: *Michigan* (2003) and *(Come on Feel the) Illinoise* (2005). He had at the time an ambition to do an album for each of the 50 states! There are thousands of songs whose titles refer to places in America, with California one of the most popular of the states:

» *Brian Wilson, "California Girls"; Led Zeppelin, "Going to California"; the Mamas and the Papas, "California Dreaming"; Red Hot Chili Peppers, "Californication"; Dead Kennedys, "California Über Alles," R.E.M., "I Remember California"; James Taylor, "Carolina in My Mind"; Joni Mitchell, "California"; the Move "California Man"; My Chemical Romance, "We Don't Need Another Song About California"; Vampire Weekend, "California English"; Katy Perry, "California Gurls."*

Songs of the states

Here are some other state-based songs:

» *The Doors, "Alabama Song"; the Bee Gees, "Road to Alaska," "Massachusetts"; Los Lobos, "Arizona Skies"; Lyle Lovett, "North Dakota; Perry Como, "Delaware"; Bob Seger, "Get Out of Denver"; Ray Charles, "Georgia on My Mind"; R. Dean Taylor, "Indiana Wants Me"; Elvis Presley, "Kentucky Rain"; Jerry Lee Lewis, "What Made Milwaukee Famous"; Mountain, "Mississippi Queen"; Neil Young, "Ohio"; Al Stewart, "Katherine of Oregon"; Elton John, "Philadelphia Freedom"; Captain Beefheart, "Moonlight on Vermont"; America, "Old Virginia"; Miranda Lambert, "Oklahoma Sky."*

The prime subjects of placename song lyrics in the US are New York, Los Angeles, and Hollywood. Cities closely associated with music, such as Memphis, Nashville, and Detroit, also feature. In the 1960s, San Francisco had numerous songs written about it when it was the capital of the hippie counterculture. Barney Hoskyns's *Waiting for the Sun: The Sound of Los Angeles* (1996) has an appendix listing songs about Los Angeles.

> *New York's architecture alone is enough to inspire a whole album. In fact, that's what happened at first—my early stuff was mostly just interpretations of landscapes."*
>
> **LANA DEL RAY TO *THE QUIETUS*, OCTOBER 2011**

Songs of New York

» *Frank Sinatra, "New York, New York"; Bruce Springsteen, "New York City Serenade"; Sting, "Englishman in New York"; Don Henley, "New York Minute"; Arrow, "New York Groove"; Barbara Streisand, "New York State of Mind"; the Pogues and Kirsty MacColl, "Fairytale of New York"; Ryan Adams, "My Blue Manhattan"; Van Morrison, "Coney Island"; Beastie Boys, "No Sleep Til Brooklyn"; Lana Del Rey, "Brooklyn Baby"; Drifters, "On Broadway"; Simon and Garfunkel, "Bleecker Street"; Nat King Cole, "On the Streets of New York"; Taylor Swift, "Welcome to New York"; Alicia Keys, "New York"; Gil Scott Heron, "New York Is Killing Me."*

Songs of Hollywood and San Francisco

» *Fleetwood Mac, "Hollywood"; the Corrs, "Queen of Hollywood"; the Eagles, "King of Hollywood," "Hollywood Waltz"; Thin Lizzy, "Hollywood (Down on Your Luck)"; System of a Down, "Lost in Hollywood"; Scott McKenzie, "San Francisco"; Flowerpot Men, "Let's Go to San Francisco"; Tony Bennett, "I Left My Heart in San Francisco"; Eric Burdon and the Animals, "San Franciscan Nights."*

Other locations in the USA

» *Neil Young, "Albuquerque"; Bruce Springsteen, "Atlantic City"; Tim Hardin, "The Lady Came from Baltimore"; Paul Butterfield Blues Band, "Born in Chicago"; David Bowie, "Panic in Detroit"; Martha and the Muffins, "Echo Beach"; Glen Campbell, "Galveston"; Albert King, "Kansas City"; Mott the Hoople, "All the Way from Memphis"; Bob Dylan, "Nashville Skyline"; Bruce Springsteen, "Somewhere North of Nashville"; Tim Buckley, "Monterey"; Loudon Wainwright III, "Ode to Pittsburgh"; R.E.M., "All the Way to Reno"; Nanci Griffith, "San Diego Serenade"; Everclear, "Santa Monica"; the Byrds, "Tulsa County Blue"; Blondie, "Union City Blue"; Glen Campbell, "Wichita Lineman"; Wilco, "Via Chicago."*

Places in the UK

Songs about places in the UK are rarer than those about the USA. Since the UK is geographically smaller, it is harder to feel that your dreams and the answer to your problems lie at the end of a few hundred miles of motorway. British musicians are also less inclined toward overt patriotism. Songs about England, for example, usually start from a sense that the theme is problematic, assuming they aren't outright attacks. Blur's album *Modern Life Is Rubbish* was an attempt to write songs about definite characters who would illustrate the romantic and sinister aspects of English life. Popular songs about England, post-1960s, tend to be skeptical, verging on cynical. This is felt strongly in punk bands like the Sex Pistols.

England

» *Oysterband, "Another Quiet Night in England"; Roy Harper, "One of Those Days in England"; the Clash, "Something About England," "This Is England"; Kate Bush, "Oh England (My Lionheart)"; Kirsty MacColl, "England"; the Waterboys, "Old England"; Billy Bragg, "I'm Not Looking for New England"; Sex Pistols, "Anarchy in the UK"; Laura Marling, "Goodbye England (Covered in Snow)."*

British songwriters have only recently started to overcome the sense that to write songs about journeys or places in the UK is bathetic. It is still unexpected to examine a CD and find a title like "Clouds Over Carlisle" or "Meet Me in Lincoln." In the British context, Carter the Unstoppable Sex Machine's "24 Minutes from Tulse Hill" is a funny allusion to Gene Pitney's "24 Hours from Tulsa," and Billy Bragg's "A13 Trunk Road to the Sea" is an unromantic British parody of "Route 66," starting in Wapping, East London.

As is the case with most countries, there are plenty of songs about the capital London and its districts, though probably more in the pre–rock 'n' roll era than after (standards like "Maybe It's Because I'm a Londoner," "Doing the Lambeth Walk," "Underneath the Arches," et cetera). In the mid-1960s, it was briefly hip to write songs about London, when it was center of the pop world (until the axis shifted to San Francisco). When England was "swinging," the New Vaudeville Band could write a hit lyric like "Winchester Cathedral" or "Finchley Central." Not now.

London and environs
» *Ed Sheeran, "Take Me Back to London"; The Clash, "London Calling," "White Man in the Hammersmith Palais"; Catatonia, "Londinium"; Gene, "London, Can You Wait?"; Ralph McTell, "Streets of London"; Blur, "London Loves"; ELO, "Last Train to London"; the Pet Shop Boys, "West End Girls"; Elvis Costello, "I Don't Want to Go to Chelsea"; Gerry Rafferty, "Baker Street"; Donovan, "Hampstead Incident"; Kirsty MacColl, "Soho Square"; the Kinks, "Waterloo Sunset"; Cat Stevens, "Portobello Road"; Ian Dury, "Billericay Dickie"; Coldplay, "Cemeteries of London"; Duffy, "Warwick Avenue"; Lily Allen, "LDN."*

English counties are not as glamorous as US states—they're smaller, and the geographical contrasts are not as pronounced. An exception is in traditional folksong, from times when people mostly travelled on foot, and often didn't meet anyone who lived further away than the nearest village (see "Scarborough Fair"). In reality, the counties of England have their own character and history; it just takes more imagination to see it. But they do not represent modernity in the way that the USA always has, and popular songs are bound up with modernity. Consequently, English counties are almost invisible in popular song lyrics (a title like Bill Nelson's "Adventures in a Yorkshire Landscape" is very rare), but towns and cities do figure.

Cities

» *ELO, "Birmingham Blues"; the Bangles, "Going Down to Liverpool"; Gerry
and the Pacemakers, "Ferry Cross the Mersey" (Liverpool); the Stone Roses, "Mersey
Paradise"; Simple Minds, "Belfast Child"; Manic Street Preachers, "Cardiff
Afterlife"; Happy Mondays, "Manchester Rave On"; Fatboy Slim, "You're Not from
Brighton"; Lindisfarne, "Fog on the Tyne" (Newcastle); Alan Price, "Jarrow Song."*

Towns and other geographical references

» *Oysterband, "The Oxford Girl"; Peter Gabriel, "Solsbury Hill"; the Waterboys,
"The Glastonbury Song"; Siouxsie and the Banshees, "Land's End"; Manic Street
Preachers, "Blackpool Pier"; Pink Floyd, "Grantchester Meadow"; Traffic, "Berkshire
Poppies"; Blur, "Clover Over Dover"; Badly Drawn Boy, "Stockport"; Robyn
Hitchcock, "No, I Don't Remember Guildford"; Doves, "Shadows of Salford";
Roy Harper, "Watford Gap"; the Fall, "Bournemouth Runner"; Arctic Monkeys,
"Rotherham"; Coldplay, "Violet Hill."*

The rest of the world

A band's tour itinerary might take them to far-flung places and new surroundings—a
rich topic for lyric writing. As Tony Wright of Terrorvision explained to *Melody
Maker*, "You get to go to so many places and meet so many people that you're
never short of something new to write about. Inspiration for the words comes
from everything we do—one day we'll be in one country and the next we'll be in
another and so we'll write a song about that."

Songs about countries other than the one you live in might be inspired by a
holiday; by current events, history, politics, the desire to go there; or because that
country represents a theme or an emotion. All countries have a geographical reality
and a cultural reality (including the country you live in). All landscapes are also
imagined; all geography is also the cultural topography of symbols and values.

These lyrics are not confined to being about the country concerned; that may
just be the backdrop to something else.

When it comes to arranging and recording a song, a country's own music
might suggest the instruments. The West Indies are associated with calypso;
Jamaica with reggae; Cuba with the music of the Buena Vista Social Club; India
with its scales, sitars, and tablas; and evoking the Far East might put a pentatonic
scale to other uses than are found in John Lee Hooker's blues.

This list of titles does not include songs in other languages. For example, Edith Piaf, Jacques Brel, Francoise Hardy, Maurice Chevalier, and Serge Gainsbourg could supply hundreds of songs about France, but in French. This book restricts itself to the Anglo-American tradition.

Canada

Songs about Canada often focus on the great outdoors and the symbolism of north. (A great book about that symbolism more widely is *The Idea of North* by Peter Davidson.)

» *Echobelly, "Canada"; Billy Bragg, "Ontario Quebec and Me"; the Byrds, "Blue Canadian Rockies"; Eliza Carthy, "Quebecois"; Violent Femmes, "Vancouver"; Jeff Buckley, "Vancouver"; Andy Williams, "Canadian Sunset."*

Central America

Here it is the heat, laid-back life, corruption, and political revolution which provide themes.

» *Incubus, Long John Baldry, "Mexico" (about the 1968 Olympics); Marty Robbins "El Paso"; Stan Getz and João Gilberto, "The Girl from Ipanema"; Jackson Browne, "Jamaica Say You Will"; Bruce Cockburn, "Nicaragua"; the Zutons, "Havana Gang Brawl"; R.E.M., "The Flowers of Guatemala"; Arcade Fire, "Haiti"; Bobby Bloom, "Montego Bay"; Billy Ocean, "Caribbean Queen"; Athlete, "El Salvador"; the Minutemen, "Untitled Song for Latin America"; Camilla Cabello, "Havana."*

South America

This continent evokes lyrics about tropical weather, political tyranny, escape, ancient civilizations, and ecology.

» *Julie Covington, "Don't Cry for Me Argentina"; Kirsty MacColl, "Columbia"; Stackridge, "The Road to Venezuela"; Pink Flag, "Brazil"; Duran Duran, "Rio"; Crass, "Sheep-Farming in the Falklands"; Martin Stephenson and the Dainties, "Boat to Bolivia"; Bob Martin, "Silver Rails to Rio"; Neil Young, "Like an Inca"; Toad the Wet Sprocket, "Chile."*

Western Europe

These countries offer much in the way of sense of place and history, and sophistication.

» *Nelson Riddle, "In Old Lisbon"; John Cale, "Andalucia"; Three Dog Night, "Never Been to Spain"; Mink Deville, "Spanish Stroll"; Joni Mitchell, "Free Man in Paris"; the 1975, "Paris"; Supergrass, "Road to Rouen"; the Verve, "Monte Carlo"; Red Hot Chilli Peppers, "Venice Queen"; Rufus Wainwright, "Greek Song"; the Rakes, "Strasbourg"; Pavement, "Zurich Is Stained"; Elvis Costello, "Luxembourg," "New Amsterdam"; the Beautiful South, "Rotterdam (Or Anywhere); Scott Walker, "Copenhagen"; Al Stewart, "Night Train to Munich"; the Associates, "White Car in Germany"; Lou Reed, "Berlin"; Billy Joel, "Vienna."*

Scandinavia and Eastern Europe

Go to the Scandinavian countries and you really are in virgin territory for lyrics. Some images you might like to think about include deep fjords, snow, pine forests, wilderness, northern lights. Go east and, despite the changing political scene in those countries, your lyrics are likely to be entering Cold War and spy country.

» *Eliza Carthy, "Sweden"; David Bowie, "Warszawa"; Joy Division, "Warsaw"; Jethro Tull, "Budapest"; Matt Monroe, "From Russia with Love"; the Beatles, "Back in the USSR"; Sting, "Russians"; Al Stewart, "Roads to Moscow"; Blondie, "Contact in Red Square"; George Ezra, "Budapest."*

The Middle East

The popular song lyric has rarely been interested in the geopolitical realities of the Middle East, preferring instead to conjure visions of an older exotic and sensual Arabia of camels, deserts, oases, and the ancient monuments of Egypt.

» *The Police, "Tea in the Sahara"; Siouxsie and the Banshees, "Israel"; the Coral, "Arabian Sand"; Kate Bush, "Egypt"; the Cure, "Fire in Cairo"; the Bangles, "Walk Like an Egyptian"; the Teardrop Explodes, "Thief of Baghdad"; the Human League, "The Lebanon"; the Clash, "Rock the Casbah."*

Africa

The obvious humanitarian needs of the continent have meant that in pop lyrics (especially charity songs) Africa is often the place of starvation, conflict and disease. It is also likely to bring political themes into focus, as was the case with apartheid in South Africa.

» *Toto, "Africa"; Bob Marley, "Africa Unite"; Gretchen Petersen, "Over Africa"; Roy Harper, "South Africa"; Bob Dylan, "Mozambique"; Billy Joel, "Zanzibar"; the Housemartins, "Johannesburg"; Kanye West, "Diamonds from Sierra Leone"; Peter Gabriel, "Biko"; Paul Simon, "Under African Skies."*

Asia

Lyrics about the Far East stress its apparent exoticism, with India and Tibet being the focus for imagined secret spiritual wisdom from the mid-1960s onward.

» *Big Star, "The India Song"; Lawrence Welk, "Calcutta"; Led Zeppelin, "Kashmir"; Cat Stevens, "Katmandu"; David Bowie, "China Girl," "Seven Years in Tibet"; Tom Waits, "Singapore"; Babybird, "Hong Kong Blues"; Tom Waits, "Burma Shave"; the Dead Kennedys, "Holiday in Cambodia"; Freddy Cannon, "One Night in Bangkok"; Deep Purple, "Woman from Tokyo"; Elvis Costello, "Tokyo Storm Warning"; Japan, "Visions of China"; Graham Parker and the Rumour, "Discovering Japan"; Coldplay, "Lovers In Japan"; Phoebe Bridgers, "Kyoto."*

The Pacific

There seem to be few lyrics about countries in the southern Pacific, perhaps reflecting their geographical isolation and remoteness from the experience of most pop musicians in the Anglo-American tradition and their relative youth as countries compared to those that colonized them. With global warming we may yet hear a few more songs about the north and south poles.

» *Smashing Pumpkins, "Galapagos"; Men at Work, "Down Under"; Manic Street Preachers, "Australia"; John Cale, "Antarctica Starts Here"; Al Stewart, "Antarctica"; Icehouse, "Great Southern Land."*

Journeys

> *Travelling is a big inspiration. Just being in motion, a train, a plane. As soon as I'm mobile, I start to write things down, usually from the first line onwards . . . If my opener doesn't work for the first verse, I usually move it to the end of the second verse."*

PAUL HEATON OF THE BEAUTIFUL SOUTH TO *MELODY MAKER*

Describe a journey, and you can sketch a lyric by stating:

- where and why it started
- where it's going
- by what means you are travelling
- where you are currently and what needs to happen to get there
- what this journey means to you
- how long it might take
- if you think you will make it
- what happens when it is finished.

That's plenty of stimulus for a lyric. In popular songs, people have walked, cruised the freeways on bikes or in cars, hitchhiked, jumped on trains, and taken jet planes. They have even been through deserts on horses that had no name!

Road songs

The road is a rich source of metaphor—you can turn the wrong way down a one-way street, or live life in the "fast lane." Life itself can be interpreted as a journey, with right and wrong turnings, as in the Isley Brothers' "The Highways of My Life."

» *America, "Ventura Highway"; Deep Purple, "Highway Star"; Joni Mitchell, "Refuge of the Roads"; Robert Johnson, "Crossroads"; the Eagles, "Life in the Fast Lane"; Edwin Starr, "25 Miles"; the Tom Robinson Band, "2-4-6-8 Motorway"; the Pretenders, "2000 Miles;" the Lovin' Spoonful, "On the Road Again"; Robert Plant, "Big Log"; Talking Heads, "Road to Nowhere"; Tom Waits, "Wrong Side of the Road"; Van Morrison, "Bright Side of the Road"; Sheryl Crow, "Everyday Is a Winding Road," the Jimi Hendrix Experience, "Burning of the Midnight Lamp"; Arctic Monkeys, "One for the Road."*

All that's required is to connect a term like "border" or "road" with an abstract noun like "love," "hope," "fear," or "doubt," as in a couplet like *I can't live this way any longer / in the borderland of doubt.* These metaphors broaden out into geographical references such as borders and compass points:

» *Ed Sheeran, "South of the Border"; Thin Lizzy, Tame Impala, "Borderline"; Dire Straits, "Southbound Again"; Elton John, "Border Song"; Richard and Linda Thompson, "When I Get to the Border"; Little Feat, "Down Below the Borderline"; ELO, "Across the Border."*

Travelers

There are many lyrics about life on the road—a topic close to the heart of touring musicians, who spend their lives moving from concert to concert. Or, as Madonna sang in *Evita*, a matter of "Another Suitcase in Another Hall." The figure of the ever-traveling man (it usually is a man) is part of the folklore of song lyrics.

» *The Jimi Hendrix Experience, "Highway Chile"; Junior Walker and the All Stars, "(I'm a) Road Runner"; Free, "Travelling Man"; Mountain, "Crossroader"; Dion, "The Wanderer"; the Who, "Going Mobile"; Bob Seger, "Travellin' Man"; Bonnie Raitt, "The Road's My Middle Name"; Roger Miller, "King of the Road"; Boston, "Hitch a Ride"; Creedence Clearwater Revival, "Travellin' Band"; Ed Sheeran, "Nina"; Bat for Lashes, "Travelling Woman."*

Traveling homeward

Lyrically, home is a "hot-button" word—a concept that is emotive for most people. We become adults as we leave home, and usually there's no going back. A vast number of people at any given time are thinking about home, wanting to get back home, or making a home. The journey home and inward is the balance to all the journeys in popular song that go away and outward.

Home might be a place, or it might be defined as something else, like a person; home can be in the country or the city. Sometimes these songs have a certain death-longing about them, as the return home can be associated with a sense of spiritual exile from heaven. You can check for this when a lyric associates rest, stasis, nightfall, or autumn, for example, with home.

» *Carole King, "Goin' Back"; the Beatles, "There's a Place," "The Long and Winding Road"; Simon and Garfunkel, "Homeward Bound"; Bruce Springsteen, "My Hometown"; Meredith Brooks, "My Little Town"; Rory Gallagher, "Going to My Home Town," Ten Years After "Going Home"; Slade, "Take Me Back 'Ome"; Andy Williams, "Home Lovin' Man"; Slim Whitman, "Home on the Range"; Arctic Monkeys, "Still Take Me Home"; FKA Twigs, "Home with You."*

Transport

" *I buy the local papers every day, and they're full of car wrecks and . . . I guess it all depends on what it is in the paper that attracts you. I'm always drawn to these terrible stories."*

TOM WAITS TO *MOJO*, APRIL 1999

Writing about people traveling can give a lyric movement. When people go on journeys, things happen; they meet other people, see new things, have new thoughts and feelings, and so on. Bruce Springsteen once pointed out that he was less interested in cars than the people *in* the cars. So, the question becomes: which mode of transport interests you at a given time of writing?

Cars

Rock 'n' roll and cars have been linked since Chuck Berry wrote tunes like "No Particular Place to Go" and "Maybellene," celebrating the joys of being young and mobile.

The birth of rock 'n' roll in the 1950s coincided with a classic period of American car manufacture, when cars got bigger and more elaborately contoured, with chrome, fins, and extravagant taillights. Chevrolets and pink Cadillacs are as much rock symbols as blue suede shoes or a guitar-shaped pool. Specific brand names also became significant:

» *Bruce Springsteen, "Cadillac Ranch"; the Clash, "Brand New Cadillac"; Hot Chocolate, "Heaven Is in the Back Seat of My Cadillac"; Gene Vincent, "Pink Thunderbird"; Chuck Berry, "Jaguar and the Thunderbird"; Janis Joplin, "Mercedes Benz"; Commander Cody and His Lost Planet Airmen, "Hot Rod Lincoln"; Prince, "Little Red Corvette"; Wilson Pickett, "Mustang Sally"; Nanci Griffith, "Ford Econoline"; the Beach Boys, "Little Deuce Coupe," "Little Honda"; 1910 Fruitgum*

Company, "Firebird"; Bob Dylan, "From a Buick 6"; Lana Del Rey, "White Mustang"; Frank Ocean, "White Ferrari"; Kings of Leon, "Camaro."

If you didn't want to be specific, it didn't matter. The idea of the car was powerful enough:

» *The Rolling Stones, "Black Limousine"; Big Star, "Big Black Car," "Back of a Car"; Dan Seals, "My Old Yellow Car"; Kristina Olsen, "The Man with the Bright Red Car"; Bachman Turner Overdrive, "Four Wheel Drive"; U2, "Fast Cars"; Beck, "Magic Stationwagon"; Gary Numan, "Cars"; Arcade Fire, "Keep the Car Running."*

Most modern cars lack not only the colors but also the glamour of their older forebears. Can you imagine writing a lyric about a gray, gas-guzzling SUV? In the age of global warming, driving a car is no longer a gesture of rebellion.

In the USA in the affluent 1950s, a car was a teenager's easiest means to circumvent adult rules about who you saw and how much you saw of them. The car was a status symbol; learning to drive was a rite of passage. As you earned more money, you could buy a bigger car. A bigger car was a way of attracting girls. Racing cars was a way of proving your manhood, as in the story narrated by the Beach Boys' "Don't Worry, Baby." The car was a place where you could live fast and die young. In reality, car wrecks claimed popular figures like Eddie Cochran, Jayne Mansfield, and James Dean.

Moving cars

Picking up the driving imagery, the Beatles wrote "Drive My Car" and "Day Tripper." Rock stars are driven around in limos, as Marc Bolan's reference to a Rolls-Royce in T.Rex's "Children of the Revolution" reminds us.

For a lyric, a car automatically evokes people, movement, and new experiences, which amounts to the chance of something dramatic happening.

» *Gene, "A Car That Sped"; Joni Mitchell, "Car on a Hill"; Bruce Springsteen, "Stolen Car," "Drive All Night"; Chuck Berry, "No Particular Place to Go"; the Jimi Hendrix Experience, "Crosstown Traffic"; Lucinda Williams, "Car Wheels on a Gravel Road"; Iggy Pop "The Passenger"; Tracy Chapman "Fast Car"; Deftones, "Be Quiet and Drive (Far Away)."*

Associated images and phrases

Cars and driving provide a considerable source for smutty sexual metaphors. "Drive My Car" and "Mustang Sally" are relatively innocent examples, but Prince's "Little Red Corvette" and Led Zeppelin's "Trampled Underfoot" are bolder. The vocabulary of cars and driving lends itself to punning metaphors, as do many related words and concepts, as the following titles indicate.

» *Meat Loaf, "Paradise by the Dashboard Light"; Alice Cooper, "Under My Wheels"; Pearl Jam, "Rear View Mirror"; the Go-Go's, "Skidmarks on My Heart"; Elvis Costello, "Five Gears in Reverse"; Jackson Browne, "Runnin' on Empty"; Joni Mitchell, "Big Yellow Taxi"; Queen, "I'm in Love with My Car"; the Dictators, "(I Live for) Cars and Girls"; Prefab Sprout, "Cars and Girls"; Paul Simon, "Cars Are Cars"; Shania Twain, "In My Car (I'll Be the Driver)"; Wilco, "Passenger Side."*

Part of the drama of driving is that things can go seriously wrong, and the appeal of the car and the open road can turn sour, as these songs demonstrate:

» *Paul Anka, "Tell Laura I Love Her"; Jan and Dean, "Dead Man's Curve"; the Shangri-Las, "The Leader of the Pack," the Beatles, "A Day in the Life" (someone ought to have noticed that the lights had changed); Bruce Springsteen, "Racing in the Streets" (speeding in a residential area); David Bowie, "Always Crashing in the Same Car" (especially careless driving); Mungo Jerry, "In the Summertime" (doing 125mph!); Dave Edmunds, "Crawling from the Wreckage"; Soundgarden, "Limo Wreck"; Catatonia, "Road Rage."*

Motorcycles and buses

Motorcycles retain their rebel image, hence the band name Black Rebel Motorcycle Club, or George Michael choosing to be photographed in a BSA jacket. Rockers in 1950s England and 1960s Hell's Angels are forever associated with rock music; the Vespa scooter, the favorite vehicle of the Mods, proved more appealing visually than in song. Truckers are also romanticized as outsiders in popular song.

» *Steppenwolf, "Born to Be Wild"; Bruce Springsteen, "Born to Run"; Chris Spedding, "Motor Bikin'"; Iggy Pop, "Motorcycle"; Manic Street Preachers,*

"Motorcycle Emptiness"; the Shangri-Las, "Leader of the Pack"; Sinead O'Connor, "Black Boys on Mopeds"; Richard Thompson, "1952 Vincent Black Lightning"; the Who, "Magic Bus"; the Beatles, "One After 909"; the Count Five, "Double Decker Bus"; C. W. McCall, "Convoy."

Trains

In lyrics, trains have different associations to cars. For a start, you don't own a train, and in the old days you could even jump aboard without paying. Trains travel long distances, so they are linked to the size of a continent like the USA. A train journey takes you far away from where you are, or it separates you from someone you love.

The most famous train in popular lyric is Elvis's "Mystery Train" (sixteen coaches long), closely followed by Glen Miller's "Chatanooga Choo-Choo." There are thousands of train songs in blues and skiffle, like Bukka White's "Panama Limited" and "Special Streamline," or Lightnin' Slim's "Mean Old Lonesome Train." There seem to be fewer lyrics about train stations, although Simon and Garfunkel's "Homeward Bound" is set at a railway station, and Wings' "Hi Hi Hi" starts at one.

» The Monkees, "Last Train to Clarksville"; Los Lobos, "The Train Don't Stop Here"; No Doubt, "Big City Train"; James Brown, "Night Train"; the Cure, "Jumping Someone Else's Train"; the Jimi Hendrix Experience, "Hear My Train A-Comin'"; the Clash, "Train in Vain"; Tiny Bradshaw, "The Train Kept A-Rollin'"; the Doobie Brothers, "Long Train Runnin'"; Elvis Presley, "Mystery Train"; Paul Simon, "Train in the Distance"; The The, "Slow Train to Dawn"; the O'Jays, "Love Train"; Gladys Knight and the Pips, "Midnight Train to Georgia"; Ocean Colour Scene, "The Day We Caught the Train"; the Sports, "Strangers on a Train"; Blink-182, "Last Train Home"; the Fall, "Victoria Train Station Massacre."

Boats and planes

Travel by ship is too luxurious and slow to fit in with the lyrics of the rock era. If a lyric uses the image of a ship, it is usually a metaphor and often unconsciously archaic (as in "Sailing," with its boat on thoroughly allegorical "stormy waters." Ship travel for pleasure, as in a cruise, is linked to the first three decades of the 20th century. There are more lyrics referring to modern sea travel in songs of the 1920s–1940s.

» *Billy J. Kramer, "Trains and Boats and Planes"; Bebop Deluxe, "Ships in the Night"; Neil Young, "Cripple Creek Ferry"; the Beatles, "Yellow Submarine"; the Beach Boys, "Sloop John B."; Rod Stewart, "Sailing"; Gordon Lightfoot, "The Wreck of the Edmund Fitzgerald"; Procol Harum, "Salty Dog"; Creedence Clearwater Revival, "Proud Mary"; the Doors, "The Crystal Ship"; CSNY, "Wooden Ships"; Nick Cave and the Bad Seeds, "The Ship Song"; Fiona Apple, "O' Sailor."*

In the late 20th century, air travel took over as a means of crossing vast distances—but this does not seem to have inspired many songwriters.

» *Joni Mitchell, "This Flight Tonight"; the Byrds, "Eight Miles High"; John Denver, "Leaving on a Jet Plane"; Elton John, "Take Me to the Pilot"; John Sebastian, "Red Eye Express"; Roy Harper, "Twelve Hours of Sunsets"; Nanci Griffith, "Outbound Plane"; Joni Mitchell, "Amelia"; the Rose Garden, "Next Plane to London"; the Motors, "Airport"; Frank Sinatra, "Come Fly with Me"; Red Hot Chilli Peppers, "Aeroplane"; MIA, "Paper Planes"; Foo Fighters, "Learn to Fly."*

Crime and punishment

Popular music has always loved the outsider—perhaps because it is itself an "outsider" from the world of high art. The past 60 years of music are rooted in rock 'n' roll—a teenager's music—and teenagers self-define as outsiders, belonging neither to the adult world nor that of children. So, the criminal as an outsider becomes something of a heroic figure. Guns, murders, love triangles, fires, riots all provide vivid dramatic material for song lyrics. They also provide dramatic images and metaphors for other types of song. Few metaphors are as "arresting" as that of a gun or gangster, as with the Steve Miller Band's metaphorical "Gangster of Love." Homicide and firearms in lyrics mean the drama and tension of life and death situations.

The general rules for committing homicide in a lyric appear to be: first, if your woman is unfaithful shoot first and ask questions later; second, make sure you have someone to tell it to; and three, be close enough to the border to make a getaway to Mexico. If you do get caught, deliver an eve-of-execution confession detailing how much you loved her, or how she done you wrong, or how you just couldn't take it (anymore).

» *The Jimi Hendrix Experience, "Hey Joe"; Queen, "Bohemian Rhapsody"; Dave Dee Dozy Beaky Mick and Tich, "Last Night in Soho"; Tom Jones, "Green Green Grass of Home"; Eric Clapton, "I Shot the Sheriff" (but the defendant pleads not guilty to shooting the deputy); Elvis Costello, "Shot with His Own Gun"; the Boomtown Rats, "I Don't Like Mondays"; Body Count, "Cop Killer"; Ice T, "Six in the Morning"; the Clash, "Guns on the Roof"; Black Rebel Motorcycle Club, "Six Barrel Shot Gun"; ZZ Top, "Six Shooter."*

Grievous bodily harm, rape, and affray are mostly treated from the view of the victim, unless the victim has turned into the representative of a despised social order:

» *The Jam, "Down in the Tube Station at Midnight"; the Prodigy, "Smack My Bitch Up"; Tori Amos, "Me and a Gun"; Nirvana, "Rape Me"; Eurythmics, "Sex Crime 1984"; the Smiths, "I Started Something That I Just Couldn't Finish"; the Clash, "White Riot"; Bobby Fuller Four, "I Fought the Law"; the Rolling Stones, "Street Fighting Man"; Kaiser Chiefs, "I Predict a Riot."*

A small number of lyrics deal with child abuse and bullying. More skill and sensitivity is now required of the lyric writer in handling such topics than was even the case in the last century:

» *Siouxsie and the Banshees, "Candyman"; Suzanne Vega, "Luka"; the Mission, "Amelia"; Pearl Jam, "Jeremy"; the Who, "Fiddle About," "I'm a Boy"; Tasmin Archer, "In Your Care"; Loudon Wainwright III, "Hitting You."*

Arson and explosives in lyrics also mean high drama. Fires often feature in a sociopolitical context of unrest:

» *The Jimi Hendrix Experience, "House Burning Down"; Elton John, "Burn Down the Mission"; the Jam, "Funeral Pyre"; the Prodigy, "Firestarter"; the Ruts, "Babylon Is Burning"; Siouxsie and the Banshees, "Burn the House Down"; Public Enemy, "Burn Hollywood Burn"; Green Day, "Letterbomb"; the Mothers of Invention, "Trouble Every Day (The Watts Riot Song)"; Stiff Little Fingers, "Suspect Device"; Alicia Keys, "Girl on Fire"; Radiohead, "Burn the Witch."*

Robbery and petty damage in lyrics are sometimes connected with teenage frustration and minor brushes with the law:

» *Kate Bush, "There Goes a Tenner"; the Clash, "Bank Robber"; Georgie Fame, "Ballad of Bonnie and Clyde"; the Smiths, "Shoplifters of the World Unite"; the Slits, "Shoplifters"; U2, "I Threw a Brick Through a Window"; Nick Lowe, "I Love the Sound of Breaking Glass"; Arctic Monkeys, "Riot Van."*

Illegal substances feature in lyrics as potent symbols of countercultural values, of living by different rules to the norm. The drugs featured vary from youth cult to youth cult, from one age to another. There are also cautionary songs about the damage caused by drug use:

» *Supergrass, "Caught by the Fuzz"; Thin Lizzy, "Opium Trail"; Eels, "Novacaine for the Soul"; the Beatles, "What's the New, Mary Jane?"; the Velvet Underground, "Heroin"; J. J. Cale, "Cocaine"; Queens of the Stone Age, "Feel Good Hit of the Summer"; the Rolling Stones, "Sister Morphine"; Black Sabbath, "Sweet Leaf"; the Ramones, "Now I Wanna Sniff Some Glue"; Neil Young, "The Needle and the Damage Done"; Grandmaster Flash and Melle Mel, "White Lines (Don't Don't Do It)."*

Courts, judges, and jail are taken as the embodiment of a social order which the rebel may be challenging. Less frequently they are seen as bulwarks against chaos. The jail break-out offers dramatic story-telling possibilities.

» *Shorty Long, "Here Comes the Judge"; 10cc, "Good Morning Judge," "Rubber Bullets"; Travis, "Re-Offender"; Thin Lizzy, "Jailbreak"; Elvis Presley, "Jailhouse Rock"; Sham 69, "Borstal Break-out"; Coolio, "Gangsta's Paradise"; the Offspring, "When You're in Prison"; Blind Lemon Jefferson, "Prison Cell Blues"; Johnny Cash, "25 Minutes to Go"; the Adverts, "Gary Gilmore's Eyes"; Dr. Feelgood, "Riot in Cell Block #9"; Motörhead, "Jailbait"; Atoms for Peace, "Judge, Jury and Executioner."*

Lyrics have also been spun round the related figures of the sheriff, the policeman, and the private detective. The sheriff is often a positive figure, the policeman is usually reviled, and the detective has a seedy glamour.

» *The Clash, "Police and Thieves"; Charley Patton, "High Sheriff Blues"; Cypress Hill, "Looking Through the Eye of a Pig"; Asian Dub Foundation, "Officer XX"; Everything But the Girl, "Good Cop Bad Cop"; the Strokes, "New York City Cops"; Bruce Springsteen, "Highway Patrolman," "American Skin (41 Shots)"; Dire Straits, "Private Investigations"; Elvis Costello, "Watching the Detectives."*

Time past and memory

When it comes to arousing emotions in the listener, there are few more potent words than "yesterday." Memory, reflections on how things used to be, old selves, past lovers—everything to do with time past is a rich subject area for lyrics. Such themes speak of universal concerns with being young, being old, maturing; with looking forward and back. This normal facet of human life is stimulated and exacerbated by the pace of modern life—the way familiar objects, activities, fashions, ways of doing things, the very buildings of our towns and cities, change seemingly before our eyes. The comments under many a YouTube video of a song from the past provide touching and eloquent proof of this.

These emotions are so strong that they can stop people hearing the real intent of a lyric. The Beatles' "In My Life" is often heard simply as a lament for the past, when actually the song's emotional calculations come out in favor of the present.

The challenge for a lyric writer in this area is to avoid easy nostalgia (as the joke goes, even nostalgia isn't what it used to be). A more interesting lyric about the past balances its attractions with genuinely good things about today. If you want a bittersweet combination of golden past with happy present, listen to a song like Love Affair's "Bring on Back the Good Times," where past joys thought lost are experienced more sharply as they are recovered in the present.

» *Stevie Wonder, "Yester-me, Yester-you, Yesterday"; the Beatles, "Yesterday"; Gene Pitney, "That Girl Belongs to Yesterday"; the Four Tops, "Yesterday's Dreams"; Simply Red, "Holding Back the Years"; Led Zeppelin, "Ten Years Gone"; Diana Ross, "Remember Me"; Mary Hopkin, "Those Were the Days"; Jethro Tull, "Living in the Past"; Sting, "Fields of Gold"; the Faces, "Love Lived Here"; Dean Martin, "Memories Are Made of This"; Barbara Streisand, "The Way We Were"; the Byrds, "My Back Pages"; Daft Punk, "One More Time."*

Historical dates

You might also consider writing a lyric about a recent historical event. These could form the subject of a song, or provide the backdrop for a personal experience. (There is more about purely historical themes further on.) Here are some titles that relate to a date, place and/or event, imagined or real, in the past 50 years.

» *The Police, "Born in the '50s"; Morrissey, "Munich Air Disaster 1958"; the Gaslight Anthem, "The Sound of '59"; the Four Seasons, "December 1963 (Oh What a Night)"; Family, "Summer '67"; the Stooges, the Vines, "1969"; Bryan Adams, "Summer of '69"; the Stooges, "1970"; the Connells, "'74-'75"; Five Grand Stereo, "1975"; Wayne County and the Backstreet Boys, "Max's Kansas City 1976"; the Clash, "1977"; Smashing Pumpkins, "1979"; Simple Minds, "New Gold Dream (81-82-83-84)"; Van Halen, "1984"; Manic Street Preachers, "1985"; Travis, "Tied to the 90s"; Blur, "1992"; Pulp, "Disco 2000."*

Dated events

Alternatively, focus on a historical event that interests you and is felt to be significant. Again, the challenge is to describe it in a compressed way. In the chorus of such a song state what it is that matters about the event; leave the verses for narrating the story. The bridge can also be used as a place where deductions can be made about the event's significance. A lyric can only be a snapshot of a big event, but snapshots can be memorable. Consider the imaginative power of a song like the Band's "The Night They Drove Ol' Dixie Down."

» *Randy Newman, "Dayton, Ohio 1903," "Louisiana 1927"; Al Stewart, "Somewhere in England, 1915," "Laughing Into 1939"; David Bowie, "1917"; John Cale, "Paris 1919"; the Who, "1921"; Aimee Mann, "Fifty Years After the Fair" (alludes to New York World's Fair of 1939); the Bee Gees, "New York Mining Disaster 1941."*

Childhood, youth, and school

Popular music is associated with youth, so it contains a huge number of songs about being young, growing up, clashing with authority figures, feeling confused, struggling with identity, and negotiating the rites of adolescence. Think of a childhood experience, good or bad, and write about it. How typical do you think it might be of many people's experiences? The innocence of childhood (children's voices on records almost always signify innocence) is itself an important theme:

» *Fiona Apple, "Shameika"; Brian Wilson, "Child Is Father of the Man"; Billy J. Kramer, "Little Children"; Tyrannosaurus Rex, "Child Star"; Page and Plant, "When I Was a Child"; Madonna, "Dear Jessie," "This Used to Be My Playground"; CSNY, "Teach Your Children"; R.E.M., "The Wrong Child"; Neil Young, "I Am a Child"; Siouxsie and the Banshees, "Playground Twist"; Jonas Brothers, "What I Go to School For"; Rumer, "Pizza and Pinball"; Air, "Playground Love."*

Where there are children there must be parents, and such relationships can be written about from both sides:

» *Bruce Springsteen, "Independence Day"; Cat Stevens, "Father and Son"; Queen, "Father to Son"; the Beatles, "She's Leaving Home"; Paul Simon, "Mother and Child Reunion"; Gilbert O'Sullivan, "We Will"; Manfred Mann, "My Name Is Jack"; Tori Amos, "Winter"; Kate Bush, "Mother Stands for Comfort"; David Bowie, "The Bewlay Brothers"; Madonna, "Papa Don't Preach"; John Lennon, "Mother"; My Chemical Romance, "Mama"; the Killers, "Daddy's Eyes."*

Then there is the subject of sexual awakening—sometimes celebrated by those who would like to take advantage of it:

» *The Yardbirds, "Good Morning Little Schoolgirl"; the Knack, "My Sharona"; Neil Sedaka, "Happy Birthday, Sweet Sixteen"; Johnny Burnette, "You're Sixteen"; the Undertones, "Teenage Kicks"; the MC5, "Teenage Lust"; the Ramones, "Teenage Lobotomy"; the Flamin' Groovies, "Teenage Head"; Wheatus, "Teenage Dirtbag"; Tori Amos, "These Precious Things."*

Conflict with parents, authority figures, and alienation from society (or what the adolescent imagines as "society") is often expressed in an anthem for the current teenage generation:

» *The Sweet, "Teenage Rampage"; the Who, "The Kids Are Alright"; "My Generation"; Nirvana, "Smells Like Teen Spirit"; Mott the Hoople, "All the Young*

Dudes"; Alice Cooper, "Generation Landslide"; T.Rex, "Children of the Revolution"; the Lovin' Spoonful, "Younger Generation"; Eddie Cochran, "Summertime Blues"; Richard Hell and the Voidoids, "Blank Generation"; Bob Dylan, "The Times They Are A-Changing"; Dion and the Belmonts, "Lonely Teenager"; Frankie Lymon and the Teenagers, "I'm Not a Juvenile Delinquent"; Taylor Swift, "Fifteen."

If you've left school, write a lyric about schooldays. If you're still at school, write about some of your experiences there, good and bad, or what it feels like to be away from school in the holiday, or what it will be like to leave forever. There are songs about school and its timetables and the joy (expressed with joyful recklessness in David Bowie's "Kooks"), of throwing away homework and going out instead. There seem to be fewer songs about college and university.

» Supertramp, "School"; Alice Cooper, "School's Out"; Chuck Berry, "School Day (Ring Ring Goes the Bell!)"; Jerry Lee Lewis, "High School Confidential"; Madness, "Baggy Trousers"; Pink Floyd, "Another Brick in the Wall"; the Darkness, "Friday Night"; Janis Ian, "At Seventeen"; Bruce Springsteen, "Growing Up"; X-Ray Spex, "Germ-Free Adolescents"; the Beach Boys, "Be True to Your School"; the Jam, "When You're Young"; the Boomtown Rats, "Mary of the Fourth Form"; the Adverts, "Bored Teenagers"; Marty Wilde, "Why Must I Be a Teenager in Love?"

Time present

" *He [Berry Gordy, head of Motown] told me to 'never write a song like it's past, always write a song like it's happening right now so people can associate with it.' So when I decided to write 'You've made me so very happy,' I said 'he's making me happy now,' even though I was very sad because I had a bad love affair, a boyfriend that walked out on me. So I said, 'I'm gonna write a song like this is the happiest day of my life.'"*

BRENDA HOLLOWAY TO THE *YTF* NEWSLETTER

Popular music likes to be fashionable and of the moment, so there are plenty of songs with the word "modern" in the title, or that otherwise celebrate the moment:

» The Jam, "This Is the Modern World"; David Bowie, "Modern Love"; Bloc Party, "This Modern Love"; Black Mountain, "Modern Music"; the Strokes, "The Modern

Age"; Sheena Easton "Modern Girl"; Madonna, "Holiday"; Bruce Springsteen, "Better Days"; the Beach Boys, "Here Today"; Smashing Pumpkins, Jefferson Airplane, "Today"; Bryan Adams, "On a Day Like Today"; Aimee Mann, "Today's the Day"; Kate Bush, "Moments of Pleasure"; Roy Harper, "Frozen Moment"; the Lovin' Spoonful, "Daydream"; Fatboy Slim, "Right Here, Right Now"; Miranda Cosgrove, "About You Now."

Time present can also be summed up in expanded form as a lyric about whatever is happening today:

» *The Kinks, "Days"; Lou Reed, "Perfect Day"; Badfinger, "Day After Day"; Haircut 100, "Fantastic Day"; Bill Withers, "Lovely Day"; Talking Heads, "Happy Day"; the Cure, "In Between Days"; Mariah Carey, "One Sweet Day"; U2, "Beautiful Day"; Altered Images, "Happy Birthday"; the Beatles, "Birthday"; "Stevie Wonder, "Happy Birthday"; Nick Cave and the Bad Seeds, "Today's Lesson"; the National, "About Today."*

Divisions of the day

Many lyrics describe something happening at a particular time of day, or what that time of day suggests by way of a mood. Each portion of the day is associated in song lyrics with a variety of activities. The Moody Blues' concept album *Days of Future Passed* went all the way through a single day in songs, recited poetry, and instrumental passages. Kate Bush's *Aerial* has a nine-song suite that extends over a day. Roger Waters's *The Pros and Cons of Hitch-Hiking* has a number of parts, each of which are titled a couple of minutes apart between four and five in the morning. Chuck Berry's "Reelin' and Rockin'" relates events as the hours go by, and Bill Haley used the clock as a structuring device in "Rock Around the Clock."

Dawn and early morning

» *Cream, "Sunshine of Your Love"; Eagles, "Tequila Sunrise"; the Supremes, "Here Comes the Sunrise"; Bette Midler, "Delta Dawn"; the Boo Radleys, "Wake Up Boo"; Wham!, "Wake Me Up Before You Go Go"; the Blue Nile, "7am"; Peter Paul and Mary, "Early in the Morning," "Early Morning Rain"; the Four Seasons, "Early in the Morning," Rolf Harris, "Sun Arise"; Radiohead, "Morning Mr. Magpie."*

Morning

» *The Rascals, "Beautiful Morning"; Joni Mitchell, "Chelsea Morning"; the Beatles, "Good Day Sunshine"; Nick Drake, "From the Morning"; the Monkees, "Sometime in the Morning"; the Verve, "Velvet Morning"; Free, "Come Together in the Morning"; Bob Dylan, "Meet Me in the Morning"; Diana Ross, "Touch Me in the Morning"; Dusty Springfield, "Breakfast in Bed"; the Lumineers, "Morning Song"; Beck, "Morning."*

Afternoon

» *The Kinks, "Sunny Afternoon"; the Starland Vocal Band, "Afternoon Delight"; the Small Faces, "Lazy Sunday Afternoon"; Supergrass, "Late in the Day."*

Twilight and sunset

» *Roy Harper, "Twelve Hours of Sunsets"; Elton John, "Don't Let the Sun Go Down on Me"; the Kinks, "Waterloo Sunset"; Sting, "Lithium Sunset"; Nick Drake, "Day Is Done"; Thin Lizzy, "The Sun Goes Down"; Fleetwood Mac, "When the Sun Goes Down"; the Chemical Brothers, "Setting Sun"; Gordon Lightfoot, "Sundown"; MGMT, "In the Afternoon"; Iron and Wine, "Passing Afternoon."*

Nighttime is the most frequently cited time because of its associations with adventure, going out, mystery, excitement, socializing, dancing, seducing, and making love.

Evening and darkness

» *Patti Smith, "Because the Night"; Bruce Springsteen, "Spirit in the Night"; the Moody Blues, "Nights in White Satin"; Lionel Ritchie, "All Night Long"; the Police, "Bring on the Night"; Paul Simon, "Late in the Evening"; Them, "Here Comes the Night"; the Doors, "End of the Night"; R.E.M., "Nightswimming"; Phil Collins, "In the Air Tonight"; Bobby Vee, "The Night Has a Thousand Eyes"; Frank Sinatra, "Strangers in the Night"; the Strokes, "Evening Sun."*

Midnight

» *The Rolling Stones, "Moonlight Mile"; Wilson Pickett, "In the Midnight Hour"; Eric Clapton, "After Midnight"; the Stargazers, "I See the Moon"; the Jimi Hendrix Experience, "Burning of the Midnight Lamp"; the Monkees, "Midnight Train";*

Ocean Colour Scene, "40 Past Midnight"; Blondie, "11:59"; David Gray, "A New Day at Midnight"; Howlin' Wolf, "Moanin' at Midnight"; Coldplay, "Midnight."

Early hours
» *Busted, "3am"; Gene, "Sleep Well Tonight"; My Bloody Valentine, "When You Sleep"; the Pretenders, "I Go to Sleep"; KLF, "3 am Eternal"; Frank Sinatra, "In the Wee Small Hours of the Morning"; the Boo Radleys, "4am Conversation"; the Strokes, "12:51"; Gary US Bonds, "Quarter to Three"; Skip James, "4 O'Clock Blues"; Johnny Winter, "Five After Four A.M."; Judy Tzuke, "Stay with Me Till Dawn."*

Days of the week

> *I stopped at a pub just outside Oxford and met the others. It was a Friday evening. I said, 'I've got this idea for a song and you'll laugh but it's the days of the week.' I thought someone must have done this before. That night we recorded it and it was finished. Saturday I got up, listened to it and thought, 'This is excellent.' I wish every song I wrote could be this easy, this dumb. Even the video only took three hours. A joyful experience. Most songs aren't like that."*
> **ROBERT SMITH OF THE CURE TO *MELODY MAKER* ON "FRIDAY I'M IN LOVE"**

> *It leans very heavily on fairy tales, especially the macabre ones that seem very innocent when you're little, but as you get older, the real meanings come out. It's got the Red Riding Hood figure in there, and these three characters that are basically part of the same person—the Monday, the Tuesday and the Sunday person. And they go through a bit of a mess in the song . . . they can only really function when they're all part of the same thing and, at the end of the song, they all come together. When they're not in sync, the person isn't functioning or happening at all."*
> **JULIANNE REGAN OF ALL ABOUT EVE ON "TUESDAY'S CHILD"**

Choose a day of the week. What associations does it have for you? Are these based on something that happened to you on that day? Do you associate a certain day with a memory, a happy or sad occasion, a mood, an activity? Develop a lyric from this idea.

In most lyrics, the days around the weekend have strong associations relating to work, leisure time, and socializing. Some writers have drawn on the proverb about children born on the various days of the week:

Monday's child is fair of face
Tuesday's child is full of grace
Wednesday's child is full of woe
Thursday's child has far to go
Friday's child is loving and giving
Saturday's child works hard for its living
And the child that's born on the Sabbath day
Is fair and wise and good and gay

There is a less well-known rhyme about which day of the week to hold a wedding:

Monday for wealth, Tuesday for health,
Wednesday the best day of all;
Thursday for crosses, Friday for losses
Saturday no luck at all.

A lyric can be structured around the seven days, as in the Cure's "Friday I'm in Love," U2's "Some Days Are Better Than Others," Sting's "Seven Days," Craig David's "7 Days," and Etta James's "Seven Day Fool."

Monday is often dreary and no fun because it's the "return to work" day. The idea of a "blue Monday" is something of a cliché.

» *The Bangles, "Manic Monday"; the Mamas and the Papas, "Monday Monday"; the Boomtown Rats, "I Don't Like Mondays"; the Carpenters, "Rainy Days and Mondays"; Fleetwood Mac, Pulp, "Monday Morning"; T-Bone Walker, "Stormy Monday"; Bobby Bland, "Stormy Monday Blues"; Fats Domino, "Blue Monday"; Nick Heyward, "Atlantic Monday"; Marillion, "Chelsea Monday"; Janis Ian, "Might as Well Be Monday."*

Tuesday has moderate appeal as the day after Monday if there has been an adjustment back into the working week.

» *All About Eve, "Tuesday's Child"; Moody Blues, "Tuesday Afternoon"; the Chairmen of the Board, "Everything's Tuesday"; Melanie, "Ruby Tuesday"; David Bowie, "Love*

You Till Tuesday"; Kristin Hersh, "Tuesday Night"; Stone Temple Pilots, "Church of Tuesday"; Cat Stevens, "Tuesday's Dead"; Eliza Carthy, "Tuesday Morning"; Cowboy Junkies, "Sun Comes Up; It's Tuesday Morning."

Wednesday and **Thursday** have registered less often in lyrics.

» *Simon and Garfunkel, "Wednesday Morning 3 a.m."; Tori Amos, "Wednesday"; the Undertones, "Wednesday Week"; Lisa Loeb and Nine Stories, "Waiting for Wednesday"; John Lee Hooker, "Wednesday Evening"; Hey Mercedes, "Our Weekend Starts on Wednesday." David Bowie, "Thursday's Child"; Cat Stevens, "Sweet Thursday"; Jim Croce, "Thursday"; Townes Van Zandt, "Like a Summer Thursday"; the Hollies, "10:15 Thursday Morning"; Morphine, "Thursday"; the Millennium, "To Claudia on Thursday."*

Friday is happy because it's the end of the week—it's a going-out night, and (if you're at school) there's probably no homework to do.

» *The Cure, "Friday I'm in Love"; the Darkness, "Friday Night"; the Easybeats, "Friday on My Mind"; the Specials, "Friday Night Saturday Morning"; Will Young, "Friday's Child"; Love and Kisses, "Thank God It's Friday"; Paul Weller, "Friday Street"; David Ackles, "Another Friday Night"; Van Morrison, "Friday's Child"; Steely Dan, "Black Friday"; Joe Jackson, "Friday"; Sam Fender, "Friday Fighting."*

Saturday is for shopping and socializing, and Saturday night can mean a raucous party, a dancing late-nighter, or a punch-up.

» *Elton John, "Saturday Night's Alright (for Fighting)"; the Drifters, "Saturday Night at the Movies"; David Bowie, "Drive-in Saturday"; Nick Drake, "Saturday Sun"; the Monkees, "Saturday's Child"; Graham Parker, "Saturday Nite Is Dead"; Chicago, "Saturday in the Park"; Sam Cooke, "Another Saturday Night"; Nils Lofgren, "One More Saturday Night"; Suede, "Saturday Night"; Eels, "Saturday Morning"; Eddie Cochran, "Weekend"; Coldplay, "Hymn for the Weekend"; Massive Attack, "Saturday Come Slow."*

Sunday morning is lying in, possibly church-going (though not often in popular lyrics); Sunday evening is calm and reflective.

» *The Small Faces, "Lazy Sunday"; Monkees, "Pleasant Valley Sunday"; Morrissey, "Every Day Is Like Sunday"; the Velvet Underground, "Sunday Morning"; Lionel Ritchie, "Easy Like Sunday Morning"; Elvis Costello, "Sunday's Best"; Blondie, "Sunday Girl"; the Shirelles, "I Met Him on a Sunday"; the Doobie Brothers, "Another Park, Another Sunday"; the Harptones, "A Sunday Kind of Love"; Rain Tree Crow, "A Reassuringly Dull Sunday"; Dillinger Escape Plan, "Sick on Sunday"; Courtney Barnett, "Sunday Roast."*

Seasons and months

The months of the year encompass the seasons with their rich symbolic overtones of birth, growth, maturity, decay and death. Traditionally, in the northern hemisphere, spring is March–May, summer is June–August, fall or is September–November, and winter is December–February (allowing for where you live, and the impact of global warming). Examples would include Future Islands' "Seasons (Waiting on You)" and Crowded House, who offered the metaphor of "Four Seasons in One Day." Needless to say, the most popular season for lyrics is summer, because, as the Beach Boys put it, "Summer Means New Love." Here are some seasonal songs:

Spring

» *Pentangle, "Springtime Promises"; Mel Brooks, "Springtime for Hitler"; Black Crowes, "The Colour of Spring"; Judy Collins, "So Early, Early in the Spring"; the Go-Betweens, "Spring Rain"; Vampire Weekend, "Spring Snow"; Mitski, "First Love / Late Spring."*

Summer

» *Mungo Jerry, "In the Summertime"; Incubus, "Into the Summer"; the Temptations, "It's Summer"; the Style Council, "Long Hot Summer"; the Lovin' Spoonful, "Summer in the City"; All About Eve, "Our Summer"; the Jimi Hendrix Experience, "Long Hot Summer Night"; Eddie Cochran, "Summertime Blues"; Cliff Richard, "Summer Holiday"; Marshall Crenshaw, "Starless Summer Sky"; the Beach Boys, "All Summer Long"; Don Henley, "The Boys of Summer"; Taylor Swift, "Cruel Summer"; Lana Del Rey, "Summertime Sadness."*

Autumn

» *Siouxsie and the Banshees, "Halloween"; Justin Hayward, "Forever Autumn"; Roger Williams, "Autumn Leaves"; the Vines, "Autumn Shade"; Peter Paul and Mary, "Autumn to May"; Procol Harum, "In the Autumn of My Madness"; Francoise Hardy, "Autumn Rendez-vous"; Yo La Tengo, "Autumn Sweater."*

Winter

» *Simon and Garfunkel, "Hazy Shade of Winter"; Tori Amos, "Winter"; Tyrannosaurus Rex, "The Throat of Winter"; the Doors, "Winter Love"; Darlene Love, "Winter Wonderland"; Leonard Cohen, "Winter Lady"; Aztec Camera, "Walk Out to Winter"; Queen, "A Winter's Tale"; Fleet Foxes, "White Winter Hymnal"; the Walkmen, "While I Shovel the Snow."*

Some of the characteristics attributed to seasons can be also associated with the appropriate months. For ideas, think also of special days that fall in certain months—Valentine's Day (February), April Fool's Day, Easter (April), Independence Day (July), Halloween (October), Guy Fawkes Night and Thanksgiving (November), Christmas (December), all of which could figure in a lyric. I have deliberately excluded Christmas songs (there are too many), but if you want to investigate them, start with the Phil Spector–produced album *A Christmas Gift to You*.

Here are songs using a month in the title—with the exception of March as no-one seems to set lyrics in March.

January and February

» *Michelle Lews, "January's Child"; Pilot, "January"; U2, "New Year's Day"; Lindisfarne, "January Song"; Abba, "Happy New Year"; Tori Amos, "Black Dove (January)"; David Gray, "January Rain"; Jeff Buckley, "New Year's Prayer"; the Breeders, "New Year"; Frank Sinatra, "June in January"; Cole Porter, "My Lovely Valentine"; ABC, "Valentine's Day"; Paul McCartney, "Valentine Day"; Lou Reed, "Christmas in February"; Foo Fighters, "February Stars"; Billy Bragg, "Valentine's Day Is Over," "The Fourteenth of February"; Oleander, "February Son."*

March

» *Julie London, "Melancholy March"; Silverstein, "The Ides of March"; Susannah McCorkle, "The Waters of March"; Journey, "Winds of March."*

April

» Simon and Garfunkel, "April Come She Will"; Pat Boone, "April Love"; Oysterband, "20th of April"; a-ha, "Soft Rains of April"; the Jesus and Mary Chain, "April Skies"; Al Jolson, "April Showers"; Prince, "Sometimes It Snows in April"; the Associates, "Tell Me Easter's on Friday"; the Black Crowes, "Good Friday"; Ron Sexsmith, "April After All"; Loudon Wainwright III, "Fool's Day Morn."

May and June

» The Bee Gees, "First of May"; Blue Öyster Cult, "Then Came the Last Days of May"; the Tremoloes, "May Morning"; the B52's, "June Bug"; the Kinks, "Rainy Day in June"; Jamiroquai, "Seven Days in Sunny June"; Heather Nova, "One Day in June"; the Wannadies, "Love in June"; the Minutemen, "June 16th"; the Decemberists, "June Hymn."

July and August

» Bruce Springsteen, "4th of July Asbury Park"; Stevie Wonder, "Hotter Than July"; Aimee Mann, "4th of July"; Fall Out Boy, "Fourth of July"; Ocean Colour Scene, "July"; Uriah Heep, "July Morning"; Neil Diamond, "Hot August Night"; Eric Clapton, "August"; Love, "August"; Funkadelic, "Friday Night, August 14th"; Counting Crows, "August and Everything After"; Taylor Swift, "August"; Florence and the Machine, "Dog Days Are Over."

September and October

» Carole King, "It Might as Well Rain Until September"; James Taylor, "September Grass"; Earth, Wind, and Fire, "September"; Big Star, "September Gurls"; Green Day, "Wake Me Up When September Ends"; Neil Diamond, "September Morn"; Kurt Weill and Maxwell Anderson, "September Song"; Fiona Apple, "Pale September"; XTC, "Harvest Festival"; the Incredible String Band, "October Song"; Amy Winehouse, "October Song"; U2, "October"; the Pet Shop Boys, "My October Symphony."

November and December

» Guns N' Roses, "November Rain"; Sandy Denny, "Late November"; Gorillaz, "November Has Come"; the National, "Mr. November"; Morrissey, "November Spawned a Monster"; the Waterboys, "November Song"; All About Eve, "December";

Taylor Swift, "Back to December"; David Gray, "December"; Wendy and Lisa, "I Think It Was December"; Edie Brickell, "Air of December"; Counting Crows, "A Long December"; Everything But the Girl, "25th December"; Roberta Flack, "The 25th of Last December"; the Who, "Christmas"; John Lennon, "Happy Xmas (War Is Over)."

Time future: dystopias, space, aliens

" *Dreams are all the promises of the future that never seem to get here."*

JIM WHITE TO *MOJO*

Another potentially interesting subject area is the future. This extends from the short term to the long term, and from the personal to the collective. Future songs at their simplest mean the lyric idea "*I'm so looking forward to seeing Marsha (or Bill) on Friday night*" (which happens to be tomorrow), or a sense of romantic foreboding, as in Marvin Gaye's "I Heard It Through the Grapevine."

People in love songs swear to love each other until mountains crumble into the sea (see Ben E. King); rivers dry up and stars fall out of the sky. The end of the world thus becomes an image for romantic loss. This long vision leads to titles like "Forever and a Day" and paradoxes like the Moody Blues' *Days of Future Passed.*

Tomorrow titles

» *The Monkees, "Look Out Here Comes Tomorrow"; the Beatles, "Tomorrow Never Knows"; Sheryl Crow, "Tomorrow Never Dies"; Badfinger, "Maybe Tomorrow"; the Shirelles, "Will You Still Love Me Tomorrow"; the Carpenters, "Our Day Will Come"; the Chiffons, "One Fine Day"; Aqualung, "Good Times Gonna Come"; Gorillaz, "Tomorrow Comes Today."*

At the furthest reach, there are lyrics about humanity and life in the distant future, including King Crimson's "21st Century Schizoid Man," Zager and Evans's "In the Year 2525," Barry MacGuire's "Eve of Destruction" and the Fifth Dimension's "Aquarius." Future lyrics can be personal—projecting an optimistic vision for lovers into the immediate future—or about society—a utopia. If the vision is of a world gone wrong, the lyric is a dystopia usually by default a protest song. David Bowie wrote more visions of the future than most, including "The Man Who Sold the World," "Five Years," "Drive-in Saturday," "Diamond Dogs," "Aladdin Sane," and others. The notorious year 1984 didn't turn out quite so bad after all. Other futuristic songs now overtaken by time include the Jimi Hendrix Experience's "1983," David Bowie's "1984," Wings' "Nineteen Hundred and Eighty-Five," Jamiroquai's "Revolution 1993," and Prince's "1999."

Space and aliens

The development of rockets and space exploration in the 1950s and 1960s, coupled with the popularity of outer-space science-fiction books, TV series, and cinema films, and the phenomenon of UFO sightings, resulted in a number of songs about aliens and spaceships.

» *David Bowie, "Space Oddity," "Life on Mars"; T.Rex, "The Visit," "Planet Queen"; Graham Parker and the Rumour, "Waiting for the UFOs"; Ash, "Girl from Mars"; Neil Young, "After the Goldrush"; Blue Öyster Cult, "E.T.I. (Extra Terrestrial Intelligence)"; Stackridge, "Purple Spaceships Over Yatton"; the Jimi Hendrix Experience, "House Burning Down," "Third Stone from the Sun"; the Byrds, "Mr Spaceman"; Peter and Gordon, "Everyone's Gone to the Moon," Elton John, "Rocket Man"; Queen, "39"; Kesha, "Spaceship."*

Smart answers: parody, response

I was criticized terribly for writing novelty songs; people were very snobbish. Although there was a tradition of humor in folk, it was exorcised in the '60s. 'Ugh, go away funny man,' they said."

LOUDON WAINWRIGHT III TO *MOJO*, DECEMBER 1993

For me, one of the greatest lyricists of all time is George Formby. His more obscure songs are so hilarious, the language was so flat and Lancastrian and always focused on domestic things. Not academically funny, not witty, just morosely humorous, and that really appealed to me."

MORRISSEY TO *NME*, 1984

I get fed up with the indie world . . . they're so somber. They have no time for humor. They can't get above themselves—they're so clearly trapped in themselves that nothing is funny. They're in pain, and that's their universe, and that's what they want the world to pay for."

LIZ PHAIR TO *GUITAR WORLD*, DECEMBER 2005

> *I don't really like a lot of bands who write lyrics about themselves all the time, wallowing in self-pity. You've gotta laugh at yourself as well. If you don't do it all comes across too melodramatic and over the top. People don't believe it."*
>
> **KELLY JONES OF STEREOPHONICS TO *MELODY MAKER***

One way to start a lyric is to write a "smart answer" to another. Shaping a response to the original gets you going on one of your own. The response can take various forms—a witty adjustment to a title, or an extended engagement with the source material. The former might not carry through into the song's meaning and theme; it could just be an eye-catching title.

If I write a song called "I Want to Hold Your Head," people will relate it to the Beatles' "I Want to Hold Your Hand," but the lyric might not take the allusion any further. What you need is an eye for a pun or a similarity of wording, for how a word changes if one letter is altered, or if a phrase is inverted, as with Joni Mitchell's "The Pirate of Penance" (*The Pirates of Penzance*) or Public Enemy's "Rebel Without a Pause" (*Rebel Without a Cause*). Sufjan Stevens's album title *(Come On Feel the) Illinoise* is a play on Slade's "Cum On Feel the Noize."

» *Freak Power, "Turn On, Tune In, Cop Out" (based on the 1960s slogan "turn on, tune in, drop out"); Carter the Unstoppable Sex Machine, "101 Damnations" (101 Dalmatians); the Hives, "Abra Cadaver" (abracadabra); Badly Drawn Boy, "Everybody's Stalking" ("Everybody's Talking"); Soul Asylum, "Somebody to Shove" ("Somebody to Love"); Dustball, "Send in the Clones" ("Send in the Clowns"); the Beautiful South, "Old Red Eyes Is Back" (a reference to Frank Sinatra, whose nickname was "Ol' blue eyes"); Al Stewart, "League of Notions" (League of Nations); XTC, "Knights in Shining Karma" (instead of "armor").*

A clever way of generating such titles is to find a well-known phrase and transpose initial letters of key words, or move words around from something familiar:

» *Kula Shaker, "Grateful When You're Dead" (referring to the band); Kirsty MacColl, "Electric Landlady" (playing on Electric Ladyland); Butthole Surfers, "Hairway to Steven" ("Stairway to Heaven"); Half Man Half Biscuit, "Trouble Over Bridgewater" ("Bridge Over Troubled Water"); the Tremeloes, "Breakheart Motel" ("Heartbreak Hotel").*

Here are some other titles that involve an element of wordplay, but done with more than just the change of a letter or two:

» *Squeeze, "Stranger Than the Stranger on the Shore" ("Stranger on the Shore"); Ryan Adams, "English Girls Approximately" (Dylan-esque); Radiohead, "Subterranean Homesick Alien" ("Subterranean Homesick Blues"); Teenage Fanclub, "Neil Jung" (Carl Jung meets Neil Young); X, "Your Phone's Off the Hook but You're Not."*

At a deeper level, choose a famous song and write a lyric taking the opposite view of the theme and/or the imagery. This need not be a parody or comic—though such an approach is a good method for generating a funny song. The Arrows' "I Love Rock 'n' Roll" (later a hit for Joan Jett) was written as an answer to the Stones' "It's Only Rock 'n' Roll (but I Like It)" because the writers took exception to the implication of the word "only." On the larger scale, this could create something like Liz Phair's *Exile in Guyville* album, a response to the Stones' *Exile on Main Street*.

Answering back

The "straight" (non-parody) approach is to choose a famous song you like and write a lyric on a similar theme. How would you translate its world into a lyric you would feel comfortable singing? What are the nearest equivalent perceptions and experiences in your own daily life? Or take a famous song and write a continuation to the situation or emotion that it represents. If the original song was about two people dreaming of escaping to another place and building a better life, your lyric could describe what happened to them when they did it.

Consider a title like the Supremes' "Love Is Here (and Now You're Gone)." Imagine the fun to be had with people's expectations if you write a love song called "Love Is Here (and Now I'm Gone)." The Jam memorably turned Nevil Shute's novel *A Town Called Alice* into "A Town Called Malice." From this we could derive a song called "Malice in Wonderland," or Smokie's pop "Living Next Door to Alice" could be wittily grunged into "Living Next Door to Malice."

Having written "Peggy Sue," Buddy Holly wrote "Peggy Sue Got Married" to continue the story. The Miracles' "Got a Job" answered the Silhouettes' "Get a

Job." Many songwriters have echoed Chuck Berry's "Johnny B. Goode," including T.Rex with "Jason B. Sad" and Mungo Jerry with "Johnny B. Badde."

» *Kaiser Chiefs, "Caroline, Yes" ("Caroline, No"); David Ackles, "Surf's Down" ("Surf's Up"); Starsailor, "Silence Is Easy" (the proverb "silence is golden"); Tears for Fears, "Brian Wilson Said" ("Jackie Wilson Said"); Billy Bragg, "I Dreamed I Saw Phil Ochs Last Night" (Bob Dylan's "I Dreamt I Saw St. Augustine"); the Detergents, "Leader of the Laundromat" (parody of "Leader of the Pack").*

Comedy songs

Writing comedy songs is an art in itself. Some comedians made a name singing comedy songs not necessarily written by them; George Formby, Flanders and Swann, Tom Lehrer, and Randy Newman are well-known for comic songs. Eric Idle and Neil Innes extended their spoof on the Beatles, *The Rutles*, across a double album, and Spinal Tap's parody of heavy rock is the most famous film to satirize rock. There were also groups like Half Man Half Biscuit and the Bonzo Dog Doo-Dah Band. The Monty Python team wrote comic songs, including a Eurovision send-up and the notorious "Always Look on the Bright Side of Life" from *Life of Brian*.

The type of comedy song where a new lyric is added to an original's music requires copyright clearance and permission; it also means you only get royalties for the words. For example, Billy Connolly parodied Tammy Wynette's "D.I.V.O.R.C.E" by rewriting the lyric but retaining the music.

» *Ray Stevens, "Bridget the Midget"; Bernard Cribbins, "Right Said Fred," "Digging a Hole," "My Brother"; Charlie Drake, "Please Mr. Custer"; the Wurzels, "Combine Harvester" (a rewrite of Melanie's "Brand New Key"); the Goons, "The Ying Tong Song"; the Bonzo Dog Doo Dah Band, "I'm the Urban Spaceman"; Tom Lehrer, "Poisoning Pigeons in the Park"; the Firm, "Star Trekkin'"; Allan Sherman, "Hello Mudduh, Hello Fadduh"; LadBaby, "I Love Sausage Rolls."*

Songs inspired by the arts

" *Read a book—any book—but to make it interesting, begin to read one that you've not read before. With a pencil underline every situation or statement in the first chapter that suggests a song idea, entering them all in your notebook."*

JIMMY WEBB

" *I had a rhythm idea with a synth line I took home to work on one night. While I was playing it this repeated 'yes' came to me and made me think of Molly Bloom's speech right at the end of Ulysses . . . I went downstairs and read it again, this unending sentence punctuated with 'yeses,' fantastic stuff, and it was uncanny, it fitted the rhythm of my song . . . [the James Joyce estate refused her permission to use the actual text] I tried to write it like Joyce. The rhythm at least I wanted to keep. Obviously I couldn't do his style. It became a song about Molly Bloom, the character, stepping out of the page."*

KATE BUSH TO Q ON "THE SENSUAL WORLD," DECEMBER 1993

One way to avoid writer's block is to draw ideas for lyrics from the arts. This means not only singers and musicians of earlier periods, but literature, painting, sculpture, theatre and films. Such inspiration could come simply as a title or a one-line allusion; it could be a character or a concept or a feeling. At its most ambitious, such a song might try to approximate the overall experience of the source work.

Painters and paintings

Paintings lend themselves well to treatment in a lyric because they are a single image. They can be taken in much faster than a novel, for example (at least on a superficial level); and, if they have any narrative element, it may be implied rather than developed, which gives the songwriter an opportunity to tell that story in a lyric (or make one up that fits the picture). The lives of artists have also formed song subjects.

» *David Bowie, "Andy Warhol"; Paul Simon, "Rene and Georgette Magritte with Their Dog After the War"; Don McLean, "Vincent" (Van Gogh); Brian and Michael, "Matchstick Men and Matchstick Cats and Dogs" (L. S. Lowry); Queen, "The Fairy Feller's Master-Stroke" (Richard Dadd); Wings, "Picasso's Last Words";*

Ocean Colour Scene, "Mona Lisa Eyes"; Marianne Faithful, "Witches Song" (inspired by Goya's drawings); Peter, Bjorn and John, "Blue Period Picasso"; Manic Street Preachers, "Interiors (Song for Willem de Kooning)."

Plays and poetry

Poetry is an artform with a complex relationship to songs, since it is the artform closest to the song lyric—so much so that the two forms are often confused. Some songs have been inspired by poems, and of course there is always the option of setting a poem to music, although you may need copyright clearance to do this in public.

» *Billy Bragg, "Walt Whitman's Niece"; Clifford T. Ward, "Not Waving—Drowning" (named after a Stevie Smith poem); the Jam, "Tonight at Noon" (named after a poem by Liverpool poet Roger McGough); Oasis, "Don't Look Back in Anger" (the play Look Back in Anger by John Osborne); Iron Maiden, "Rime of the Ancient Mariner" (Coleridge); Rush, "Xanadu" (the poem "Kubla Khan" by Coleridge); Joni Mitchell, "Slouching Towards Bethlehem" (W. B. Yeats's "The Second Coming"); the Waterboys, "The Stolen Child" (W. B. Yeats); Dire Straits, "Romeo and Juliet"; Lou Reed, "Romeo Had Juliette"; Adam Cohen, "Cry Ophelia."*

Writers and fiction

Many songwriters find prose fiction stimulates ideas for songs. Traveling musicians have plenty of time to read when they are on the road. Sometimes they don't even need to read the whole work. Matt Berninger of the National confessed to *Pitchfork*, "Most of the time, I'm quoting back covers and bookshelves, not necessarily books."

Kate Bush's hit "Wuthering Heights" evokes the romantic intensity of Emily Bronte's novel, but, as she admitted, "It was a real challenge to *précis* the whole mood of a book into such a short piece of prose." Without being specific to one book, Elvis Costello's "Watching the Detectives" conjures up the *milieu* of pulp fiction and film noir.

In 1987, in connection with his album *Nebraska*, Bruce Springsteen revealed that he had been reading William Price Fox, author of the novel *Dixiana Moon* and numerous short stories. The song "Open All Night" was inspired by Fox's writing. Springsteen revealed in 1996 that he got into short story writers like

James M. Cain, Jim Thompson, and Flannery O'Connor; his album *The Ghost of Tom Joad* draws on John Steinbeck's classic novel, *The Grapes of Wrath* (1939). In 1986, Morrissey told the *NME*, "I've never made any secret of the fact that at least 50 per cent of my writing can be blamed on Shelagh Delaney, who wrote *A Taste of Honey*."

Skills you might pick up from a creative writing course are certainly transferable to song lyrics. As Sufjan Stevens explained to the *Creative Independent* in 2017, "I developed my songwriting voice in the tradition of fiction writing, using techniques that I learned in writing workshops. I'd just apply all of those techniques to songwriting. I conditioned myself to really "show, don't tell" and to use active verbs and dynamic nouns and be as specific as possible."

» *10,000 Maniacs, "Hey Jack Kerouac"; Metallica, "For Whom the Bell Tolls" (story by Ernest Hemingway); America, "Watership Down" (novel by Richard Adams); Ash, "Day of the Triffids" (novel by John Wyndham); Graham Parker, "Just Like Herman Hesse"; Genesis, "Unquiet Slumbers for the Sleepers," ". . . In That Quiet Earth" (Emily Bronte); Billy Bragg, "The Man in the Iron Mask" (Alexandre Dumas); Belle and Sebastian, "The Loneliness of the Middle Distance Runner" (alludes to Alan Sillitoe's novel The Loneliness of the Long Distance Runner); John Cale, "Paris 1919" (alludes to A Child's Christmas in Wales by Dylan Thomas); Prince, "The Ballad of Dorothy Parker"; Modest Mouse, "Bukowski."*

Famous people and historical events

Many songwriters have periods where they either don't want to write about themselves or are bored with doing so. One way out of this is to write about famous and infamous characters from history, and historical events. Here's how to approach it:

- Choose a character who made an impression on the world who interests you. Be sufficiently open-minded and curious about the world and one will find you.
- Get to the root of why they interest you. That will be the personal core of the song which takes it beyond a mere exercise.
- Research this person. Read about them, watch a film about them. Biographical entries in any good encyclopedia make a useful starting point.

- Don't overdo the note-taking—you're gathering material for a lyric, not a novel.
- List short phrases that encapsulate the person and their life, what they did, how others saw them. Out of these phrases may become the title and the beginning of a lyric.
- Can you distil the essence of this person's life in an image or a phrase? This could be the chorus or refrain.
- Is there a sequence of events which typify this character? You can't tell the whole story in detail of a person's life in a song lyric. But a narrative element will give the lyric drama.

One such historical figure might be the escapologist Harry Houdini (1874–1926), the subject of Kate Bush's song "Houdini," not only because of his escape stunts but because his life touched on the question of life after death, as Bush explained to the *KBC* newsletter: "He and his wife made a decision that if one of them should die and try to make contact, that the other would know it was truly them through a code that only the two of them knew. . . . It is such a beautiful and strange story that I thought I had very little to do, other than to tell it like it was. But in fact it proved to be the most difficult lyric of all the songs [on her album *The Dreaming*] and the most demanding." This lyric also suggested the photography for the album sleeve on which it was released.

If a person or event is really well-known, their name only has to appear in the title or hook for the meaning to be clear, as is the case with Elvis Costello's "Two Little Hitlers" and Abba's "Waterloo." You may need to consider whether listeners in different parts of the world will understand the historical references. Elvis Costello knew an American audience wouldn't grasp a reference to 1930s British fascist Oswald Mosley in "Less Than Zero." He rewrote a verse so that Oswald became Lee Harvey Oswald, alleged assassin of JFK.

» *The Smiths, "Some Girls Are Bigger Than Others" (Antony and Cleopatra); Supergrass, "Richard III"; Orchestral Manoeuvres in the Dark, "Joan of Arc," "Enola Gay"; Nico, "Genghis Khan"; Boney M, "Rasputin"; Joni Mitchell, "Amelia" (pilot Amelia Earhart); Simon and Garfunkel, "So Long Frank Lloyd Wright"; the Magnetic Fields, "Death of Ferdinand De Saussure"; Morrissey, "Jack the Ripper"; Belle and Sebastian, "Marx and Engels"; Neil Young, "Cortez the Killer"; Bill*

Hayes, "The Ballad of Davy Crockett"; Beastie Boys, "Paul Revere"; Five Grand Stereo, "David Bowie"; Weezer, "The British Are Coming."

Writers sometimes use a famous person simply as a colorful comparison. Ben Folds Five released a song called "Julianne" in which the first line compares a girl to Axl Rose. Bananarama's "Robert De Niro" is another example. A famous person as an image carries a certain ambience. When sketching a lyric this ambience can act as a magnetic field, attracting other ideas into the imagined space, and stepping over any initial feeling you may have of not knowing precisely what you want to say. Film stars and recent politicians often serve this purpose well.

Film stars
» *Sheryl Crow, "Steve McQueen"; Elton John, "Candle in the Wind" (Marilyn Monroe); Madonna, "Vogue"; Kim Carnes, "Bette Davis Eyes"; Blue Öyster Cult, "Joan Crawford"; Underworld, "Bruce Lee"; Bauhaus, "Bela Lugosi's Dead"; Madness, "Michael Caine"; Carly Simon, "You're So Vain" (reportedly about Warren Beatty); Billy Bragg, "Ingrid Bergman"; Fall Out Boy, "Uma Therman"; Gorillaz, "Clint Eastwood."*

Politics and politicians
» *R.E.M., "Exhuming McCarthy"; Manic Street Preachers, "The Love of Richard Nixon"; U2, "MLK," "Pride (in the Name of Love)"; Chicago, "Harry Truman"; Mercury Rev, "Lincoln's Eyes." John F. Kennedy's assassination influenced the Byrds, "He Was a Friend of Mine"; Phil Ochs, "The Crucifixion"; the Beach Boys, "The Warmth of the Sun"; Peter Gabriel, "Family Snapshot"; Marvin Gaye, "Abraham, Martin and John"; Tori Amos, "Jacqueline's Strength."*

Musicians
" *I liked [Buddy] Holly because he spoke to me. He was a symbol of something deeper than the music he made.*
DON MCLEAN, WHO WROTE ABOUT HOLLY'S DEATH IN "AMERICAN PIE," TO *LIFE*

It's hardly surprising that songwriters might want to honor singers, bands, and musicians they admire. On the 2020 Fleet Foxes album *Shore*, the song "Sunblind" alludes to musicians admired by Robin Pecknold, including Bill Withers, John

Prine, Elliott Smith, Judee Sill, Nick Drake, Otis Redding, Jeff Buckley, Curtis Mayfield, and Jimi Hendrix.

Usually, there is a certain length of time before such songs are written, partly to establish that the subject is of an importance to deserve a song, and to wait until they belong to a different generation. Otherwise, there is the risk that the singer or band providing the homage might look as though they were too close to the subject, which would call into question their originality. There is an assumption that to write a song about another musician means you secretly want to be them, even if this isn't the case.

Songs inspired by Elvis Presley

Elvis Presley's status as the "king of rock 'n' roll" and his relatively early death have made him popular as a subject of songs. In many lyrics he symbolizes loneliness in the midst of worldly success, or the cost of fame (see also David Bowie's "Fame").

» *Dire Straits, "Calling Elvis"; Kate Bush, "King of the Mountain"; Gillian Welch, "Elvis Presley Blues"; Thin Lizzy, "The King Is Dead"; Jimmy Webb, "Elvis and Me"; Belle and Sebastian, "A Century of Elvis"; Manic Street Preachers, "Elvis Impersonator: Blackpool Pier"; Kirsty MacColl, "There's a Guy Works Down the Chip Shop Swears He's Elvis"; These New Puritans, "Elvis."*

At the other end of the popularity scale, writing a song about a musician is a means to draw attention to someone whose music has, in your view, been neglected, either because their career went into decline, or (as with many professional songwriters) they were never known to the public in the first place.

Such songs can excite curiosity in a generation too young to have known the music first time round. Don McLean's "American Pie" begins as an account of his sadness at the death of Buddy Holly in February 1959, and then turns into an allegory on the 1960s. There is an increasing frequency of these songs as popular music since the 1950s develops a sense of its history and tradition and the key players in it. This would apply to songs like the Boo Radleys' "Jimmy Webb Is God," Barenaked Ladies' "Brian Wilson," and the Replacements' "Alex Chilton" (of Big Star).

Even if you don't want to create a whole lyric about a musician, they can sometimes make for an effective allusion or detail. T.Rex's "Ballrooms of Mars" namechecks Bob Dylan, John Lennon, and the disc jockey Alan Freed, and the album *The Slider* (1972), to which it belongs, has other songs that mention the filmmaker Pasolini and the New York street musician Moondog.

» *Billy Bragg, "Levi Stubbs' Tears" (lead singer of the Four Tops); ABC, "When Smokey Sings" (Smokey Robinson); Big Audio Dynamite, "James Brown"; Dexys Midnight Runners, "Jackie Wilson Said," "Oh Geno" (Geno Washington); Ian Dury, "Sweet Gene Vincent"; Buddy Holly, "Bo Diddley"; Happy Mondays, "Donovan"; Neil Young, "From Hank to Hendrix"; Oasis, "Cast No Shadow" (written about Richard Ashcroft of the Verve); John Martyn, "Solid Air" (for Nick Drake); Free, "My Brother Jake" (about guitarist Paul Kossoff); George Harrison, "When We Was Fab"; David Bowie, "Song for Bob Dylan"; Maroon 5, "Move Like Jagger"; Wilco, "Bob Dylan's 49th Beard."*

Going slightly further afield, songwriters occasionally mention performers and composers in fields of music such as jazz and classical music. Writing lyrics about jazz musicians is, of course, terribly hip. The standout hit of this kind is Stevie Wonder's "Sir Duke," a tribute to Duke Ellington, which also mentions Ella Fitzgerald, Glen Miller, Count Basie, and Louis Armstrong.

Lyrics about classical figures often vent popular music's resentment toward high culture, as in Chuck Berry's "Roll Over Beethoven" and Roy Wood's "Bend Over Beethoven." A few exceptions include Kate Bush's "Delius (Song of Summer)," Siouxsie and the Banshees' "The Last Beat of My Heart" (Shostakovich), Eurythmics' "Beethoven (I Love to Listen To)," and Falco's "Rock Me Amadeus" (inspired by the film *Amadeus*, about Mozart).

Songs about songs

When songwriters get stuck for a subject, they sometimes fall back on describing what they do—and so we get lyrics about songs and wanting to write a song. Many of these lyrics are suffocatingly self-conscious. For a start, admitting out loud that you're not feeling inspired doesn't make for an inspiring lyric. Such a lyric can look smugly self-engrossed, with an inflated sense of musical talent. Some of these lyrics are so portentously self-absorbed that they invite not sympathy for the songwriter's predicament but the response, "So, you can strum three chords and write a song—ever looked at a score by Stravinsky? See a difference?" There is also a sense that a song about a song is a form of postponement, just as a story about telling stories puts us one remove from a story. The waiter reading the menu is no substitute for the food.

More meaningful is when music itself becomes a metaphor for other types of harmony, such as that felt between lovers. This lyric motif can also be used in spiritual songs, where music is an expression of cosmic harmony, part of the order of things. This goes back at least as far as Greek philosophy and the belief in the "music of the spheres." Both these musical metaphors themes can be found in the Who's output, the first in "Getting in Tune," and the second in "Pure and Easy." The tenacity of Pete Townshend's pursuit of this notion of the universal power of music, during the years 1968–73, is probably unparalleled by anyone in rock music.

In addition to songs glorifying the singer/songwriter and his or her art, there are truckloads of songs celebrating music-making, there are songs about instruments, and, last but not least, songs about specific genres such as rock 'n' roll.

The guitar man and the band

In the mid-1950s, when the electric guitar became the symbol and voice of rock 'n' roll rebellion, the guitarist became a folk hero who could make huge amounts of money and wield a magic spell over increasingly large audiences. The quintessential lyric on this topic is Chuck Berry's "Johnny B. Goode," a narrative about a country boy who learns rhythm by imitating trains and whose rise to fame is prophesized by his mother. The extended sense of the *electric* guitarist as a "shaman" is encapsulated in the Jimi Hendrix Experience's "Voodoo Chile." Here are songs about singers, players, bands, and their rise and fall.

» *Chuck Berry, "Johnny B Goode"; Dire Straits, "Sultans of Swing," "Walk of Life"; Bread, "Guitar Man"; the Carpenters, "Superstar"; David Bowie, "Ziggy Stardust"; Elton John, "Bennie and the Jets"; Oasis, "Rock N' Roll Star"; Hole, "Rock Star"; the Byrds, "So You Want to Be a Rock 'n' Roll Star"; Nickelback, "Rockstar"; the Moody Blues, "I'm Just a Singer (in a Rock and Roll Band)"; Bruce Springsteen, "Where the Bands Are"; Grand Funk Railroad, "We're an American Band."*

The guitar

It isn't surprising that the guitar should be venerated as an object of beauty, of longing (if you're young and can't afford a Fender or a Gibson), of power, of sex appeal, and as a route to riches. The guitar is also sometimes anthropomorphized, as in the Beatles' "While My Guitar Gently Weeps" and Bon Jovi's "My Guitar Lies Bleeding in My Arms," so that it becomes the embodiment of the singer's emotions. Bruce Springsteen's recent "House of a Thousand Guitars" celebrates the power of music to create community in difficult times.

» *Taylor Swift, "Teardrops on My Guitar"; Townes Van Zandt, Moody Blues, Susan Werner, "Blue Guitar"; Loudon Wainwright III, U2, "Red Guitar"; XTC, "My Brown Guitar"; Pete Townshend, "Sheraton Gibson"; Squeeze, "F-Hole"; Bebop Deluxe, "Sunburst Finish"; David Sylvian, "Dobro"; Neil Young, "This Old Guitar"; the Magnetic Fields, "Acoustic Guitar"; Joe Brown, "Talking Guitar"; Billy Bragg, "This Guitar Says Sorry"; Amanda Palmer, "Guitar Hero."*

Other instruments and accessories

" *I think of a beautiful sax like a human being, a sensuous shining man being taken over by the instrument. The perfect setting was this smoky bar in Berlin with nobody listening except me in a corner."*

KATE BUSH TO *SOUNDS* ON "THE SAXOPHONE SONG"

Even if you don't want to write a whole lyric about an instrument, it could suggest a central metaphor for a situation. The black and white keys of a piano were taken as an image of racial harmony in the McCartney and Wonder song "Ebony and Ivory." There are proverbial phrases linked with instruments, such as a phrase like "second fiddle." The lyrics of Sly and the Family Stone's "Dance to the Music" introduce the musicians and their instruments one by one. For comic purposes so does the Bonzo Dog Doo-Dah Band's "The Intro & the Outro," name-checking Adolf Hitler on vibes! Such lyrics obviously invite the inclusion of the instrument in the arrangement, or the effects device in the case of R.E.M.'s "E-Bow the Letter."

» *Kate Bush, "Violin," "The Saxophone Song"; Nick Drake, "Cello Song"; David Gray, "Wurlitzer"; the Who, "Squeeze Box," "Success Story" (on the trials of*

*recording); Squeeze, "Farfisa Beat"; Freddie and the Dreamers, "Susan's Tuba";
Mantronix, "Bassline"; the Stone Roses, "She Bangs the Drums"; Bob Dylan, "Mr
Tambourine Man"; Gomez, "Love Is Better Than a Warm Trombone"; Björk,
"Headphones"; Genesis, "Guide Vocal"; Wilco, "Heavy Metal Drummer"; Alana
George, "Your Drums, Your Love."*

Stage songs and crowd-pleasers

One particular self-referential lyric celebrates live performance and holds
a mirror to the audience. It is the sort of lyric in which the word "tonight"
looms large and rock bands ask their audiences if they're ready to rock. This is
a crowd-pleasing move, a "we're all in this together" gesture, even if the song
sounds contrived and self-conscious.

The showbiz recognition of the performer as entertainer can clash with rebel
counter-establishment pretensions, as expressed in the Who's "Join Together."
This list also includes several songs about festivals.

» *The Who, "Long Live Rock"; Bryan Adams, "Kids Wanna Rock"; Wings, "Rock
Show"; Led Zeppelin, "The Ocean"; Status Quo, "Rockin' All Over the World";
Alice Cooper, "Hello Hurray"; Chuck Berry, "House Lights"; Queen, "We Will
Rock You"; Robbie Williams, "Let Me Entertain You"; AC/DC, "For Those About
to Rock"; Mountain, "For Yasgur's Farm" (about Woodstock); Joni Mitchell,
"Woodstock"; Echo and the Bunnymen, "Altamont"; David Bowie, "Memory of a
Free Festival."*

General paeans to rock

Here is a short list of songs with "rock" or "rock 'n' roll" in the title. The phrase
can among other things be shorthand for having a good time, having sex, or
playing 12-bars at high volume.

» *Chuck Berry, "Rock and Roll Music," "Sweet Little Rock and Roller"; Ian Dury,
"Sex & Drugs & Rock & Roll"; Joan Jett and the Blackhearts, "I Love Rock 'n'
Roll"; Led Zeppelin, "Rock and Roll"; Billy Joel, "It's Still Rock 'n' Roll to Me"; the
Rolling Stones, "It's Only Rock 'n' Roll (But I Like It)"; Mott the Hoople, "Golden
Age of Rock 'n' Roll"; Johnny Winter, "Golden Days of Rock and Roll"; Argent,
"God Gave Rock and Roll to You"; Black Rebel Motorcycle Club, "Whatever*

Happened to My Rock and Roll"; Danny and the Juniors, "Rock and Roll Is Here to Stay."

The song can be a metaphor for an old relationship. There are songs about couples who have adopted a song because they heard it when they met. This becomes "their" song, and said song becomes devastating after a breakup. Cue a subject for a lyric. Motown writers Holland-Dozier-Holland were audacious enough to draw attention to repeating their own musical formulae with the Four Tops when they wrote "It's the Same Old Song" as a love song.

» *Elton John, "Sad Songs (Say So Much)"; Jim Croce, "I'll Just Have to Say I Love You in a Song"; Roberta Flack, "Killing Me Softly With His Song"; B. J. Thomas, "(Hey Won't You Play) Another Somebody Done Somebody Some Wrong Song"; Travis, "Sing"; M, "Pop Muzik"; Genesis, "Abacab"; Wings, "Silly Love Songs"; Elton John, "Your Song"; the Who, "Guitar and Pen," "All This Music Must Fade"; John Miles, "Music"; the Beatles, "Only a Northern Song"; Smokey Robinson, "Melody Man"; Coldplay, "Yellow"; My Chemical Romance, "We Don't Need Another Song About California"; Phoebe Bridgers, "Garden Song."*

Classical references

To add a touch of pretension and grandeur to your lyric, borrow a structural term from the vocabulary of classical music. Suitable terms include melody, overture, opera, serenade, rhapsody, suite, symphony, and references to keys. The Moody Blues named an album after the mnemonic for the musical stave: *Every Good Boy Deserves Favours*. With the exception of the word "melody," there is no connection between song form and any of these large-scale musical structures.

» *ELO, "10538 Overture," "Concerto for a Rainy Day"; the Righteous Brothers, "Unchained Melody"; the Verve, "Bitter Sweet Symphony"; the Supremes, "I Hear a Symphony"; the Beach Boys, "Winter Symphony"; Keith West, "Excerpt from a Teenage Opera"; David Gates, "Suite: Clouds, Rain"; Wilco, "Pieholden Suite"; Lindisfarne, "Train in G Major"; Billy Bragg, "Way Over Yonder in the Minor Key"; Red Hot Chili Peppers, "Mellowslip Slinky in B Major."*

Politics and protest

" *When I started writing these new songs, I was listening to a lot of political programs on BBC Radio 4. I found myself . . . writing down little nonsense phrases, those Orwellian euphemisms that our government and yours are so fond of. They became the background of the record.*"

THOM YORKE OF RADIOHEAD TO *ROLLING STONE*, 2003

" *When I see contemporary songs quoted by contemporary music critics, they say, 'This is a great lyric,' and they'll isolate a line, and I'll think, What's great about that? There's no nourishment in that line. There's not even alliteration or linguistic color, you know? 'Everybody's gay.' You know—it's a statement, but there's not art. . . . is it all distilled down to its simplest essence and therefore it's valid? Or do people just not know how to express themselves very well?*"

JONI MITCHELL TO *MOJO*, AUGUST 1998

The state of the world offers an endless source of potential lyric themes, and eventually most songwriters are tempted to have their say about something that annoys them. Writing a protest song makes you feel you have said something significant in the larger scheme of things. The challenge is not to allow this satisfaction to eclipse the more relevant one of artistic judgement. No matter how right you think you are about the issue, the first concern must be artistic: is this a good lyric? Good intent does not guarantee artistic success, nor is it a measure of it.

War and violence

The 1960s counterculture's opposition to the Vietnam War brought about a rock version of the protest song. As far as topics go, the songwriter can count on an audience thinking that war and violence are bad things, so, in protest lyrics, these are safer subjects than most. Some of the best examples include:

» *Edwin Starr, "War"; Marvin Gaye, "What's Going On"; Bob Dylan, "Masters of War"; Happy Mondays, "Altogether Now"; John Lennon, "Give Peace a Chance," "Happy Xmas (War Is Over)"; Peter Gabriel, "Games Without Frontiers"; Bruce Springsteen, "Born in the USA"; Country Joe and the Fish, "I Feel Like I'm Fixin' to Die Rag"; Paul Hardcastle, "19"; Frankie Goes to*

Hollywood, "Two Tribes"; Jimi Hendrix's Band of Gypsies, "Machine Gun"; U2, "Bullet the Blue Sky," "Sunday Bloody Sunday"; Black Sabbath, "War Pigs"; Radiohead, "2 + 2 = 5"; Green Day, "American Idiot"; David Bowie, "How Does the Grass Grow."

Poverty and unemployment

Unemployment and poverty touch a chord of identification and sympathy in the majority of people. Not everyone has fought in a war or been gunned or bombed, but almost everyone knows what it is to at least fear poverty.

» Marvin Gaye, "Inner City Blues"; the Isley Bros, "Harvest for the World"; George Harrison, "Bangla Desh"; Band Aid, "Do They Know It's Christmas"; the Police, "Driven to Tears"; the Specials, "Ghost Town"; Grandmaster Flash and the Furious Five, "The Message"; Tracy Chapman, "Talkin' 'Bout a Revolution"; UB40, "One in Ten"; Elvis Presley, "In the Ghetto"; Wilco, "Poor Places."

Environmental issues

Few traps are so powerfully sprung for the unwary songwriter as writing a song with a "message." "Message" songs are bywords for slogans and platitudes over which a sticky goo of generalized sentiment has been poured. The notion of writing a song with a message is itself flawed, because it implies a simplistic relation of form and content. It suggests once you get the "message" you can throw away the song as if it were a sweet wrapper. This should be borne in mind by songwriters who want to tackle current ecological issues. The earliest ecological protest songs date from the 1960s and chiefly concern pollution rather than the then unknown global warming:

» Joni Mitchell, "Big Yellow Taxi"; Marvin Gaye, "Mercy Mercy Me (the Ecology)"; the Four Tops, "That's the Way Nature Planned It"; the Moody Blues, "A Question of Balance"; Pete Seeger, "Where Have All the Flowers Gone?"; Spirit, "Nature's Way"; Cliff Richard, "Silvery Rain"; Radiohead, "Idioteque"; Anohni, "4 Degrees"; Billie Eilish, "All the Good Girls Go to Hell."

Politics and power

In the early 1960s, the heyday of protest, both Bob Dylan and Phil Ochs wrote protest songs about Medgar Evans, although Dylan is alleged to have said to Ochs, "You're not a songwriter, you're a journalist." Songs about politics and protest were more visible in the 1960s than at any time since, because popular music itself was undergoing a revolution.

Initially, such songs were associated with folk music (itself allied to a variety of left-wing causes) and singers such as Woody Guthrie. It reached a bigger audience than the folk clubs because of the involvement of singers like Pete Seeger, Bob Dylan, and Joan Baez. Only five years after the Beatles had gone to #1 all over the world with "She Loves You," they were recording "Revolution." Since then, political songs have emerged from punk, new wave, rock, heavy rock, and rap.

» *Pete Seeger, "We Shall Overcome"; Elvis Costello, "Night Rally"; the Who, "Relay"; Buffalo Springfield, "Ohio"; the Rolling Stones, "Street Fighting Man"; the Police, "Invisible Sun"; Peter Gabriel, "Biko"; the Specials, "Nelson Mandela"; the Beatles, "Revolution"; Thunderclap Newman, "Something in the Air"; U2, "Mothers of the Disappeared"; Billy Bragg, "There Is Power in a Union"; the Chi-Lites, "(For God's Sake) Give More Power to the People"; Plastic Ono Band, "Power to the People"; the Temptations, "Ball of Confusion"; System of a Down, "Hypnotize."*

Alert to the turn rock was taking, soul music of the late 1960s increasingly reflected the trials and aspirations of frustrated African Americans, the civil rights movement, and black power.

» *Stevie Wonder, "Heaven Help Us All"; James Brown, "Say It Aloud (I'm Black and I'm Proud)"; Public Enemy, "911 Is a Joke"; Billie Holiday, "Strange Fruit"; Tracy Chapman, "Across the Lines"; Bob Dylan, "The Ballad of Medgar Evans"; Eminem, "White America"; Curtis Mayfield, "Miss Black America"; Artists United Against Apartheid, "Sun City"; Sam Cooke, "A Change Is Gonna Come"; Prince "Sign 'O' the Times"; Kendrick Lamar, "Swimming Pool (Drank)": Manic Street Preachers, "IfWhiteAmericaToldTheTruthForOneDayItsWorldWouldFallApart."*

Writers perceived as deviating into protest can get into commercial difficulties. In the 1970s, Jackson Browne established himself as a singer/songwriter writing about love and loss, but in the 1980s he released many songs that dealt with broader themes. When his 1993 album *I'm Alive* was released, Elektra issued an ad subtitled "Jackson Browne Resurfaces" (the sleeve was his head emerging from water). Apparently, to return from protest songs was to come up for air. The ad reassured the prospective buyer that these were love songs reflecting recent events in Browne's personal life. The subtext was, "Hey, it's okay, it's safe to buy *this* one—he's not doing political protest stuff now."

Keep a sense of perspective with the protest song. Why should the ability to strum chords mean you have answers to great political and social questions?

Aware of the absurdity lurking in this scenario, songwriter Barry Mann released a single in 1968 called "Young Electric Psychedelic Hippy Flippy Folk and Funky Philosophic Turned on Groovy 12-String Band," which satirized the desire of performers to comment on anything and everything and the eagerness of the media to listen to them.

A guide to writing protest lyrics
Here are some things to bear in mind when writing protest lyrics:

- To make big issues seem real, a lyric must be grounded in human particulars, because they flesh out the abstraction.
- Be clear where you stand, but humanize your doubts or make a virtue of them.
- Look for the details from which the theme emerges. This makes it easier for people to relate to the lyric.
- Be wary of assuming a stance of personal moral superiority.
- If you want to write a chant that crowds can take up, keep things simple, as in "Power to the People" or "Give Peace a Chance."
- Having your heart in the right place won't save a crude or incompetent lyric.

Fantasy and myth

> *[Genesis] were writing songs that were surreal, escapist, not your average lyric. And that's all well and good until you've got to sing them. We were listening to some of our old live tapes, and 'bread bin' was in one of the lyrics. You try and sing 'bread bin'—it's a difficult word to put anything to."*
>
> **PHIL COLLINS TO *MOJO* ON TAKING OVER VOCALS IN GENESIS**

> *I grew up in the suburbs, and it was all very prosaic and dull . . . as a writer, fantasy is really an excellent vehicle for expressing ideas in their purest sense, without any preconceptions. There's nothing better than having your own made-to-order extra-terrestrial world."*
>
> **NEIL PEART OF RUSH TO *UNCUT***

> *You can have your own mythology scene. Or write, you know, fiction. Complete fiction though, you know . . . the way I write things, I just write them with a clash between reality and fantasy mostly. You have to use the fantasy in order to show different sides of reality."*
>
> **JIMI HENDRIX TO BBC RADIO, DECEMBER 1967**

If you want to have a break from the real world, write a lyric which is fantasy or based on myth. Inspiration could come from fantasy stories, science-fiction, or children's stories. A lyric does not have to be crudely realistic to be truthful about life or the human condition, or to express feelings. Fantasy songs can express emotions obliquely. Like dreams, they relate to our inner lives and unconscious. Speaking to the *Irish Independent* in 2019, Ezra Koenig of Vampire Weekend insisted, "It always hurt my feelings when people would say that Vampire Weekend's lyrics were nonsense. They're not nonsense. They're impressionistic."

The fantasy lyric received a strong impetus in the 1960s. This was partly due to the influence of psychedelia and the books hippies venerated, notably J. R. R. Tolkien's epic *Lord of the Rings*. Between 1968 and 1970, Marc Bolan wrote five albums worth of songs based on a Tolkienesque world of elves and wizards. Tolkien also influenced Led Zeppelin's "Ramble On" and "Battle of Evermore," and provided the title for "Misty Mountain Hop." Other key fantasy texts included C. S. Lewis's *Chronicles of Narnia*, Lewis Carroll's *Alice in Wonderland*, and books by Ray Bradbury. The Beatles' "I Am the Walrus,"

Jefferson Airplane's "White Rabbit," and Elton John's "Mona Lisas and Mad Hatters," all allude to Carroll.

Nursery rhymes and children's stories

Children's songs often have a fantastical element. Nursery rhymes can also be reset and given an adult meaning, or lend an image to a title.

» *Adam and the Ants, "Prince Charming"; Robert Plant, Joss Stone, the Firm, "All the King's Horses"; Sam the Sham and the Pharaohs, "Li'l Red Riding Hood"; Squeeze, "Pinocchio"; Stevie Ray Vaughan, "Mary Had a Little Lamb"; Death in Vegas, "Aladdin's Story"; Kate Bush, "In Search of Peter Pan"; Radiohead, "Tinker Tailor Soldier Sailor Rich Man Poor Man Beggar Man Thief."*

Fantasy

Glam rockers like David Bowie, Roxy Music, progressive bands like Genesis (*The Lamb Lies Down on Broadway*), Hawkwind, Pink Floyd, Yes, and Rush (see *2112*) often invented fantasy stories. Tubeway Army's "Are Friends Electric" is based on Philip K. Dick's novel *Do Androids Dream of Electric Sheep?*

More sinister fantasy informed the lyrics of heavy rock groups. Metallica and other metal bands draw on the stories of H. P. Lovecraft for songs like "The Call of Kthulu," while Alice Cooper made up horror stories of his own for *Welcome to My Nightmare.*

Inexperienced young songwriters, especially in rock bands who lean toward sword and sorcery, often unconsciously default to fantasy lyrics of courtly love imagery derived third hand from an idealized Middle Ages. This stuff is comprised of castles, lakes, magic woods, swords, maidens, ladies, queens, kings, fools, jesters, wizards and witches, soldiers, crystals, et cetera. Gordon Lightfoot's "If You Could Read My Mind" is interesting in this connection because it has some of this imagery, derived from paperback romance, but undercuts it. The details are ascribed to a film or book that the speaker and the woman he's addressing have seen or read. It's a clever lyric that includes within itself the act of interpretation.

Fantasy itself as a psychological habit can be the subject of a lyric. The Jam's "Billy Hunt" and Pink Floyd's "Arnold Layne" and "See Emily Play" are about people lost in fantasy. The Temptations "Just My Imagination (Running Away with Me)" is a good example of the way that lovers are fantasists; the entire lyric leads the listener to make a false interpretation of the situation being described.

» *Hawkwind, "In Search of Space"; Pink Floyd, "Astronomy Domine"; Queen, "Seven Seas of Rhye"; the Beatles, "Lucy in the Sky with Diamonds," "Magical Mystery Tour"; King Crimson, "The Court of the Crimson King"; Bob Dylan, "Mighty Quinn"; David McWilliams, "Days of Pearly Spencer"; Rory Gallagher, King Crimson, "Moonchild"; Iron Maiden, "Seventh Son of a Seventh Son"; Genesis, "Eleventh Earl of Mar"; Rush, "The Temples of Syrinx"; All Time Low, "Somewhere in Neverland."*

Greek and Roman myth

If you don't feel you could invent a fantasy world, there are always Greek and Roman myths—the root of Western art and literature for centuries. They have been recycled and interpreted by writers, painters, sculptors, composers, etc. A myth can provide a parallel for the situation you're writing about.

Greek and Roman myths are often considered too highbrow for chart lyrics, so there have been few hits with such references. Prog-rock bands—who want their music to be viewed as art, not ephemeral pop—have fewer reservations about working such myths into songs. For them, it could signal that they were serious musicians. Nevertheless, chart-wise Sting alluded to the two rocks Scylla and Charybdis in "Wrapped About Your Finger," a reference to the Sirens who tempted Odysseus occurs in Radiohead's "There There," and there is an allusion to the Trojan horse in Manfred Mann's "5-4-3-2-1."

» *Led Zeppelin, "Achilles Last Stand"; the Herd, "From the Underground" (Orpheus and Eurydice); Nick Cave and the Bad Seeds, "The Lyre of Orpheus"; Cream, "Tales of Brave Ulysses"; the Hollies, "King Midas in Reverse"; the Incredible String Band, "The Minotaur's Song"; Wishbone Ash, "Persephone"; the Waterboys, "The Pan Within"; Mercury Rev, "Hercules"; David Bowie, "Pallas Athena"; Wings, "Venus and Mars"; Ash, "Aphrodite"; Procol Harum, "Pandora's Box"; Iron Maiden, "The Flight of Icarus"; Al Stewart, "Helen and Cassandra"; XTC, "Jason and the Argonauts"; Elvis Costello, "Poor Fractured Atlas"; Laura Marling, "Undine"; Arcade Fire, "It's Never Over (Oh Orpheus)."*

If the song can stand it, classical references add grandeur. Otherwise, try juxtaposing a classical reference with the everyday, as Dylan sometimes did in the mid-1960s, and as did Prefab Sprout ("Venus of the Soup Kitchen") and Mercury Rev ("Goddess on a Highway"). A soup kitchen and a highway are the last places you would expect to find an immortal being. The most popular figure from classical myth (unsurprisingly) is Venus, the goddess of love.

Outside of classical stories, Randy Newman wrote an album of songs about the Faust myth, and Dylan titled a song "Isis" after an Egyptian deity. No self-respecting heavy-rock band is without its tableau of riffing Viking pillage, following Led Zeppelin's "Immigrant Song."

The supernatural

> *Well, we all have demons inside. I've witnessed a lot of self-destruction in the world I'm in, and writing about it is my way of dealing with it."*
>
> **LUCINDA WILLIAMS TO *MOJO***

> *I'd pick up the guitar, come up with a riff, and go, 'That sounds a bit evil.' The words had to fit that mood."*
>
> **TONI IOMMI OF BLACK SABBATH TO *MELODY MAKER***

Most ghosts and demons in song lyrics are strictly metaphorical. Such imagery is an easy-to-apply shorthand for the trauma of lost love, or to describe self-destructive impulses, as the Lucinda Williams quote makes clear.

These days, everyone is "haunted," everyone has their "personal demons." In this connection, see Kristin Hersh's "Your Ghost," or Here Come the Tears' "The Ghost of You." Songs such as "Haunted" and "Bring Me to Life" by Evanescence are typical of a type of overwrought lyric saturated with gothic imagery of dying, being undead, bleeding, screaming, being pulled down, of salvation and deliverance.

Astrology has provided some colorful titles and vivid imagery for songs. Both Paul Weller and R.E.M. have used the concept of the "Saturn Return," which refers to a 29-year astrological cycle alleged to reflect our struggles to mature. Deep Purple did "Maybe I'm a Leo," and astrology is implied in song titles like "Cancer Moon," "Scorpio Girl," et cetera, and Albert King's "Born Under a Bad Sign."

ESP, parapsychology, prophecy, synchronicity, and out-of-body experiences have all been fruitful lyric subjects.

» *Al Stewart, "Nostradamus"; Kate Bush, "Strange Phenomena"; Paul Kantner and Grace Slick, "Your Mind Has Left Your Body"; the Police, "Synchronicity"; Ash, "Astral Conversations with Toulouse-Lautrec"; Buzzcocks, "ESP"; Stevie Wonder, "Superstition."*

Sometimes, songwriters want to spook their listeners, make them curious, or revel in occult power by proxy. The blues and R&B have a long tradition of stories of doing deals with dark forces to get what you want, a legend attached to Robert Johnson ("Hellhound on My Trail"). If you like this sort of thing, check out Dr. John's album *Gris-Gris*. It was okay for Jimi Hendrix to claim he was a "voodoo chile" but harder if you were born in the deep south of Sussex.

» *Fleetwood Mac, "Black Magic Woman"; the Rattles, "The Witch"; Donovan, "Season of the Witch"; Jethro Tull, "The Witch's Promise"; Redbone, "Witch Queen of New Orleans"; Fleetwood Mac, "Rhiannon"; the Eagles, "Witchy Woman"; John Mayall, "I'm Your Witchdoctor"; John Kongos, "Tokoloshe Man"; the Darkness, "Black Shuck"; the Prodigy, "Voodoo People"; Boney M, "Voodoonight"; Aerosmith, "Voodoo Medicine"; Siouxsie and the Banshees, "Voodoo Dolly"; Coldplay, "Magic."*

It is no surprise, given rock music's long history as the voice of rebels, that it should contain many songs about the archetypal rebel, Satan, and hell. The use of occult imagery in lyrics by early heavy-rock bands like Black Sabbath and Black Widow at the start of the 1970s had by the 1990s created a whole genre of the stuff.

» *Atomic Rooster, "Devil's Answer"; Van Halen, "Runnin' with the Devil"; the Rolling Stones, "Dancing with Mr. D"; the Crazy World of Arthur Brown, "Fire"; Meat Loaf, "Bat Out of Hell"; Chris Rea, "Road to Hell"; AC/DC, "Highway to Hell"; Saxon, "Beyond the Grave"; Iron Maiden, "The Number of the Beast"; Blue Öyster Cult, "Don't Fear the Reaper"; Ozzy Osbourne, "Mr. Crowley"; Black Widow, "Come to the Sabbath"; P. J. Harvey, "The Devil"; Kanye West, "Devil in a New Dress."*

Spirituality

> *I was told that if I insisted [on the title 'Deal with God'] the radio stations in at least ten countries would refuse to play it because it had 'God' in the title—Spain, Italy, America, lots of them. I thought it was ridiculous. Still, especially after The Dreaming, I decided I couldn't be bloody-minded. You have to weigh up the priorities."*
> **KATE BUSH TO Q ON "RUNNING UP THAT HILL"**

> *I think I felt good about incorporating sex-and-death imagery, especially if I found it in the Old Testament. That felt good to me. That felt kind of cool. That felt kind of rock 'n' roll."*
> **BLACK FRANCIS OF THE PIXIES TO *MOJO***

The main use of positive religious imagery in song lyrics has been as a metaphor for romance, as in Belinda Carlisle's "Heaven Is a Place on Earth," the Elgins' "Heaven Must Have Sent You," Tavares' "Heaven Must Be Missing an Angel," and Madonna's "Like a Prayer." Falling in love is the most common experience of expanded consciousness, however flawed or transient; as Amen Corner posed it, "If Paradise Is Half as Nice." The Monkees' "I'm a Believer" was romance as conversion.

Ultra-romantic lyrics appropriate the imagery of religion and drain it of any metaphysical meaning. It is possible to write a lyric that can be interpreted as a love song or as religious (devotional). During their first four albums, U2 were very good at this. Images for this kind of ambiguity include terms like "soul," "salvation," and "angel."

Fleetwood Mac, Madonna, Jimi Hendrix, and Bruce Springsteen all wrote songs called "Angel," and there have been plenty along the lines of B.B. King's "Sweet Little Angel," or Roxy Music's "Angel Eyes." The biggest song of Robbie Williams's career is "Angels," a new-age scenario in which God never puts in an unwelcome appearance. This sort of vague belief, which asks nothing of the ego, is acceptable to a mass audience in a way that traditional or more defined belief generally is not.

Back in 1971, George Harrison fused East and West, combining "hallelujah" with "hare Krishna" on "My Sweet Lord," a #1 in the UK and the USA, without his credibility suffering. But that was because you can't argue with an ex-Beatle with near-guru status, a great slide solo, and a Phil Spector production that's almost a religious experience in itself.

The power of music is sometimes sufficient to overcome a tepid reaction to religious lyrics. The Strawbs' hymn "Lay Down" was helped by the Les Paul power chords that punctuate the verses. Back in the mid-1960s, the Byrds took several verses from Old Testament text *Ecclesiastes* into the chart with Pete Seeger's "Turn Turn Turn." For many years, U2 closed their set with "40," the words of which come from Psalm 40, and Boney M had a hit with "The Rivers of Babylon," another Old Testament text.

By contrast, consider the critical disdain that affects Cliff Richard's mainstream religious material, and that nearly eclipsed even Bob Dylan during his evangelical phase. No such critique has ever touched the Rastafarian songs of Bob Marley ("Exodus," "Redemption Song") which are treated as beyond criticism. Gospel is, of course, always liable to generate a hit by virtue of its emotive and declamatory style (as with the Edwin Hawkins Singers' "Oh Happy Day"), and it is viewed as "authentic" because of its connection with the blues. A different standard is applied to, say, Cat Stevens singing "Morning Has Broken" than is applied to Marvin Gaye singing about saving the children. To many, John Lennon's humanist anthem "Imagine" is more palatable, and it remains one of the most popular "belief" songs ever written.

Biblical references

A song can use spiritual imagery without being about religion, but there are a few artists whose prior critical reputation has enabled them to use more Christian imagery than would normally be considered "hip." Bruce Springsteen, who came from a Catholic household, put Biblical allusions in songs like "Adam Raised a Cain," "Pink Cadillac" (Adam and Eve), "Lion's Den" (Daniel), "The Promised Land," "The Price You Pay" (Moses and the chosen land), and "Ice Man" (the flaming sword that guards the garden of Eden mentioned in *Genesis*). The story of Cain and Abel occurs in many songs (see Elvis Costello's "Blame It on Cain"). The Doors' song "Break on Through" contains the phrase "The gate is strait, deep and wide," which is Biblical. The second verse of Leonard Cohen's "Suzanne" alludes to Jesus's miracle of walking on the water, and Elvis's "Hard-Headed Woman" refers to Samson and Delilah, and Adam and Eve.

» *Billy Bragg, "King James Version"; Mott the Hoople, "Roll Away the Stone"; Gretchen Peters, "Like Water into Wine"; David Bowie, the Boo Radleys, "Lazarus";*

Elton John, "Where to Now St. Peter?"; Bob Dylan, "Gates of Eden"; Badly Drawn Boy, "40 Days, 40 Nights"; Depeche Mode, "Judas"; the Stones Roses, "I Am the Resurrection"; Virgin Fugs, "The 10 Commandments"; Aphrodite's Child, "The Four Horsemen"; 10,000 Maniacs, "Noah's Dove"; Joni Mitchell, "The Sire of Sorrow (Job's Sad Song)"; Arcade Fire, "Neon Bible"; the Killers, "Joseph, Better You Than Me."

The 1960s counterculture bequeathed Eastern terms like Zen, nirvana, and karma to pop's language, and Van Morrison's songs include other esoteric terms like "astral" and "dweller on the threshold." T.Rex's "Cosmic Dancer" and CSNY's "We Have All Been Here Before" are both about reincarnation. The Police's "Secret Journey," Kate Bush's "Sat in Your Lap," and the Waterboys' "The Glastonbury Song," are all about pilgrimage. More general songs about belief or lack of it include:

» *John Lennon, "God"; David Bowie, "Word on a Wing"; Norman Greenbaum, "Spirit in the Sky"; Led Zeppelin, "In My Time of Dying"; the Wallflowers, "God Says Nothing Back"; Joan Osborne, "One of Us"; the Byrds, "Jesus Is Just Alright With Me"; Wishbone Ash, "The King Will Come"; the Who, "Bargain," "Pure and Easy"; Depeche Mode, "Personal Jesus"; George Harrison, "Awaiting on You All," "Give Me Love (Give Me Peace on Earth)"; the Police, "Spirits in the Material World"; Blind Faith, "Presence of the Lord"; Judee Sill, "Jesus Was a Cross Maker"; Wilco, "Jesus Etc."; Kanye West, "Jesus Walks"; Coldplay, "God Put a Smile Upon Your Face"; Tom Waits "God's Away on Business"; Frank Ocean, "Godspeed."*

songwriter interviews

nick cave

Interviewed by Simon Smith

Nick Cave's favorite lyrical themes—death, violence, religion, love, and a mythic view of the American South—have found expression backed by the abrasive art punk of the Birthday Party, and latterly the increasingly melodic Bad Seeds. Cave has also written novels and film scripts.

» *How important are song titles, in terms of their connection with the lyric?*
Hugely important. When there isn't an appropriate one, we would end up quite deliberately using titles such as "The Witness Song" or "The Ship Song." These have quite a resonance for me, in the same way as I've always like "The Something Blues." There's an immediate recognition to that. You know what you're getting.

And, talking of blues, John Lee Hooker is, to me, the greatest of the blues lyric writers. There's something incredibly subtle and deeply rooted. And it's improvised, and you can tell it's just come out of him sitting there and doing a free rant, but it goes to places that you wouldn't imagine. It's spine-tingling. He gives himself a lot of space to create the whole picture. There's a whole trance, hypnotic thing both to the music and the lyrics. If you half-listen to John Lee Hooker it can be kind of meaningless, but if you listen to what he's actually singing about, it's riveting.

He has probably influenced me more than any other lyricist. I mean, Bob Dylan hasn't really influenced me much, in the sense that he's just too good. If you try to write a song like Bob Dylan, it just sounds sub–Bob Dylan. Once you try to mimic it's a real sign of desperation.

» *Although, as you said earlier, you do start out trying to emulate stuff that you like.*
Well, you carry on doing that to certain a degree. It's been difficult recently because I've been trying to get words together, and you just get snatches of something, like a half idea for a song. This can spiral into a feeling that you have nothing to say. I was looking through a lyric book for the last album, and it was interesting to see that some of these very successful songs started out of the most inane thoughts.

» *Wasn't "There She Goes, My Beautiful World," from* Abattoir Blues, *about having lost your muse?*
Yeah. Exactly.

» *When did you first start to write lyrics?*
Well, I'd always written poetry, for as far back as I can remember. It was kind of a private vice, and I didn't really tell anybody about it. I grew up in a country town in Australia, and it wasn't something that you shouted from the rooftops.

» *Not a manly pursuit?*
No, you didn't indulge in that kind of behavior. Incredibly suspect. I can still remember some of it, not the actual words but what they were about. Love stuff—so nothing's really changed. When I joined a band later [Boys Next Door] we did a lot of covers—initially Sensational Alex Harvey Band and Alice Cooper—then we started creeping in a few of our own songs. I think I was mostly just interested in words.

» *So the words came first?*
Yes. I mean, I had nothing to say. I was trying to cling on to anything that half resembled a song. Most of the efforts aren't worth spending any time on. What you initially try to do is find a voice for yourself. You try to do anything you possibly can, and the only way you can judge it is if it resembles something else that you like. And after a while you begin to find your voice and you try to work on that. It's about finding an authentic voice and developing that from record to record, and that never stops.

» *You seem to have reached a point where you are recognizably yourself. There is, after all, a school of Nick Cave.*

I guess. However, the difficulty is to continue to find that authentic voice, but one that is sufficiently developed from the last record. I'm really in that process at the moment, in the early stages of writing a new record, and I'm sitting around not having written any songs for a year with absolutely nothing in my head whatsoever. The difficulty isn't actually in writing the lyrics themselves it's in finding the voice again, but one that doesn't sound like the one that you had on the last record

» *Taking that further, over your career you have employed themes that have gone across a number of albums. For instance, in The Birthday Party and earlier days of The Bad Seeds there was the more obviously Southern Gothic-influenced material and the prison songs. This all seems to have changed dramatically after* Murder Ballads *(1996) when you released* The Boatman's Call *(1997), which introduced a more obviously autobiographical element to your lyrics—in particular people latched on to the P. J. Harvey element [Harvey and Cave had had a relationship around this time]—and there was less character play in the songs.*

Yeah. Well, I wouldn't do that kind of earlier material now. Things did change, and I'm really pleased that they did. I think there's a dividing line there. A lot of people who liked my music prior to that change possibly didn't like it so much after. There's a more confessional element that I dabbled in on *Boatman's Call*, but over the next couple of records that dropped off, because it's kind of a dead-end street. I mean, to rely totally on what's happening in your life is not always the best food for songs, particularly when day after day life is pretty much the same.

What I felt really happy about with the last record [*Abattoir Blues / The Lyre of Orpheus*, 2004] was that it achieved a balance, in that I felt that wasn't writing anything that wasn't true to myself, but at the same time it was an artistic statement as opposed to a list of grievances.

» *Who would you say has influenced you most over the years?*

I'd have to say they aren't songwriters for the most part. There are a few poets— Ted Hughes, W. H. Auden, Robert Lowell, Philip Larkin, Thomas Hardy— and they've had a general influence on me. As for the lyric writers that I rate,

I'd say Bob Dylan, Leonard Cohen, Mark E. Smith, John Lee Hooker, early/mid-period Van Morrison, Shane MacGowan, people who I feel are really great with words.

» *You had a novel published [*And the Ass Saw the Angel, *1989] and have written film scripts [*The Proposition, *2005], including an unused script for* Gladiator II. *Is there any parity with what you do with lyrics and prose and scriptwriting?*
Only that I find other forms of writing far easier than lyrics. Lyric writing is really hard, the hardest thing that I do. It's really f***ing hard, and writing a script is really f***ing easy.

» *Some of the problems with lyric writing must come down to how traditional a route you want to take—whether to use rhyme, for instance.*
All the poets I'm really affected by use rhyme. I've never been able to get into a lot of American post-war poetry, which just sounds like endless ravings and witterings.

» *So you're not a Ginsberg fan?*
No, although he's probably better than some of the others. He uses more formal structure than some of those guys. The more it breaks down and the more those rules are thrown away, the less affecting it is for me. I'm not really interested in people's opinions or ideas—I'm certainly not interested in my own—rather the problem of putting what you want to say into some kind of formal structure.

» *How about having your lyrics printed on album sleeves, so people can read them as pieces in their own right? Not every songwriter is happy to do that, but you always have.*
It probably would've been better if I hadn't, perhaps. But there was a certain tradition, in the days of progressive music—and I grew up with that—where part of listening to music was poring over the lyrics, no matter how f***ing stupid they were. The cover and all its elements were an important part of the experience, and this is lost now. You don't even know song titles anymore.

» *Is there any influence of place on your writing?*
Your habits change from place to place and the influences of other people on you change. But I wasn't swapping countries for inspiration.

» And what about the religious element in your work?

I always found the idea of God interesting and mysterious, linked very strongly to my creative side, so it seemed something I could place in my work. But I probably wouldn't do it anymore.

» And you've always had a great line in swearing. It always sounds natural, not as if you're doing it to shock.

Yeah. Well, I'm pretty foulmouthed. I'm quite conscious of it, though. I mean, it just seems to work.

» There's a lot fear and violence in your lyrics, and characters who create fear around them. "Deep in the Woods" [The Bad Seed EP by the Birthday Party, 1983] is a case in point, where a woman is murdered and then you in character come out with the line "I took her from rags right through to stitches." Hilarious.

Well, I would of thought that most of that stuff was comic to begin with, and I hope it was seen that way. I guess it's the comic element that I'm most interested in, because it's the stuff that feels really good to write, though you can't always say it. It sits in your notebook for a while, and you kind of warm to it a bit and you slot it in. These things, the outrageously comic lines, are the ones I end up enjoying most.

» Like Leonard Cohen. Those who write him off as a bedsit miserabilist aren't hearing the humor. And it's always been there, even in the early stuff.

Yeah. Have you listened to any of those albums recently? They're so dark, particularly *Songs of Love and Hate*. But there's a humorous element, and I really like that record—but I wouldn't like all records to be like that. Such sustained cruelty. "*There's a funeral in the mirror / And it's stopping at your face.*" That's funny.

keith
reid

Interviewed by Tom Seabrook

Unusually for a non-performing, behind-the-scenes lyricist, Keith Reid is actually an integral member of a band. Along with pianist and vocalist Gary Brooker, Reid formed Procol Harum in 1967 as a vehicle for the duo's songs. The band's first recording was of a slice of abstract lyricism Reid titled "A Whiter Shade of Pale," which Brooker set to a tune loosely based on Bach's "Air on a G String" from the Suite No. 3 in D Major. It went on to become one of the most successful singles of all time. Other Reid/Brooker-penned Procol Harum hits include "Homburg," "Conquistador," and "Pandora's Box."

» *Do you want to write, or do you have to write?*

Definitely something I want to do, and chose to do. I don't have to do it. Although I don't think it's a bad thing when people have to write to earn a living. That's a very valid impetus for doing things. I write now because I really want to, and I need to. It's an outlet. If I didn't have this, I'd probably have a lot of frustration.

» *Do you have a set pattern for writing lyrics?*

I go through phases. I get inspired, or something happens—you hear something, read something, see something—and that triggers a response. And the response in my case is to put words down on paper. Whenever I get an idea I'll make some notes, but won't necessarily turn that straight into a song. But I'll accumulate ideas, and then if I feel like writing a song, I'll turn it into a song.

» *Do you ever force yourself to write, or do you wait for inspiration to come?*

I don't sweat it too much. I've come to realize that you go through periods: sometimes you go through a period of months where it seems like every day you get ideas, and it all feels very creative. And then you go through periods where nothing seems to spark your imagination. So now, I can go through a couple of months where nothing really happens, and it doesn't bother me. Because I know that something will happen, and it does. But having said that sometimes I will just go and put something down on paper, but generally I let it happen, because I know it will at some point.

There used to be a time when I'd rely on keeping an idea in my head for a while, but nowadays I can't remember them. Now I write them down. But it's a funny thing: I only write [ideas] down in pencil. Because it's only an idea. Then I let it germinate. I don't ink it in . . . I only ever type a song out when it's finished. I suppose it's a bit like with a painting; when you start it's just a sketch, and then as you think about it more, you color it in.

You discover the song as you write it. You get an idea, but there's no way of knowing what the whole song's going to be about. An idea develops, and then you discover in the writing of it what it is. You get surprised by the stuff that comes out. I see where it is, where it takes me. I don't have much of an idea.

» *Is there anything that you feel you shouldn't write about?*
No. I firmly believe that you have to try to be honest and truthful, and that's the only . . . You have to follow the internal logic to the end, so that there's a sense of truth. You have to be very truthful, whatever line you're pursuing. You might chose at the end of the day not to let something see the light of day, but while I'm working, there isn't anything I wouldn't write about.

» *Nothing that you wouldn't want put out into the public domain?*
Well . . . a few months before 9/11 I wrote a song called "American Ugly," and I really thought it was a good piece of writing. But then 9/11 happened, and I thought, *Bang goes that one*. It was just close to the bone. I was going to use it for a record, but you can't.

» *Not as close to the bone as something like "Bomb the Pentagon" by Primal Scream, for example.*
I don't know that song, and I don't know why they wrote that line. It depends whether they meant it. I wouldn't do anything if I didn't mean it, and I wouldn't write anything for effect. I would never write anything to be controversial.

» *But if you thought something "controversial," would you write about it?*
If I honestly felt it, and honestly meant it, I wouldn't back away from it. But at the end of the day, I might decide "this is insensitive" and put it in the drawer. With

"American Ugly," events overtook me. But I wouldn't write anything specifically to cause outrage.

» *Do you write with the singer that you're working with at the time in mind? When the rest of Procol Harum say, "We're going to do a new record," for instance, do you go back over what you're written in the meantime and see what's suitable, or do you start work on a new "Procol Harum project"?*

That's a good question. For the last record that we did, when we started saying we were going to do it, I really sat down and wrote songs for that record. I suppose I was writing for that record, but it isn't a particular style of writing. Procol Harum was formed as a band to do the songs Gary and I had written. So I think of them as my records—as me expressing myself.

» *So do you write differently if you write for other people?*

Yes, actually I probably do. When I'm working with another artist, I try to get into their head. Experience has told me that if I don't get into their head, then what I come up with isn't going to work for them. You try to find out what they're thinking and try to relate to them. So, in a way, when I'm writing songs for Procol Harum, I'm purely expressing myself. But when I write with and for other artists, I'm trying to see what they're feeling, and trying to add my take on that.

» *A lot of songwriters like the words to be attached to the music, as a single entity, but you published a book of your lyrics, so you must be fairly comfortable with the words on their own?*

I am actually. They always have to work on a piece of paper for me to pass them on and have them set to music. If they don't look good on paper, I throw them away.

» *How much importance do you attach to the title of a song?*

Here's the thing . . . for years and years, I never used to have a title. It always came last, which is why, with a lot of Procol Harum songs, the title is some kind of summation of what the song is about. It used to be the last thing. More recently, the title can be the first thing that comes along. It's been there at the beginning, it's been there at the end. I don't have any rules.

» *How about the first line? Is it important to start with a bang?*

I never used to give it any thought. The first time I ever gave that any thought was a few years ago when I read an interview with George Michael, where he said that his first couple of lines have to have a lot of impact. That never occurred to me, because I try to make every line important. But I know that people do.

» *Do you think about rhyme and rhythmic patterns as you write?*

You have to have a rhythmic pattern—that's why you're writing songs and not something else. Rhyme is very important. There's always some sort of rhyming scheme. It can be odd—there's a Procol Harum song called "A Salty Dog" [from *A Salty Dog*, 1969] where I had the idea of writing something circular. But there's always a pattern, and that's very important to me.

» *Which of your lyrics are you most proud of?*

That's difficult. But I remember thinking that some of the lyrics to "Grand Hotel" [from *Grand Hotel*, 1973] were pretty damn clever. I did some rhyming there that I wasn't trying to do, so which wasn't contrived. There's a couplet—"*Dover sole, and oeufs mornay / Profiteroles and peach flambé*"—that I thought was pretty good! I didn't work on it—it just came out. And I thought, to blow my own trumpet, *That's as clever as Noel Coward!* There's also "A Salty Dog," which I think is the most direct piece of writing I've written. I don't believe I could be more self-revealing. That's as direct and as honest as I think it's possible to be.

» *That goes back to what we saying about writing with other people in mind.*

I've never censored myself. Gary was very good. If I gave him something, and he could set it to music, he'd sing it. He didn't seem to mind, and I suppose in a way we were a band, so it was valid for him to sing my lyrics. But I've certainly found, writing with other people, that they may not want to sing what I'm thinking—they may feel uncomfortable because it doesn't reflect where they're coming from.

» *What other songwriters do you admire? Who did you look to when you first started?*

When I started to write I emulated Bob Dylan. He was my inspiration. I wanted to write like him, definitely. After a while I started to find my own voice. There are other writers that I've admired—Randy Newman, Joni Mitchell—but I didn't emulate them, because they were my contemporaries. Any great work is inspiring—music, painting—but Bob Dylan was the only songwriter who inspired me to the point of emulation.

» Brian Eno has said that the hardest thing in modern music is to write a great lyric. Do you agree?
Yeah, I think so. As a lyricist, I find that when I write with other musicians, they have tracks coming out of theirs ears. It's much easier to write music, particularly nowadays with computers, than to write words. You can get away with crap lyrics if you have a good beat! But, saying that, a great piece of music is also very hard to write.

» Are there any terrible lyrical clichés that you try to steer clear of?
There actually aren't, because you can always subvert them. That's something that I've done. There is no cliché that you cannot subvert. You can even have fun with "moon" and "June," the greatest cliché of all time. You can take the greatest cliché, and then the next two lines can be something brilliant. Clichés are there to be exploited, that's my advice to a songwriter! There's nothing that you can't use to your advantage.

» Are lyrics these days less important than they used to be?
Yes and no. If you're a student of music, and you look at the golden age of classic songwriting, it seems that now people can get away with a lot more. There is nothing that can't be a hit song now. You can repeat the same phrase over a loop—you can write three words, and that'll be it, which I guess you couldn't do, in the 1930s, before computers. Even going back to the golden age of song, people got away with some rubbish, but now, at the touch of a button, you can make a sound than sounds impressive. You can get away with more.

aimee
mann

Interviewed by David Simons

As the bass-playing singer/songwriter for Boston's 'Til Tuesday, Aimee Mann
had a hit with her very first try, *Voices Carry*, in 1985. Her solo albums include
Whatever, I'm with Stupid, Bachelor No. 2, and *The Forgotten Arm*. Nine of her
songs were used in the soundtrack to the 1999 film *Magnolia*.

*» What's an example of a lyric you've altered to fit the meaning of the song, but
maybe kept the initial premise?*
For the opening line to "Red Vines," [*Bachelor No. 2*] instead of, "*They're all
still on their honeymoon / Just read the dialogue balloon*," I'd originally written,
"*They're all still on their honeymoon / It's Underdog Day Afternoon*." [*laughs*] Which
I thought was a bit much, although for a while there I was going to call the record
Underdog Day.

A while back I was reading this Fiona Apple interview and she was talking
about making poetry by cutting out headlines from newspapers. So I thought,
That sounds like fun. So I tried that, and I wound up with a couple of the lines
for "Calling It Quits" [*Bachelor No. 2*, 2000] that way. I kept working at it like
that, and writing stuff down at the same time, until it took a shape that meant
something to me. Then I just went back and threw out all the other stuff that was
just wordplay.

*» You've had quite an assortment of cowriters over the years. "That's Just What You
Are," for instance, was a song Jon Brion had started, then you came in and wrote the
bridge and finished it off. Is that your favorite way to collaborate?*
A lot of times Jon would do that—just hand me a little chord progression and
some words and melody, or some kernel of an idea. And I just always found his
music very inspiring, so it was very easy for me to make a whole song out of
that. "Amateur" [*I'm with Stupid*] was like that as well—a lot of it was already
there, I just had bring it to the end. The other thing about Jon is that he would
always tell me right away what the concept of the lyric was—and I'd always know

immediately what he was talking about. Like with "That's Just What You Are," he's referring to someone who's always acting like a jackass and won't do anything about it; you know, *That's just how I am, and I can't change*, that sort of thing. I could relate to that!

» *So, coming into it like that, where you've already got the road map, seems like the most preferable way to go.*
Yeah, and it's definitely a lot more fun. Because there's already something there for you to follow.

» *What about writing with Elvis Costello? Same thing?*
It's actually just the opposite with me and Elvis—that's a case where I'll have to come up with the initial framework. Like on "The Fall of the World's Own Optimist" [*Bachelor No. 2*], I had, like, a verse and a chorus, but I couldn't come up with any words for the verses. So then he came along and wrote this whole B-section to the chorus, which was really great—it takes the song in this whole other direction. And then he added in the verse lyrics, which I then had to tailor to get back to the original topic.

» *It sounds very similar to the way he worked with McCartney.*
Yeah, I'll bet it was. Because that seems to be a very effective method for him.

» *Your husband, Michael Penn, has helped out instrumentally on your various efforts, and yet there are no Mann/Penn songwriting credits.*
We don't really collaborate, mostly because we both like to work in the same style. Also, Michael has a harmonic sensibility that's totally different from mine. He just goes to chord changes that are kind of foreign to me, even though it doesn't sound foreign when you're listening. Still, it's hard when you're writing with someone, and he's going to this chord change and you're thinking, *Wow, I would never go there*. But of course he can get away with it on his own, because he's got the melodic ideas and the arrangements already in his head—he knows exactly where it's going once it's time to record.

» *Do you two at least sit down and exchange ideas?*
Every now and then there'll be a song that he's working on that'll be close enough

to my style of writing, that I'll come in and say, "Look, why don't you try this chord progression," or, "Why don't you do this thing in the middle." And he'll give me advice as well—particularly if I'm stuck, I might ask him what he thinks, and he'll come up with some chord that I hadn't thought of. But in general, I don't think we really click as writers.

» *One thing you and Michael have in common is the ability to come up with really inventive lyric ideas. "I swore you off, but you climbed back on," for instance, from "Long Shot"—some people would labor over a line like that for weeks. Did you?*
It depends on how bad my writer's block is [*laughs*]. I find that by jotting down ideas in a notebook—which I'll occasionally do when I want to get into the writing process—really helps, it's the kind of thing I should probably utilize more than I actually do. For me, it's usually just a matter of writing down topics, rather than individual phrases. But something like that can really jump-start the creative process—especially when you don't feel like writing at all.

» *In "It's Not Safe," you wrote about an "idiot who keeps believing in luck." Was that you?*
In this business, people often say one thing and do another. And for a long time I guess I did believe—until I finally reached the point where I stopped believing and just got out. I'm now satisfied that I can't do anything to make it better, I just equate it with anybody who's ever had to get out of a bad relationship. Believe in luck? Sure, you can be like Annie, you know, the sun will come out tomorrow, but that's crazy. I'd rather be perky and optimistic on my own behalf—and whatever happens, happens.

david crosby

Interviewed by Sid Griffin

As a founder member of the Byrds, and a constant around which various permutations of Graham Nash, Neil Young, and Steven Stills haved formed, David Crosby is one of rock's key figures. His songwriting fuses folk, pop, jazz, and Indian influences, with his lyrics encompassing the personal and social in equal measure.

» *Do you have a particular routine to get into when you know you want to sit down to write lyrics?*

No, but that's an interesting item there. I have always wished I could write the way Bob Dylan writes where he gets up in the morning and starts writing on his typewriter and here come the lyrics. He's done this his whole life and I have never been able to do this and wish I was able to.

What I have found is that very often when I am going to sleep there is the period where the verbal crystallization level which is talking to you right now starts to slow down and go to sleep and another level which is more like an imaginative, intuitive level that is capable of making longer leaps of connection . . . that level gets a shot at the steering wheel for a minute and I will be almost asleep and suddenly words will start to come and I will have to wake up, turn on the light and start to madly scribble on something next to me.

And I remember asking a science fiction author that I love, William Gibson, if he had ever experienced that, and he said, "Yeah, all writers know this . . . we call it *The Elves Take Over the Workshop*, and that's why all good writers have a pad and pen next to their bed." I didn't know that. Yet sometimes the entire song will come out in one blurb: words, music, title, and it definitely happens to me. Sometimes it is just the words and if I don't have a musical inclination with it I will call James [his son James Raymond, the R in CPR] or Nash or one of other people I write with. Mostly James, these days. We work together quite a bit on all the CPR music. The result has been a bunch of good music, some of the best I have ever written.

» *Paul Simon is notorious for rewriting and rewriting his lyrics to get them perfect. Other writers largely stick with what they were inspired to write the first time. Where do you stand on this?*

I do much more than I did when I started. When I started, I would just scribble it down and that was it, that was pretty much it. Then sometimes, you know, somebody would suggest something which would improve it, Nash in particular here; but generally I used to go with what I got start off the bat.

Then, when I started using a computer, all of a sudden I found I was a much better editor of my own work because I could take this out, put it up here, take that out, put it down there, move that up to here as the facility a computer gives you to work with your lyrics is tremendous. I did a whole lot more editing, polishing, experimenting and crafting after I started putting down my lyrics on computer.

» *How old were you when you started writing songs? Were you playing the coffee houses back in LA?*

Yes, I started writing when I was maybe 19 or 20 years old, something like that. The first song I ever wrote was called, I think, "Across the Plains," and it was not very good. I'm glad my early efforts happened but . . . the first song I ever wrote which was a decent song was probably "Everybody's Been Burned" which The Byrds did [*Younger Than Yesterday*, 1967].

» *What about "I See You" by the Byrds? You're not keen on some of your other earlier songs?*

Nah, I think "Everybody's Been Burned" was probably the first really good one. It was kind of a torch ballad but it was jazzy and you could do a lot of things with it.

» *Which of your lyrics are you most proud of and why?*

Hmmm, this is a tough question. You know, I like the lyrics to "Wooden Ships" quite a bit, I like the lyrics to "Guinnevere" [*Crosby, Stills, and Nash*, 1969] quite a bit, I like the lyrics to "Déjà Vu" [Crosby, Stills, Nash, and Young's *Déjà Vu*, 1970], but probably the ones I really like would be later ones from CPR: say "Somehow She Knew" [*CPR*, 1998]. "In My Dreams" [*CSN*, 1977] is one of my best sets of lyrics. "Dream for Him" [CSNY's *Looking Forward*, 1999] is good; I think "At the Edge" [*CPR*, 1998] is probably one of my very best sets of words. You have to read that last one; I just think they are really good words, and the same for "Angel Dream" [*Just Like Gravity*, 2001]. I think "Angel Dream" is one of my very, very best sets of words.

» When writing a lyric sometimes you are telling a story and sometimes you clearly have a message you want to get across. What is the difference between the two?
The difference is, I feel the "telling the tale" songs have served me better. I wish that when I had a message to deliver I could be more circumspect and do it in a story form. I think that generally is more effective. You look at some of the story ones and they seem to do the job better, like "Monkey and the Underdog" [*Just Like Gravity*] and when I just talk directly to you sometimes it is just not as effective. Let me put it this way: I wish I could write more story songs. Like "Cowboy Movie" [*If I Could Only Remember My Name*, 1971].

» Do you find certain themes or interests in songwriting that you feel comfortable returning to?
I find with great regularity I wind up talking about dreams. I am not sure how this happens, but they seem to loom very large in my lexicon of subject matter. To put it in a broader scope, I write mostly about love. I write about love found, love lost, love explored, love unrequited, love treasured . . . that's really what I write about most.

» One theme of yours I like is the sea and sailing.
That's quite natural. They say "write from what you know," and obviously it has been a huge part of my life. The sea and sailing are just fantastic metaphors for situations in real life. I've sailed since I was 11 so that means I have been sailing for 53 years!

» At what stage in the songwriting process do your lyrics form? Are you a title first guy like Pete Townshend usually is or does it take a guitar riff first or what?
There is no set way with me. It happens every which way. Very often for me it is the words first as they are the hardest part but many times it has been words and music at the same time and a few times it has been music first. And some of those latter times it has been music I have developed over years, literally years.

There are a number of cases where I have had a theme where I have played it on the guitar a very long time before it finally gels into a song. There then is obviously cowriting. I love to cowrite with other writers because you spark each other, and you wind up going someplace you would not have gone. Look at "Yvette in English," [*Thousand Roads*, 1993] which I wrote with Joni [Mitchell], a song which definitely came out a way I would never have had it go . . . look at "Hero" [*Thousand Roads*] with Phil Collins or all of the stuff I have written with James. I really love writing with somebody else, it is probably my most favorite way.

» *Are you like Dylan in the lyrics are most important or are you, with your unusual guitar tunings and sophisticated harmonies, more of a melody man when writing songs?*

That's a tough question. It varies from song to song. Some songs the lyrics are definitely more important. You get a song like "They Want It All" [*Crosby and Nash*, 2005], the whole thing is in the story I am telling you about Enron, as the music doesn't really matter at all other than as a canvas to paint on. In general, though, the music is so important in being the context, which allows you to deliver the words and deliver the emotion and the emotional context the words need. Although I think it is harder to write memorable words than it is to write memorable music. Good, memorable lyrics anyway.

» *Is there any way you know you can find inspiration or it is waiting for the moment when it comes to you?*

Other people can just do it. The only thing I can do is make a space for it. Pick up an instrument . . . I keep a couple of guitars right next to my bed, I am looking at 'em right now, and I play them to sort of tickle the old muse button and see if there happens to be a muse flying by. So at least you are making a space for it to happen. I have always wished I could write on demand. [*Adopts silly voice*] "Hey, write a song about the Eiffel Tower!" [*Sings in music hall voice*] "It's big and built in a hole and it's tall and it's GREEAAATTTT!" I can't, though. I have never been able to write songs on demand.

» *Are there popular music clichéd images or themes you try and avoid yourself? You know, references or metaphors you cringe from when you hear them?*

I try not to think about that. Because it will cripple you as a writer from going for the very heart or throat of something good or bad when you want all your emotional avenues open. You shouldn't say, "Gee, Paul Simon already used that image." I don't want to think like that, I want to go to the heart of the thing I am trying to communicate and not worry about someone saying there has already been a tune with horses in a rainstorm in it. I don't really care. Because all of this has been said before and all of it has been played before. The best melody I ever came up with no doubt some poor South American peasant with a flute played 4,000 years ago. There is no really new stuff, so why worry? Go for the heart of the thing anyway and don't worry about anybody else having used it.

» *You are unique as a songwriter with your use of modal tunings, science-fiction images, sophisticated church and jazz harmonies, your shying away from repeating a big anthemic chorus every verse . . . has this uniqueness helped or hurt you?*
Good question! In general, I think it helps to have a willingness to push the envelope and try to do new things. It generally helps you, though every once in a while you can get a little far out and you shock the people around you. I remember when I was in the Byrds and I did "Mind Gardens" [*Younger Than Yesterday*] and the people around me thought I had surely skipped a beat and were sure I was gonna go completely bonkers any second. That was pretty strange. But I liked it. And I liked the fact it did two or three brand new things that other people weren't doing. Same for "Critical Mass" or some songs on my first solo album, *If I Could Only Remember My Name*, like "Tamalpais High (at About Three)" or "Song with No Words (Tree with No Leaves)."

» *In terms of the business and the music industry, do you feel you get respect from your fellow writers?*
Fellow writers respect, yes. The industry's respect, no. What the music industry wants is a clone of whatever is top of the charts. The last thing they want is innovation, they couldn't give a f*** less about that because they are like a school of fish in that they are all following each other, and they don't want to do something new. It scares them; anything new totally befuddles them and scares them. That is the music industry. They are absolutely not okay with art or trying to do new art; it has nothing to do with what they want to do.

My peers, on the other hand, yes. People will come up to me and say, "Man, that one tune such-and-such . . . how did you do *that*?" So I tell them what it was I did or played to get the song as they heard it. The strange guitar tunings helped me out a tremendous bit here. I learned a tremendous amount from Joni and a tremendous amount from Michael Hedges. I think Michael Hedges just about split my skull open when I heard him. Also a Bulgarian folk music LP from the 1950s, that really had a huge influence on me. I heard that when I was in the Byrds. I got turned onto that and Ravi Shankar—bang, bang, right in a row—and that screwed with my mind a great deal.

» *When you are writing a song, how important is the title to you? You've had some offbeat titles to your tunes.*
Yeah, "Tamalpais High (at About 3)" is one. Just the album title *If I Could Only Remember My Name* is one. I was told that was too long a title. I don't think titles are too important, I think the content is the deal, though sure, I have fun with titles just like other writers do.

» *How important is the first line of a song in drawing the listener in?*
Oh, crucial. The first couple of lines are the entry point for the journey you want to take the listeners on; this is where you get them to step on the train in the first place. They are crucial.

» *Would you spend more time on the opening of a song just to get them on the train?*
Not usually. The opening lines of the song are frequently the first piece of inspiration that comes to the writer, and they usually come pretty fast. The place where it takes more honing and crafting is later on in the song when the writer is trying to sustain that level of inspiration and craft which flowed so effortlessly at the top of the song. You have to have a sensible journey to the song with a beginning, middle and an end. The ends of songs are very critical too.

» *How do you feel about rhyming? Some of your songs scan very well as poetry, and some are free verse.*
"Mind Gardens" certainly didn't rhyme! I like rhyming and generally my songs rhyme but sometimes I toss it to the winds and don't bother.

» *When you do rhyme, do you stay with it until you feel your rhymes are perfect?*
Nothing's perfect. Rhyming is a sub-artform in itself, a really strong part of great songwriting. It is fun to be clever with it and fun to do it. What I really like is making the rhyme happen before the end of the line. Do two lines which scan

out, the second line rhymes and ends then there would be a tag and end of two or four or six more words after that. I like that. Then there is internal rhyming within the line of the song.

Now, many times I will do as in the song "Games" [*Graham Nash/David Crosby*, 1972]. The word "more" rhymes with the word "war" at the end of a line, and then I sing "*don't you know that*," which is just a tag after the line of the song. And I like doing that.

» *When you are writing songs are there traps to avoid which you have fallen into before?*
Yes. Yes. And I think probably the biggest one for me is preaching. Sort of pontificating. I don't like it when I catch myself doing it. It drives me bats. What I want to do is tell you a little story that has the truth which I am trying to get across buried in it, but sometimes I am so pissed off I talk right to you. And that would be "They Want It All" [*Crosby and Nash*, 2004] or that kind of a song. Which is, you know, less sophisticated and is kind of a punch in the jaw; but sometimes that is how you feel.

» *Can the popular song lyric deal with any particular subject?*
Yes. There are absolutely no rules.

» *Have you tried to push the envelope out here as well?*
Yeah, I mean as I said I mostly write about love, but you can write about anything. "Just Like Gravity" [CPR, 2001] is a good example. It is literally a song about gravity. Literally, seriously, about gravity. It is not about something else.

» *Which other songwriters do you admire today?*
Let me give you a list. Joni Mitchell. Bob Dylan. Randy Newman, Jackson Browne, Neil Young, Graham Nash, Bonnie Raitt, Nickel Creek, James Taylor. Michael Hedges's songs on *Watching My Life Go By* stunned me, they were such beautiful songs . . . and Shawn Colvin almost above everybody except Joni. Shawn Colvin just knocks my dick in the dirt. She is a brilliant writer, and I wish to God I was as good as her.

andy
partridge

Interviewed by Todd Bernhardt

XTC first came to attention as part of the British new wave of the late 1970s. Their meandering, interrupted career hasn't bought great wealth or fame. It has, though, produced much fine pop music, the lion's share of it written by the band's guitarist and singer Andy Partridge—a man usually characterized as an English eccentric in the Ray Davies mold.

» *Your lyrics give the impression of being highly crafted, and work on several different levels. How much of this is intentional, and how much is "happy accident"?*
Lyrically, I love word games. I love them in literature, in poetry, and in song lyrics. I love the fact that the same bunch of words can mean so many different things, through a different inflection, or another way of looking at it. I never look at anything straight-on—I also look at it from the back, then from above, then from underneath, then I want to slice it open and see what's inside.

That said, I don't think there are "happy accidents" with the lyrics, because I sweat blood to get them! They are by far the toughest things to feel happy about. The music is a lot easier. I'm constantly wrestling with my "editor." I never had an editor at one time, but I've grown one over the years, and he's become too important. I have to find ways of killing him off, or putting him to sleep until I need him.

» *Are there any tricks you've come up with?*
It's tough, because the older he gets, the more ornery he gets, and the more aware he is of ploys to put him to sleep. It's really useful having an editor, because it's great for shaping up raw material, but I find the editor's getting so strong, he's not letting raw material be born.

To make raw material, you have to be a bit stupid and have no restrictions, so you can grab anything and use it. The "idiot creative you" might say, "If I stick this together, that could make one of those!" But the editor says, "You're never going to use that piece, put it down."

» Or, "You or other people have said this before"?

Oh, that's the hat he wears: *You've done this before. You've said this before.* That's the death of inspiration. I *hate* the idea of repeating myself.

» Do you remember writing your first song, and, if so, what was it?

I do. I must have been about 14, and it was truly awful. It was called "Please Help Me," and was obviously a cry from my anguished teenaged soul. It went something like [*in whiny teenage voice*], "*Please help me / I'm drowning in a sea / Please help me.*" Something like that is the first mark you make in the exercise book of life. You know you're going to go wrong, that it's going to be surpassed immediately, so it's best to get it out of the way. It was my —is it called meconium? You know, baby's first turd? My musical meconium [*laughs*].

» Lyrics or music first? Is there a pattern?

No, there is no pattern. Sometimes I mess around with chords, and they suggest something, like the sea, or clouds, or a box—anything. I'm a bit synesthetic when it comes to that—I can hear sounds, and think, "That's just like fog, or a wet day in November." Often, the lyrics come because I'm trying to explain the synesthetic nature of chords –the picture that they're painting.

"Easter Theatre" [*Apple Venus Volume 1*, 1999] was like that. Very brown, muddy, ascending chords that made me think, "This sounds like something pushing up through the ground –like new buds, ooh, it's Easter." And before I knew it, I'd vomited up the reason for a song.

The tone of an instrument also can suggest things, like on "Chalkhills and Children." [*Oranges and Lemons*, 1989]. There's the little melodic figure at the beginning, which I thought sounded medieval and earthy, combined with placid, droning high keyboard chords, which sound like you're floating—so it suggested floating over a land. The lyric came out of my efforts to mentally grasp what this piece of music was about.

Sometimes it's the other way around. I'll write a poem or a piece of prose, and then think, "Gosh, that wouldn't make a bad song." "Summer's Cauldron" [*Skylarking*, 1986] was like that. So is a song that's coming out on my latest *Fuzzy Warbles* disc, "2 Rainbeau Melt." It started as a poem, then I improvised music around the poem. But it's rarer, doing it that way.

» *Except for a very few songs, such as "Your Dictionary" from* Apple Venus Volume 1, *you don't seem to be a confessional lyric writer. Is this intentional?*

I think I am confessional, but I dress up in masks. When I say "she" or "he" or "those," I probably mean me. When I say "them," I might mean me and her, or when I say "you," I might even mean me! You play all the characters in the little production yourself, and you supply their voices, but so it doesn't look wrong, you give them masks of other people. Because you've got a mask on, you can be more truthful.

» *Does this enable you to learn things about yourself that you might not otherwise have known? For example, if you look at the lyrics on* Nonsuch, *it's interesting that that it was recorded before your divorce.*

I know—it's *impending*. I do that quite a lot. I like looking back at lyrics where I can go, *Oh, my goodness, look what you've said! You didn't realize it at the time.* I recently wrote something called "I Gave My Suitcase Away." Although I wrote it intending it to be for someone else—a woman who wanted songs on the subject of coming back to live in England and not going away again—I realized a few weeks later that it's *totally* my sentiment. It's good to surprise yourself.

» *Does your writing change when you write for someone else?*

Yeah, because you're freer. You can grab any old rubbish, thinking, "I haven't got to sing this!" It's a way to discover stuff you might not look at for yourself—I suppose it's another way of fooling the editor. You might come away with something really good, and really truthful, about yourself and your opinions.

» *Who would you say were your biggest influences lyrically?*

Probably Ray Davies, and Lennon and McCartney. They're the top three. Ray Davies just because—I mean, look at the lyrics to "Autumn Almanac," one of my favorite ever songs. It's this weird, disjointed look at English life through one of those lenses that shatters it up into lots of little pictures. I love the woodiness of it, and the creakiness of it, dusty and dank—much like England.

» *He and you, actually, are often cited as deliberately English lyricists.*

I don't try to be English. I guess because I am, it comes out English. But I don't sit down and think [*affects terrible Dick Van Dyke–style English accent*] "Cor blimey, can I put a Union Jack and a beefeater's outfit on, Mary?"

» *But it sounds like it's not anything you've ever run away from, while some people, who might have been reaching for wider acceptance, might have said, "Maybe I shouldn't use this word because people in the USA or Japan might not know what it means."*

No, I think it's important to be who you are. That's the strongest asset you can have.

» *How do you feel about rhyming? Is that important to you?*

I think lyrics are best when they have an internal tempo, and little internal rhymes. I always try to create a push/pull tension with internal rhymes. Not necessarily at the end—you might put a lazy or fake red-herring type rhyme at the end, but all the tension is internal. It's quite a ballet, if you get it right.

I love the old Hollywood *Wizard of Oz* thing, where they bend things to fit, fantastically, clumsily. I find that really exciting. "*What if it was an elephant? I'd wrap him up in cellophant! What if it was a rhinoceros? Imposseros!*" [*laughing*] It's not even a real word, but you know what he's going for. I like bending the English language until it screams.

» *So, Broadway musicals and things like that also influenced you?*

Oh yeah. As a kid, there were two good things on the radio. There were show songs, or novelty songs—Spike Jones, or stuff like the Playmates' "Beep Beep," or "The Mole in the Hole" by the Southlanders, or "Big John" [by Jimmy Dean, 1961]—anything with sped-up voices, too much reverb, weird sound effects. That's what I was bombarded with until Beatles songs started creeping on to the radio.

» *Is anything off-limits for you, lyrically?*

Well, I like sex. Everyone in the world likes sex! So why are there no songs that talk directly about sex? The ones that do are just laughably awful. "I want to sex you up" is pretty banal. I wish I could write about sex in a direct way. I do write about sex a lot, but it's so heavily metaphorized that you might not know what the hell I was talking about.

» Are there clichéd images or themes that you think are particularly horrible?
"Baby." If I use "baby"—which I don't think I have at all—it would have to be very ironic. I also don't use the word "guy," so if that goes into a song, it's probably for a certain effect. I don't mind "Old Englishisms" though, because I actually use them occasionally.

» Do you think that you have, lyrically, a "voice"? Is there such a thing as an Andy Partridge lyric, or do you try to avoid that?
That's an odd one, because I still don't know what it is! I like to think I might be achieving it, but maybe that's a little pomposity, because I'm dealing with the English language and a finite amount of words, and it's probably been said so much better by people like Shakespeare, Arthur Miller, Kurt Vonnegut, and other greats.

I do like the idea that with most of my lyrics –not all of them –you could sit and read them, and they'd feel good as a spoken thing. That's important to me. I want the lyric to be able to be stripped away from anything that is interdependent with it, and still work. Like a really nice watch—if you took the watch apart, each piece would still be beautifully made.

paul
buchanan
Interviewed by David Sheppard

The Blue Nile are the thinking fan's cult group. By delivering just four albums of poised electro white soul in more than 20 years, the band have created a mystique around themselves. At their heart is singer/songwriter Paul Buchanan, whose evocative impressions of the strangeness and beauty of ordinary things account for much of the band's enduring appeal.

» *You are obviously concerned with imagery. But are there any clichéd images or themes that make you cringe when you hear them in other people's writing, or traps you try to avoid when writing lyrics?*

I never cringe at other people's lyrics. Clichéd images and themes are one thing, but I hope that I hear the lyrics with the correct intent, so if something is throwaway, I accept it as such. I really cannot think of one howler that sticks in my craw. I truly don't think like that.

A popular song lyric can be about anything—I think they are. There are obvious traps with songwriting—I don't feel a rhyme has to be perfect, for example. It's more important to avoid self-parody and just being contrived in any way.

» *How old were you when you wrote your first song, and why did you write it?*

I was about 15 when I wrote my first song, in my room, sitting on the edge of the bed after the dishes were done. For a while songwriting meant simply rearranging the chords from whichever song I had just learned and making up a new song from there. There was no one thing that inspired me to write songs, it was more a case of "them" not "it." I probably only realized that I had some facility for songwriting about the time I lost it!

Songwriting has never really been a diary for me, more a kind of memory. I do look back over the songs and recognize the narrator—though I think that's more to do with us [the Blue Nile] being stringent about the tone of voice we used in recording the vocals. Certain themes, situations and motifs do recur in my songs, however: conversations between men and women; the city; buildings; lights; nighttime and daytime; hope; the countryside outside the city . . . I think they're just my favorite ideas, though I wonder increasingly about their legitimacy.

» Do you have a routine for writing lyrics?

I don't really have a routine for songwriting at all. I write too many things down. Inevitably, the best ones chose their moments and are simple. I do redraft and revise things, but only a little.

The Blue Nile albums always take a while to make, but some songs are written quickly, often in one sitting. In fact, there are quite a few that were written like that. "Because of Toledo," or "The Days of Our Lives" are two from the last album [High], but I can think of a few others. Often, I write 80 percent of the song in one go and enjoy doing the rest later; sometimes I write a verse or so too much.

I've read what Tom Waits once wrote about songwriting being like trying to carry water in your hands and I'm aware of this idea that songs preexist on some metaphysical plain and songwriters are merely the conduits through which the muse flows. I do sort of believe in it. It seems too grand to lay claim to songs as an abstract currency in my own case, but I can assure you my job has been mainly staying out the way if something passable occurs.

» At what stage in the songwriting process does the lyric form?

For me, the various elements of a song form at approximately the same time. The lyrics, the chords and melody and most importantly the rhythm of the phrasing, those things have to be working in unison for me for it to be a song.

» How important do you think lyrics are in songwriting?

Lyrics will always have a considerable primacy on one level for me, but then I'm very vain! Lyrics aren't always the main thing. Obviously, for Bob Dylan and his ilk, the words are pretty central—I guess in some hip hop too. But in a lot of pop music lyrics aren't really that important at all.

I don't think a good lyric outweighs the music that frames it. There must be synergy between words and music. I actually think phrasing, as it varies from singer to singer, is crucial to how a song works. Sometimes, of course, the words must take precedence. Even the sound of the words or the way you can make them feel with your voice might be more important than the melody in a particular part of the song. I like it to be cumulative. Words and music should serve each other.

Is a great lyric the combination of the personal and the universal? Perhaps, though I think forthrightness is the real key. A wonderful line is *"What's it all about, Alfie?"* I'm throwing that in. The next line is also a winner: *"Is it just for the moment we live?"* [from Burt Bacharach and Hal David's "Alfie"]. I like the line *"All the stars that never were / Are parking cars and pumping gas"* [from Bacharach and David's "Do You Know the Way to San Jose"]—it's just good, isn't it? I like to draw out observations of everyday life. Mind you, I will never express a fraction of what I see every time I go out for a walk. I suppose I do file images away then and re-evoke them later in songs. My efforts are so trivial I won't expound further!

I don't think it's the writer's job to stand outside life and merely observe it. The standing to one side bit I'm really not sure of: perhaps it's part of the process but I'm not convinced that it's a good thing. I think that inhibits the writer's ability to empathize with and express to his fellow citizen. Maybe he's just projecting his own illusions onto people? As a writer, I'm really not trying to alienate or misinterpret anyone. I want to be popular for God's sake!

I am influenced by lyricists and authors—too many to go into detail, really. Honestly, everybody and everything is an influence. People I hear on the subway; a letter from the eighteenth century; the lettering on an old book; anything . . .

» *How much importance do you attach to a title?*

Song titles are important, but they're not always obvious from the start. "Tinseltown in the Rain" [from *A Walk Across the Rooftops*] was just a line in a song I'd written. It was Robert [Bell, Blue Nile keyboardist] who saw it as a title. It's emphatic. I think first lines in songs are more important—I think good songs tend to have good first lines; it's not a very encouraging place to be stumbling.

» *Which of your lyrics are you most proud of?*

A favorite lyric of mine would be this, from "Easter Parade" [*A Walk Across the Rooftops*]:

In the bureau, typewriters quiet
Confetti falls from every window
Throwing hats up in the air,
A city perfect in every detail
Easter Parade.

I like the shape; I like the stillness that song was trying to evoke.

rodney
crowell

Interviewed by David Simons

Rodney Crowell spent the 1980s writing hits for the likes of the Oak Ridge Boys, Willie Nelson, and ex-wife Rosanne Cash, while waiting patiently for his own solo career to take flight. That finally happened in 1988, when Crowell scored an unprecedented five straight #1 country hits, culled from his breakthrough release, *Diamonds and Dirt*. Crowell continues to write stark, conversational, largely autobiographical songs of a kind that Nashville has long since abandoned.

» *Country music has a story-telling and narrative tradition, but many of your songs contain lyrics that are very personal and autobiographical, particularly the material from* The Houston Kid *(2001) onward.*

Everyone's always telling you, "Write what you know." For me, there's this poignant vividness about that early part of my life. With *The Houston Kid*, I just felt like I'd found a thread that had meaning—the perspective of the kid who's grown up and starts to take stock.

» *Do you consider how those types of song will come across on stage while you're putting them together?*

Well there's no doubt that these songs really lend themselves to live solo performance –on the record, they're very dry and immediate. And the storytelling aspect is definitely something that you want to present stripped-down and austere—very much like Springsteen's *Nebraska*.

» *Though most of the material on* The Houston Kid *seems directly autobiographical, you also tell other people's stories, for instance in a song like "Highway 17," about a father's criminal actions and his effect on his young children.*

I think it's important to be able to take artistic liberties on occasion. Yet growing up I was surrounded by that kind of behavior; it was just part of the lay of the land. I certainly never went to prison, but I knew plenty of kids who did. So I'd just grafted their experience into my own.

» Though you've often worked with collaborators, you seem to avoid the writing-by-appointment style that's so prevalent in Nashville.

From time to time I've taken my chances and made a few songwriting appointments, but by and large they just don't work for me, because I don't really enjoy it. Whereas when I'm collaborating with a guy like Will Jennings, it's completely different. Will's an artist in the sense that he's a student first and foremost, he's very literate, and funny as well.

» The same seems to hold true for another of your writing partners, Guy Clark.

Guy and I often get together and just sit around telling jokes, and if you can laugh with someone for the first 10 or 15 minutes before you start writing, then it really isn't like work.

» For a lot of people, the sign of a great lyric is its ability to express a whole range of emotions.

"Stuff That Works," which I wrote with Guy, is like that. It works on so many different levels. On the one hand there are lines in there that are heartfelt serious: *"Stuff you feel, stuff that's real."* But then we were coming up with things like, *"I've got a new used car that runs just like a top,"* and we were laughing over that.

» I imagine that a good collaborator can act as "editor" as the storyline evolves.

And that was really the case with that particular song. After we'd started it, Guy went home and I began putting together this whole laundry list of "stuff that works," just hundreds of things. And the next day Guy comes back and he starts going through this massive list of items, and he's like, "Nope . . . nope . . . not that one . . . I don't think so . . . forget it . . ." And he was able to whittle it down to the essentials.

» The stuff that worked!

Right. You see, with Guy, there's so much gravity . . . if there's such a thing as a "songwriter's songwriter"—and I've been called that on occasion—but for me, Guy's the one. He can just get all the shit out of the way and just distil it right down to the plop! [*laughs*] I always felt that way about Dylan, or Townes Van Zandt, and Springsteen as well. Those are the kinds of writers whose subject matter holds up under any circumstances—those words just speak for themselves.

» A lot of songwriters, particularly in Nashville, tailor their subject matter to a specific individual.

I could work like that if I had to, but I really don't write that way. A lot of people write from the point of view of another person; their mindset is to simply provide material for a recording artist. Whereas I just don't think of myself as being outside of the song. The thing I've found is that when I successfully write for myself, it works for anybody.

» Do words or ideas pop into your head spontaneously, or do you have to be in "writing mode"?

You never know when a great idea is going to hit. This one particular time I was coming into LA from the airport, and I was in the back of a cab on the freeway, just me and my guitar. At one point this car bolts right by and cuts off our cab. And the cabby, who's pretty irate, just looks at the guy and blurts out, "Man, you give me the blues in the daytime!" And I'm like, "Um, you wouldn't happen to have a pen on you?" [*laughs*] There I am on this highway, and I start scribbling down the words to "Blues in the Daytime" [*But What Will the Neighbours Think*, 1980]—right onto the back of that guitar! I practically had the song finished by the time I got to the studio. When I got out, the cab driver looks over at me, smiles and says, "You will send me the check now, won't you?"

chuck d
and paris

Interviewed by Tamara Palmer

As front man of the multi-platinum-selling group Public Enemy, Chuck D is widely considered one of the greatest and most influential lyricists in the history of rap and hip-hop, and one of the key figures in bringing a social and political consciousness to the genre. At the time of this interview, he had recently made *Rebirth of a Nation by Public Enemy Featuring Paris*, having challenged the controversial rapper/producer Paris to write a new album project for him.

It takes a lot of trust for a world-renowned lyricist to perform an entire album written by another person, even if it's someone who is also an accomplished writer, but that's exactly what happened here. The resulting album retains the group's spectacularly bombastic beat style while also preserving its lyrical stance.

» *Why is it important to you to know about so many of today's songwriters and to study them all closely?*
CHUCK: I made very much a promise early on; whatever situation or craft or industry I had to be in, I was going to know it thoroughly. I wanted to go into the sports world, as a sportscaster, and I knew everything it took about the sports that I happened to be into. But then on the music front, I made sure that I went into that with as much pomp and circumstance as I treated sports. I needed to know about the importance of musicians, the songwriters, the labels.

» *Reaching back into your earliest musical memories, who were the people that first made you pay attention to the lyrics?*
CHUCK: Well, number one, I'm a different aberration of sorts, because I grew up as a child of the '60s. It was like being in the right place at the right time at the right age. In the '60s, you grew up with the meshings of soul coming up out of rhythm and blues, and rock 'n' roll formatting itself.

When I grew up, the earliest part I can remember is Ray Charles, James Brown, and Motown on one end—and they felt like family members. And on the other you had the Beatles and "I Want to Hold Your Hand." But by eight, nine, and ten years old, the lyrics happened to mean a lot more. Like Sly and the Family Stone, when they said "Stand" or "Thank You (Falettinme Be Mice Elf Again)," or "Sing a Simple Song" or "Everybody Is a Star." The titles meant volumes. And when I became a songwriter later on, I always made sure that I wrote from the title on down, because the title hooks you into a theme. But that was pretty much the promise that came out of a competition of songwriters that raised the standard in the craft to the point where I don't know if you can get a better time of songwriting than 1964–1974. Because it's when we had a war, we had assassinations, we had confusion. But the music clarified a lot of different things that weren't said in the news and in society itself.

» *Do you think we're going to see some of that spirit that over the next few years, as we're seeing musical reactions to events like the war in Iraq and Hurricane Katrina?*
CHUCK: The words spoke volumes back then because you didn't have the aspect of visuals. People weren't interacting with things as much then, and inside the words were a million stories. The words still mean so much today, but they add into anthems. It's the imagery that means so much more than the words or the song itself. So I don't know if it will go backward. But I will tell you this much: when you attach the words to a visual, it takes on aspects that really defy comparison. Sometimes the pictures speak a thousand words, but if you have the words dictating the pictures, now that's something else.

» *The Public Enemy album* Rebirth of a Nation *is quite a different approach for you on the songwriting front. Paris wrote 95 percent of the lyrics, which is not something that people would expect of a hip-hop lyricist of your repute.*
CHUCK: I think, often, that the mistake made in rap music is that people feel that a vocalist should write their own lyrics. That's been a major, major mistake in hip-hop, because not everyone is equipped to be a lyricist and not everyone is equipped to be a vocalist. I don't think just because someone can write well that they can [perform well] on the microphone. I think if you don't have a voice that stands out and you don't have a style, you're better off writing for somebody else.

My knowledge of the history of songwriting says how the hell can you be in music, when the best songs of all-time were written by somebody else for a particular vocalist? I really pride myself on being a vocalist, so why can't I vocalize somebody else's writings? And then, I've got volumes of things that I've written myself. Of course, I can always push myself to write something I didn't write before, but you really can't change yourself, outside of yourself being yourself. Therefore I think a lot of artists could afford to have other people write for them and just put this rap ethic bullshit down that it's taboo.

» *A lot of people in the hip-hop community seem derisive of stuff that is ghostwritten, or written by someone else, like the collaborative effort can't be great work in itself.*
CHUCK: That's just bullshit. Isaac Hayes is one of the greatest songwriters of all time—he's in the Rock and Roll Hall of Fame because he's a songwriter. Isaac Hayes's songs as an artist are interpretations of Burt Bacharach and other great artists that made him shine to another level. Hayes was a great singer, a great artist and entertainer, *and* he wrote songs for Sam and Dave. Come on, if you write songs for Sam and Dave, you're more than capable of writing songs for yourself. But Isaac chose to do songs that were beautiful interpretations [of other's work]. It lessens the load and extends the artistry. A lot of rappers could *definitely* afford to do this.

PARIS: When we did *Rebirth of a Nation*, I basically had to become Chuck in order to understand his cadence, different intonations, and things he had done before. His particular style really influenced me when I was first starting out, and I wanted to capture some of those classic Public Enemy elements on this project. I took my cues from previous tracks musically, and then there was a particular type of [vocal] flow that I took my cues from and certain techniques that I emulated.

» *How do you balance the desire to be entertaining with the need to be educational in your songs?*
CHUCK: A certain level of performance has to go into the words itself . . . the words can actually mean a lot just from the strength of the title. [James Brown's] "This Is a Man's World": inside the fabric of the song itself, it gives you that little bit of an ironic twist. I don't think a lot of irony and wit is being played with as much, because you have a dependency on the visuals. When I tried to make videos in the beginning, I tried to make the video give you what the song *didn't*

say. Hearing the song gives you a visual, but I'm not going to try to show you exactly what the song says; only what it doesn't say. But then, you have to be a twisted individual to try and f*** around with that in the first place! I always wanted to do something contrary and not the easy move. Matter of fact, I always wanted to make the difficult path in songwriting; not the obvious. I wanted to actually take people through twists, where sometimes there's booby-trapping, and all of a sudden a song blows up on them: "I didn't know it was about that!" I always wanted to do different things with songs, like almost put a timer on it and turn it and run and then people are dancing and then find out what the song is about. Or when you're able to do mirrors with it: it says one thing, but it mirrors another. And then there's *another* mirror that takes it into another realm that you didn't even figure out.

» *I don't know about you, but there will be songs I've heard my entire life and then one day I'll hear something in it that gave it a whole new meaning to me.*
CHUCK: Oh, of course. "Puff the Magic Dragon," that's a prime example. I remember that as a kid. It was a kindergarten/first-grade song, and then you start thinking, *Puff the magic dragon.* So that's what makes words powerful, when they take on other identities and double-entendres take place. And that's one of the dangers of when you're trying to make something really over-obvious, because you're not playing with the gift of songwriting. But then again, the gift of songwriting never had the luxury of brilliant filmmaking alongside of it being a key component.

PARIS: I got into this because I love hip-hop. Actually, I really love music more than I love hip-hop. My love for hip- hop has kind of died out. That's ecause the majority of the hip-hop I hear isn't talking to me. It's not saying what I want to hear from it. We come from an era where Afro-centricity was not an exception to the rule, and now it's absolutely the exception to the rule. And it's not even just Afro-centricity—anything that reflects consciousness and something other than escapism. Now, that's all that there is. All of it is escapism or something negative, from gangsterism to stripping. None of that has to do with my reality, and none of it has to do with the reality of the overwhelming majority of people who listen to the music. It's just marketed to people as though that's the way that it's the supposed to be, that this is the norm.

We reject that stance. We reject the corporate pimping of our culture. We demand more from our entertainment. Music is what dictates the streets. Hip-hop doesn't respond to the street, the street responds to hip-hop. So whoever is the gatekeeper of the material that makes it on the TV and the radio is the one that determines the course of the culture.

Chuck and I were talking about this earlier. It's never been easier to make a living—a good living—in being a buffoon. And so it is absolutely necessary for us to provide balance and to be heard.

acknowledgments

Some quotations are taken from *Songs* by Bruce Springsteen (Virgin, 2003), Fred Bronson's *The Billboard Book of Number One Hits* (Guinness, 1992), Jim Irvin and Colin McLear's *The Mojo Collection* (Cannongate, 2000), Sean Egan's *The Guys Who Wrote 'Em: Songwriting Geniuses of Rock and Pop* (Askill Publishing, 2004), Berry Gordy's *To Be Loved, Smokey: Inside My Life* by Smokey Robinson with David Ritz (Headline, 1989), Nelson George's *Where Did Our Love Go* (Omnibus, 1985), Hank Bordowitz's *Billy Joel: The Life and Times of an Angry Young Man, Innocent When You Dream: The Tom Waits Reader* edited by Max Montandon (Orion, 2006), "The Making of Pet Sounds" booklet included in *The Pet Sounds Sessions* (Capitol 1996), Jimmy Webb's *Tunesmith: Inside the Art of Songwriting* (1998), and *Songtalk*, the journal of the National Academy of Songwriters in Hollywood, collected in *Songwriters on Songwriting*, edited by Paul Zollo (Da Capo Press, 1997). Also cited are back issues and online archives of *Beat Instrumental*, *The Creative Independent*, *Guitar World*, *Guitarist*, *Interview*, *Life*, *Making Music*, *Melody Maker*, *Mojo*, *Pitchfork*, *Q*, *The Quietus*, *Rolling Stone*, *Smithsonian Magazine*, *Sounds*, *Songwriting Magazine*, *Uncut*, *The Word*, and the *YTF Motown Collectors* and *Kate Bush Club* newsletters.

Thanks to Tom Seabrook for his work on this new edition. For their involvement in the preparation of the first edition I would like to thank Nigel Osborne, Tony Bacon, John Morrish, Mark Brend, Simon Smith, David Simons, Sid Griffin, Todd Bernhardt, David Sheppard, and Tamara Palmer.

about the author

Rikky Rooksby is a guitar teacher, songwriter/composer, and writer on music. He is the author of *How to Write Songs on Guitar* (2000, revised 2009, 2020), *Inside Classic Rock Tracks* (2001), *Riffs* (2002, 2010, revised 2021), *The Songwriting Sourcebook* (2003, revised 2011), *Chord Master* (2004, revised 2016), *Melody* (2004), *Songwriting Secrets: Bruce Springsteen* (2005), *How to Write Songs on Keyboards* (2005), *Lyrics* (2006, revised 2021), *Arranging Songs* (2007), *How to Write Songs in Altered Guitar Tunings* (2010), and *Songs and Solos* (2014). He contributed to *Albums: 50 Years of Great Recordings, Classic Guitars of the Fifties, The Guitar: The Complete Guide for the Player*, and *Roadhouse Blues* (2003). He has also written *The Guitarist's Guide to the Capo* (Artemis, 2003), *The Complete Guide to the Music of Fleetwood Mac* (revised ed. 2004), *Play Great Guitar* (Infinite Ideas, 2008), 14 Fastforward guitar tutor books, and transcribed and arranged over 40 chord songbooks of music, including *The Complete Beatles*. His entries for many rock musicians appear in the new *Dictionary of National Biography* (OUP), and his published interviews, reviews, articles, and transcriptions in *Guitar Techniques, Total Guitar, Guitarist, Bassist, Bass Guitar Magazine, The Band, Record Collector, Sound on Sound, Shindig!*, and *Making Music*. His memberships include the Society of Authors, Sibelius One, and the Vaughan Williams Society. Visit his website at www.rikkyrooksby.com for more information.